C000131862

Explaining Free Will

A New Approach

Using Independence Indeterminism

A Novel Naturalistic Metaphysics for an
Open Creative Universe

Michael Elstob

Explaining Free Will

Edition 1.04

ISBN 9781790603268

The author may be contacted by email through

cmelstob@btinternet.com

Printed and distributed by Amazon.

Table of Contents

i

iv

Preface

The problem of free will and determinism has been with me for over forty years. I started out as a committed determinist, but in creating a resolution to the problem I have ended up with a view of the living and human worlds as being directively and creatively originative, and far from being wholly deterministic.

My first degree was in physics and my PhD research (Elstob 1975) included the creation of a deterministic computer simulation model of the rules and influences that seem to govern how ordinary police detectives in the UK decide upon their activities. However, over the years following completion of my PhD and as I became involved in research and teaching as a lecturer in cybernetics at Brunel University, I became increasingly dissatisfied with what determinism demands we accept: that our lives have a closed future and that there is no place for genuine creativity anywhere in the universe. It was this increasing dissatisfaction that led me to turn away from determinism and seek a naturalistic account of openness and creativity.

Early on I focused on how certain kinds of systems – particularly information and meaning processing systems – may give rise to emergent properties that are not reducible solely to the lower-level properties of the components that realise the systems (see, for example, Elstob 1984, 1986, 1988). But deterministic ideas that I was not able to abandon kept defeating me. Quantum indeterminacy coupled with chaos theory seemed to provide a way forward but at bottom all that was on offer was an uncontrollable indeterminacy that made creative origination and a person's future too much up to chance for my liking. Then, slowly, it dawned on me that I was looking in the wrong place: that what I needed to do was not to look for a scientific answer but rather to come up with an alternative set of concepts to determinism – concepts that would tell us the future is open, and that the universe has a place for creativity, and for free will. I realised that many attempts had been made to do this but that most had had to incorporate mysterious and/or extra-natural properties or entities, while what I wanted was a set of concepts as naturalistically acceptable as those underlying determinism yet even simpler and more

v

readily believable so that they might eventually come to be adopted in place of determinism.

In the 1990s my thinking became increasingly focused on the idea that the world has a pervasive looseness – that there are gaps within and between the causal networks of existence. I eventually began to understand this looseness in terms of the independence that seems to exist between many things. I came to see that if things are changing truly independently then this would imply that how they are changing with respect to one another must entail some indefiniteness because true, not just apparent, independence of change means there can be no determinate relationship that links, governs or describes how they are changing relative to one another. My development of this idea led me to a very different metaphysical picture of the natural world than that offered by determinism.

"Independence indeterminism" is the name I have given to this new metaphysical picture – an account of which I make public for the first time in this book. I have chosen the term independence indeterminism because this metaphysics identifies a type of indeterminism that is a direct consequence of assuming that true independence of change is extremely common. I argue in the book that because of the simplicity of this assumption and because people (including scientists) act in the world as if it were true (and for other reasons considered later), that we should adopt independence indeterminism in place of determinism.

Although this book has much to say about independence indeterminism and its support for belief in our universe being open and creative, I have chosen to mainly focus on one application of this new metaphysics – namely, how it helps explain free will. I have done this not only because reflection upon my PhD research led me to become consumed by the possibility of genuine free will, but also because I wanted an important and relatively well-contained problem involving openness and creativity upon which I could focus my thinking.

Structuring the argument in a way that the reader may easily follow has proved difficult, not only because the book presents many new and unfamiliar ideas that are strongly interrelated but also because I am trying to achieve two somewhat different aims. On the one hand my aim is to introduce independence indeterminism. However, much of what I want to say on this matter is not directly relevant to the issue of free will. But on the other hand, I need to discuss issues related to free will that are not directly relevant to independence indeterminism. The reader will see that I have decided to pursue these two aims by interleaving discussion on these main topics more or less equally within some chapters, and by devoting other chapters mainly to one topic rather than the other. I hope the reader will bear with this approach – an approach that I believe works better than dividing the book into to a first part on independence indeterminism, followed by a second part on free will.

The book is not a work of popular philosophy, but nor is it a highly technical treatise. Nevertheless, because many of its key ideas are new, it does require careful and thoughtful reading. However, it is aimed at quite a wide readership – one that extends considerably beyond, but includes, those participants in the free-will debate.

Acknowledgements

I thank those many people – too numerous to name here – that have been interested in this project, and have been patient while I attempted to explain what I what trying to do.

For repeated discussions about this project and related matters – in some cases discussions that have extended over a long period – I thank Mustafa Ali, Tony Cockett, Steve Cockett, David Davidson, Leo Elstob, Chris Fenwick, Graham Ellsbury, Tatia Tambouratzis, and Martin Watson.

I especially thank Shelia Harri-Augstein, Laurie Thomas, and Michael Weir for providing detailed comments on early drafts of this book.

Finally, I thank my wife Jill. Her down-to-earth and common-sense comments have always been helpful. And in particular she has often reminded me that "you can't prove it, it's just a matter of what you believe" – which is right because my thesis is a metaphysical one, and it can't be proved or disproved and must remain a matter of personal belief. But also Jill has always been wholly supportive of my work on this project.

1 Setting the Scene

1.1 Introducing Independence Indeterminism

1.1.1 The problem of free will – whether or not we are capable of creative self-determination and can genuinely "make our own fate" – has remained unresolved for well over 2000 years. In this book independence indeterminism is used to help resolve this problem, and in the remainder of this section this new way of thinking is introduced. After clarifying in section 1.2 some ideas used throughout the book, sections 1.3 and 1.4 provide some background to the problem of free will. Section 1.5 introduces the key idea of creative origination, and section 1.6 discusses the view of the human self that is adopted in the present work. The chapter ends with an outline of the remainder of the book.

1.1.2 Independence indeterminism is a new but simple naturalistic metaphysics that is proposed as a replacement for determinism – which currently is generally (and usually tacitly) assumed to be the way the world works. This new metaphysics is based on a single assumption: namely, that **true independence of change is extremely common in the universe.** This is something that is believed by (almost) everyone in their daily doings, and it underpins the way science operates. As will be argued, accepting this assumption implies that the universe has a partly open future and a place for origination (i.e. for the non-predetermined emergence of things), and for creativity (i.e. for the emergence of *novel* or *non-prefigured* things). Determinism, on the other hand, is not a new metaphysics but a very well-established one; and one that implies the future is completely predetermined and therefore closed. This means determinism offers no possibility for anyone to genuinely originate or create anything and so they cannot truly "make their own fate". Indeterminism is the denial of determinism: it is the idea that some future events are not yet fixed – that they are not predetermined. However, many people who believe in indeterminism also believe that all non-predetermined future events can only arise as a matter of pure chance which means – because no-one can influence pure chance – that with this sort of indeterminism people cannot properly "make their own fate". However, as will be argued, under independence indeterminism not all origination is a matter of pure chance since this metaphysics has a place for the "directed origination" of some future events – and indeed for the "directed *creative* origination" of some things.

1.1.3   With truly independently running changes any of them might proceed differently with respect to how the others are running because, by talking of *truly* independently running changes, there can be nothing that links, fixes, governs, or describes how the changes proceed with respect to one another. This is an absolutely fundamental point since it is something wholly incompatible with determinism. As an example, consider three fairly arbitrarily chosen ongoing changes taking place nearby as I write this: namely, the wind gusting around the house; what some particular earthworm under the lawn is doing; and what is happening inside the engine of a car moving along the road outside. If these are *truly* independently running changes then how any one of them proceeds will not be linked to or related in any determinate way to how the others are proceeding. This is what is meant by *true* independence of change. Determinism presents a very different view because it does not accept that these changes are running *truly* independently, even though they may appear to be doing so. Rather, according to determinism (as modern philosophers think of it) there is no true independence of change anywhere because this metaphysics takes everything that happens to be part of one totality of change in which the state of the universe at one instant together with the laws of nature fixes (i.e. fully determines) what the state of the universe will be at the next instant, and so on forever. So, according to determinism, the three ongoing changes just mentioned must be accepted to be proceeding in perfect lockstep, even though this is not apparent to human observers.

1.1.4   Independence indeterminism understands existence to be loosely connected, with change generally being compartmentalised and with many gaps within and between the causal networks that exist. What this means is that under independence indeterminism most things are understood to be getting on with their business independently of most other things. Science confirms this view in two main ways. Firstly, science assumes that the experimental findings or observations it reports may be confirmed, or possibly refuted, by re-establishing the relevant conditions and then repeating the experiment or observation. That is, it is accepted that only certain conditions affect what will be found, not everything, and that as long as these conditions are re-established the same results will be obtained. Or put another way, it is accepted that scientific findings are independent of most of what exists and only depend upon a relatively few aspects of existence. Secondly, and supporting the point just made, all the laws of science that have so far been established refer only to certain aspects of existence, and not to everything. This suggests that whatever is going on that is not mentioned in the laws runs independently of (i.e. does not influence) the things that are mentioned.

1.1.5   The view that independence indeterminism provides is one partly envisaged (but not clearly established) by the philosopher of science Karl Popper when he wrote: 'Our universe is partly causal, partly probabilistic, and partly open: it is emergent.' (Popper 1982, p. 130) But even this view – one far less radical than what independence indeterminism implies – is strongly at odds with the deterministic view that many people accept without question as being true. For example, in his book *The Free Will Delusion – How We Settled for the Illusion of Morality*, James Miles writes: 'If it all comes down to biology and environment our behaviour would be said to be deterministic – would be an inevitable outcome – because biology and the environment are themselves recognised as deterministic systems.' (Miles 2015, p. 7) However, under independence indeterminism biology and the environment are *not* recognised as deterministic systems, as the following discussion shows.

1.1.6   Perhaps the most important consequence of the assumption of true independence of change is that interactions between things that previously were changing (or running) truly independently of one another must be understood to be originated interactions – that is, non-predetermined events. Interactions of this sort shall be referred to as "independence interactions". A simple example will help to make clear why independence interactions are always originated events. Imagine the event of a particular raindrop falling on a particular place on your head on a particular occasion. Now consider a period some time before the occurrence of this event – say, the period between 5 and 10 seconds earlier – when it would seem reasonable to assume that true independence of change existed between the motion the raindrop was undergoing and the motion of your

3

head. With *truly* independently running changes there is nothing linking or governing how the changes are proceeding with respect to one another, and nothing ensuring they are changing in some sort of hidden lockstep. This means that during the period concerned nothing exists that determines whether or not the raindrop and your head will come into future interaction. Which means that the event of them actually coming into interaction is originated and not predetermined. This is true of all independence interactions: their future occurrence remains indeterminate as long as the things involved are changing truly independently of one another. Of course, most things that are changing truly independently of one another are very unlikely to ever interact. For instance, referring to the example given above, it is highly unlikely that the earthworm under the lawn and the engine in the car will ever interact. Nevertheless, independence interactions do seem to be very common – as instanced by the very common occurrence of raindrops falling on people's heads. If this is accepted, as it is under independence indeterminism, then this means that very many future events – i.e. those that are independence interactions – are originated events. Which means that under this new metaphysics it is not correct to say that 'biology and the environment are themselves recognised as deterministic systems' since these two domains involve a great many independence interactions. Put in more familiar terms, independence indeterminism takes chance events to be real, whereas under determinism they are taken to be only *apparently* real since they are considered to be the result of (generally very complex and dispersed) deterministic processes whose overall operation we cannot follow.

1.1.7   What independence indeterminism leads to is the conclusion that existence is fundamentally open with a great many future events yet to be originated. It recognises that causal networks are common but it argues, unlike determinism, that there are causal gaps within and between these networks. Additionally, it offers what has not been available before: namely a thoroughly naturalistic account of how humans (and animals to a more limited extent, and possibly in the future some artificial entities such as robots) may self-directively, and in certain cases creatively, *originate* important aspects of their lives. Independence indeterminism does not deny that order, dependence, interdependence, and causal connectivity are familiar features

4

of existence, and that many happenings run in a more or less determ-inistic way. For instance, once an independence interaction has actu-ally occurred, what then ensues often runs in a more or less determ-inistic way as the things involved interact with one another. For ex-ample, once a raindrop lands on your head what then happens to the drop largely unfolds in a more or less deterministic way – a way that science has gone a considerable way to understanding.

1.1.8   Independence indeterminism is a process metaphysics and as such it rejects the existence of unchanging instantaneous states of the universe, which is a fundamental assumption of determinism. The process approach is an unfamiliar way of thinking because so many things can be observed that do not appear to be changing. However, when science looks closely it sees that, below the surface, nothing is absolutely static. Taking process, or change, to be funda-mental has a very long history. The philosopher Nicholas Rescher writes: 'The Greek theoretician Heraclitus of Ephesus [535-475 B.C.] – known even in antiquity as "the obscure" – is universally recog-nized as the founder of the process approach.' Rescher goes on to say that Heraclitus thought of Nature as 'a manifold of opposed forces joined in mutual rivalry, interlocked in constant strife and con-flict.' (Rescher 1996, p. 9) This view is not adopted by independence indeterminism, but the key idea of all process thinking – that change is the fundamental feature of existence and that unchanging instant-aneous states of existence do not exist – is adopted.

1.1.9   Under independence indeterminism, although all inde-pendence interactions are originated events it is not accepted that all such interactions are undirected or chance originations because it re-cognises that some of them are directively produced. That is, some independence interactions are taken to be "directed originations" produced by the activity of a "directive system": a system that adjusts its actions in the light of independently occurring events in order to achieve or maintain some "directed outcome" (e.g. a goal). For in-stance, in order to achieve their goal of catching prey, predators must appropriately adjust their actions in the light of the evasive actions of their (partly) *independently* moving prey. And in order to achieve their goal of arriving safely at their desired destination, car drivers must appropriately adjust their actions to take account of *independently* arising and changing road and traffic conditions. And, as a further example, directed independence interactions are involved in all ball-sports because the players strive to interact with the generally *inde-pendently* moving ball in such a manner as to produce certain desired effects. However, it should not be thought that under independence indeterminism "directive activity" and directed outcomes may only be produced by purposive agents because they may also be originated by completely automatically operating directive systems. For example, the directive activity of a thermostatically controlled home heating system consists of its switching the heating on and off in response to independently varying weather and other conditions in ways that tend to maintain the directed outcome of a roughly constant temperature in the home.

1.1.10   Independence indeterminism is not compatible with de-terminism. However, determinism is a very long-standing and well-entrenched metaphysical position so why should people abandon it and adopt this new view? The main reason for doing so is that once it becomes clear that two important metaphysical views are fundament-ally incompatible it seems right that people should try to decide between them, and pick the stronger one. Usually people appeal to three principles to help them decide. Firstly, they tend to favour the metaphysics that accords most strongly with the beliefs they rely upon in living their everyday and professional lives. Here independ-ence indeterminism scores over determinism because it would be very difficult for people to abandon the (generally tacitly held) belief that most things run independently of how most other things are running, whereas it would be less difficult to abandon the rather ab-stract assumptions upon which determinism (as formally understood by most contemporary philosophers) is based. Secondly, if one view rests on simpler ideas and assumptions than the other then people tend to favour it. And here again independence indeterminism scores over determinism since it rests on the single simple idea and assump-tion that true independence of change is extremely common in the universe. In sharp contrast, determinism (as formally understood) rests on two highly abstract ideas and assumptions: namely, that there is a definite and unchanging state of the totality of existence at each instant of time, and that there are fixed laws of nature that com-pletely determine how the state of the totality of existence at one in-stant is transformed into the state of the totality of existence at the next instant. Thirdly, people tend to favour that view which is most able to account for the important phenomena that they believe exist in the world. Here also independence indeterminism does better than determinism because, among other things, it has a place for directed (and creative) origination, and for free will, whereas determinism has no place for these things. Given that independence indeterminism seems to have more going for it than determinism, it would be appropriate to ask why determinism was not replaced by independence indeterminism years ago? The answer is not clear (but some possible reasons are mentioned in section 6.1). However, it may be simply that no-one has previously thought through what the very commonly held belief in true independence of change actually implies.

1.2   Some Clarifications

1.2.1   The term "metaphysics" is being used in the dictionary sense of 'The systematic study or science of the first principles of being and of knowledge; the doctrine of the essential nature of and fundamental relations of all that is real.' (*Webster's Dictionary* 1998) The word itself comes 'from the Greek for "after natural things", that is, what comes after the study of nature.' (*Concise Routledge Encyclopedia of Philosophy* 2000, entry on 'metaphysics'). The term "naturalistic metaphysics" is used to indicate a doctrine based on assumptions beyond definite empirical confirmation or denial that addresses the essential relations, properties, and activities of the natural world – a world which is seen as forming a 'single sphere without incursions from outside by souls or spirits, divine or human, and without having to accommodate strange entities like non-natural values or substantive abstract universals.' (*Oxford Companion to Philosophy*, Honderich 1995, entry on 'naturalism'). In being such a metaphysics independence indeterminism competes on an equal footing with naturalistic forms of determinism.

1.2.2   It has proved difficult to define what free will is. The view adopted and developed in this book is that it is an ability that allows a human (or more generally a psychological agent) "to make their own fate" – not completely and in every respect, but to a significant degree. That humans have this ability is a widely held belief, as is confirmed by a study in 1998 by the *International Social Survey Programme* which asked approximately 39,000 people drawn from 34 countries various questions about religion and related matters, including whether they agreed or disagreed with the statement: "We each make our own fate." Just over 65% agreed or strongly agreed. This suggests that a majority of people, at least nowadays, believe that much of the course of their lives is largely up to them to shape and create and is not something wholly determined by circumstances (past and present), or by others, or solely through luck or fate.

1.2.3 For us to be able to "make our own fate" we must be self-directed originators. This is a more demanding requirement than it may seem because to be *originators* we must be the first cause of at least some of the things we do. That is, the causal chains (or networks of influence) upon which at least some of our actions depend should start within us and not have their roots outside us or in the past. And the requirement that we be *self-directed* originators is also very demanding because it means that our self must be exerting directional influence over the production of our originated doings in such a manner that we may legitimately claim that they are *our* originations and not purely the result of indeterministic chance events arising inside or outside us over which we have no control.

1.2.4 Given its central role in the argument being developed, more must be said about what "origination" is being taken to mean. Something (e.g. an object, a property, an event, a process) is taken to be *originated* if at some point prior to its existence (but after the creation of the universe) the universe was such that at that point the later existence of this something was not necessitated (i.e. predetermined). This definition means that an entity is taken to be originated if, even in a most indirect and/or far-past way, its existence depends upon some entity that was itself originated. However, in addressing the issue of free will participants in the debate are mainly interested in 'fresh', or "de novo", originations and not 'stale' ones. That is, the main interest is in originated things whose existence was not necessitated until relatively shortly before they actually came to be. For instance, participants tend to be interested in decisions that are originated because of the decision process itself being originative rather than because, say, the factors that led a person to decide as they did were originated long ago by social and other influences that conditioned the person to decide as they did.

8

1.2.5 Self-directed origination is something that many people don't accept as being possible. Among such people are those belonging to the following main groups. Firstly, there are those who believe that God is the only true originator, and that He determines everything that happens – which means that no natural agent can be the self-directed originator of anything, let alone their choices, moral or otherwise. Secondly, some people believe that the universe runs wholly deterministically, with no origination taking place anywhere. Thirdly, even though they may accept that some indeterminacy might exist within the universe, there are those who think that all natural agents operate completely deterministically, like a very complex machine or computer, and that as such everything they do, and everything that happens to them internally, is completely determined by their current circumstances and their present internal condition, so leaving no room for them themselves to actually originate anything. Fourthly, there are people who believe that quantum indeterministic events in the brain may lead to the de novo origination of some mental happenings – such as the formation of some ideas or the making of some decisions – but who argue that these cannot be counted as *self-directed* originations because what makes them originations are indeterministically arising quantum events that are not under the agent's control or influence. And fifthly, there are people who think that fate – whatever its basis and however it works – inexorably fixes everything that is significant that happens to a person, meaning that even if they could self-directively originate some minor aspects of their lives they could never change any of the really important events that fate dictates must occur.

1.2.6 In the past – that is, prior to the present work – one thing that has made the existence of free will such a difficult thing for many people to accept has been the lack of a naturalistically acceptable account of directed origination, and self-directed origination in particular. This has led many people to believe that this power must be of divine or supernatural origin. Such a divine power and what it gives us has been described by the Renaissance humanist scholar, Giovanni Pico della Mirandola, who wrote in his work *Oration On the Dignity of Man*:

> We have made thee neither of heaven nor earth, neither mortal nor immortal, so that with freedom of choice and with

honour, as though the maker and moulder of thyself, thou mayest fashion thyself in whatever shape thou shalt prefer. Thou shalt have the power to degenerate into the lower forms of life, which are brutish. Thou shalt have the power out of thy soul's judgement, to be reborn into the highest forms, which are divine. (Pico dela Mirandola 1486)

But if God gave us the power of self-directed origination then He gave us the power to perform evil as well as good acts, and the question then arises why a perfect being should wish to make room for evil in His universe. This, and other problems, have made free will a difficult matter for theologians and although several deeply argued positions have been developed and promulgated none has gained universal acceptance. However, since the concern of this book is with naturalistic accounts of free will little attention will be given to this great body of work.

1.2.7   Science is an obvious place to look for a naturalistic account of self-directed origination, but unfortunately, given its present metaphysical orientation, science cannot provide much help. The physics that emerged during and after the Renaissance was thoroughly deterministic and because of its huge success the idea of the universal application of determinism became strongly rooted in the scientific mind. This led to the widely held naturalistic view that the universe is essentially a giant piece of very complex clockwork – albeit a piece of clockwork that was, perhaps, set up by God and is obeying laws given by Him. The dominant position of determinism in physical science remained largely intact until the 1920s when quantum mechanics was developed and microscopic (i.e. atomic and sub-atomic) indeterminacy came to be firmly established within mainstream scientific thinking. However, not all physicists accepted this new view and some – Einstein being the most famous with his belief that God does not play dice – worked hard to find a fully deterministic account of the empirical findings of quantum physics. Although in recent years various alternative accounts have gained support, the so-called Copenhagen interpretation – that an irreducible indeterminacy exists within the quantum world – probably still retains the backing of the majority of scientists. And because this is so this is the view adopted throughout this book, except where stated otherwise.

1.2.8   However, even if the majority of present-day scientists accept that quantum indeterminacy is a fundamental feature of nature and so accept that the absolute or all-pervasive determinism of classical physics is not correct, most of them point out that this indeterminacy is generally only significant at the atomic and sub-atomic level of existence and that it intrudes very little into the macroscopic level. This means that those scientists who are concerned with macroscopic happenings generally believe they are able to proceed with their investigations under the assumption that what is going on happens deterministically. In particular this means that workers in the life and human sciences generally believe they are dealing with "adequately determined" phenomena. Bob Doyle says 'Adequate determinism is the kind of determinism we have in the world. [That is,] Macroscopic objects are adequately determined in their motions, giving rise to the appearance of strict causal determinism' (Doyle 2011, p. 392). Various other terms have been used – e.g. "near determinism" (Honderich 1988, p. 8). However, in the present work, the term "macroscopic determinism" shall be used for the belief that determinism is very largely true within the macroscopic realm. Belief in macroscopic determinism is widely held and in consequence it is commonly thought that everything that happens in a person's life must be deterministically produced. However, using the definition of origination mentioned earlier and sticking with mainstream scientific views, it is easy to show that this is unlikely to be the case.

1.2.9   Although, generally speaking, the macroscopic world is well insulated from the indeterminacy of the microscopic world, macroscopic devices have been constructed that amplify certain quantum indeterministic events in such a way that they give rise to macroscopic events which must then themselves be counted as originations. A relatively familiar example is a Geiger counter, an instrument for measuring the intensity of radioactivity in a particular location. A Geiger counter works by detecting (and then greatly amplifying to produce an audible click and/or the advance of a counter) the effects of the decay of a single radioactive nucleus – an event that occurs indeterministically, according to the mainstream view. In fact, many different sorts of devices have been developed for detecting and amplifying quantum indeterministic events and, among other things, such devices may be used to originate streams of numbers that have the property of being randomly distributed. Such streams of truly originated random numbers (that is, truly originated according to the mainstream view of quantum mechanics) have various uses in science, engineering, industry, and commerce. Indeed, there are some internet sites (e.g. the HotBits Service) that make such streams available free of charge. Consider a situation, therefore, in which someone uses the output of one of these sites as the basis for selecting the numbers for their lottery ticket, and let us further suppose that they happen to be lucky enough to win a large prize. Such a win is likely to make a big difference to the person's life and the changes involved will all count as originated events (according to the definition of origination given earlier). However, if macroscopic determinism is true, then these changes will be stale originations because they will all derive deterministically from the de novo originations (i.e. the disintegration of atomic nuclei) that led to the production of the random numbers which were used by the winner to construct their lottery entry.

1.2.10   This example demonstrates that intrusions of microscopic indeterminacy into the macroscopic realm may lead to a vast number of subsequent stale macroscopic originations. There is nothing special about these stale originations: they behave just like any other things or happenings of the same type. This is an important point because, under independence indeterminism, independence interactions must be regarded as originated events. However, they are usually not *novel* types of origination. Indeed, many independence interactions are of a type that occurs so commonly that it is convenient to think of them as being "type-determined originations" relative to the domain in which they arise. For example, instances of raindrops falling on people's heads count as type-determined originations because this type of independence interaction is almost certain to occur in situations in which people are out in the rain.

1.3   Standard Positions on Free Will

1.3.1   Free will has been recognised as a problematic concept for well over two thousand years. Belief in determinism, in its various forms, has long been seen as the source of most of the trouble since it has seemed to many people that free will cannot possibly be compatible with a world in which an agent has no power to originate anything. However, random indeterminacy has also long been recognised as not enough to give people a sort of free will worth wanting since they have no control over what it produces.

1.3.2 Quite early in the history of the debate – according to Susanne Bobzien (1998), beginning with the work of Chrissipius (c280-207 BCE) – a robust attempt was made to argue that determinism is not as much of a problem as many people thought. The argument was made that what really matters is not that people have a free *will*, but rather that they have the freedom to do what they want, or will, to do. That is, as long as what a person is doing is what they desire to do then they should not really be bothered if the source of their desire lies outside themselves – for instance, that it comes from their given nature and/or from how they have been conditioned by society. This position, known as compatibilism (or soft determinism), has been the dominant one in the free-will debate from early modern times when naturalistic philosophers started to examine the problem. Thomas Hobbes is often taken to be the father of modern compatibilism and in his great work *Leviathan* (Hobbes 1651), he wrote:

> LIBERTY or FREEDOM, signifieth, properly, the absence of opposition; by opposition, I mean external impediments of motion; and may be applied no less to irrational, and animate creatures, than to rational. For whatsoever is so tied, or environed, as it cannot move but within a certain space, which space is determined by the opposition of some external body we say hath no liberty to go further.
> [...]
> And according to this proper, and generally received meaning of the word, a FREEMAN, *is he, that in those things, which by his strength and wit he is able to do, is not hindered to do what he has a will to do.* [...] from the use of the word *free-will*, no liberty can be inferred of the will, desire, or inclination, but the liberty of the man; which consisteth in this, that he finds no stop, in doing what he has the will, desire, or inclination to do.

1.3.3 The great strength of compatibilism is that there appears to be no logical reason why the universe should not operate fully deterministically and in so doing give rise to human behaviour as we know it in all its physical, biological, social and psychological detail.

The key point is not to understand determinism too simplistically and too restrictively. In particular, determinism need not mean that a 'dominoes-world' view has to be adopted of what human persons are and how they operate and behave. Daniel Dennett, a leading contemporary compatibilist, makes this important point clear in his book *Elbow Room – The Varieties of Free Will Worth Wanting*. He writes:

> The fear that this chapter [entitled Self-Made Selves] has focused on is the fear that no naturalistic theory of the self could be given that sufficiently distinguished it from a mere domino in a chain. We do not want to be mere dominoes; we want to be moral agents. Let us review what has been found to be special about naturalistically conceived selves. Only some of the portions of the physical universe have the property of being designed to resist their own dissolution, to wage a local campaign against the inexorable trend of the Second Law of Thermodynamics. And only some of these portions have the further property of being caused to have reliable expectations about what will happen next, and hence to have some capacity to control things, including themselves. And only some of these have the further capacity of significant self-improvement (through learning). And fewer still have the open-ended capacity (requiring a language of self-description) for "radical self-evaluation." These portions of the world are thus loci of self-control, of talent, of decision making. They have projects, interests, and values they create in the course of their own self-evaluation and self-definition. How much less like a domino could a portion of the physical world be? (Dennett 1984, p. 100)

1.3.4   Clearly, the portions of the world that Dennett describes in the last few sentences are human persons, or similar beings. Throughout his book, and in his subsequent writing on free will, what Dennett is trying to establish is that determinism doesn't take away anything that really matters to us, and nor does it directly disallow any of the mental and other capacities that we feel we possess and which we greatly value. However, what determinism does deny is that a person can "make their own fate" in the sense of being able to self-directively *originate* important aspects of their life.

1.3.5   Strongly opposed to the compatibilists are the incompatibilists. Incompatibilists do not accept that free will is simply a matter of an agent being able to freely do what they want to do since they believe that an agent must also be able to freely *originate* what they want to do. Incompatiblists fall into two main groups: the hard determinists or pessimists, and the libertarians. The hard determinists believe that if determinism is true then free will cannot exist (and most of them also believe that determinism is indeed true so they don't believe free will exists at all in the natural universe). An important subgroup of the hard determinists deserves to be distinguished. Members of this group are sometimes called illusionists because while they don't believe we have free will they do believe that we have an almost immovable *illusory* belief in our possessing it – a belief that, because it may be genetically and/or socially determined, we cannot easily abandon even if rational argument is able to convince us that it is a false belief.

1.3.6   Libertarians are incompatibilists because, like all incompatibilists, they believe free will cannot be compatible with determinism, or indeed with undirected indeterminism. But unlike other incompatibilists they have a deep and resolute belief in the existence of free will, which means they believe the natural universe cannot be absolutely deterministic in its operation and must have room for self-directed origination. Libertarians constitute a large group but because they have always struggled to find a convincing naturalistic account of self-directed origination they have often advocated views that push the boundaries of what almost all scientists and many other people are able to accept. For example, one widely pursued approach argues for what is known as agent causation. This is the idea that certain agents possess the power to cause things to happen *without* this causal power beings reducible to chains of causal events within the agent and its environment. That is, agent-causal powers are seen to be emergent in the sense of not being reducible. However, it has been difficult for those libertarians who subscribe to such a view to find a convincing naturalistic account of agent-causation that is compatible with mainstream scientific thinking. Nevertheless, there have been recent attempts to give naturalistic libertarian accounts of free will that are compatible with mainstream scientific thinking, and some of these are discussed later (see sections 5.3, 5.4, and 5.5). One serious

15

weakness shared by all these attempts is that the de novo originations that are involved are quantum indeterministic ones, and as such cannot be influenced or directed by anything, including an agent's self. What is needed, and what independence indeterminism is able to provide, are sources of de novo origination that arise from the way the agent actually operates – for instance, that arise as a result of directed and non-directed independence interactions among the various parts of the agent's self. What this means is that an agent, in so operating, will itself be the originator of causal chains and so be functioning in an agent-causal manner.

1.3.7   Although "The problem of free will" has been, and still is, actively debated and worked on, it is important to point out that it is an invisible problem for most people most of the time. That is, it is a problem that has little explicit presence in the lives of most people. However, it would be a mistake to say it is therefore a problem of no human significance. It would be a mistake because the position that a person or a community holds on what free will is and whether or not humans possess it does have an important influence. This has long been recognised, as the following passage from the entry on 'free will' in the *Catholic Encyclopedia* (1909) makes clear.

> The question of free will, moral liberty, or the liberum arbitrum of the Schoolmen, ranks amongst the three or four most important philosophical problems of all time. It ramifies into ethics, metaphysics, and psychology. The view adopted in response to it will determine a man's position in regard to the most momentous issues that present themselves to the human mind. On the one hand, does man possess genuine moral freedom, power of real choice, true ability to determine the course of his thoughts and volitions, to decide which motives shall prevail within his mind, to modify and mould his own character? Or, on the other, are man's thoughts and volitions, his character and external actions, all merely the inevitable outcome of his circumstances? Are they inexorably predetermined in every detail along rigid lines by events of the past over which he himself had had no sort of control? This is the real import of the free-will problem.

1.4 On Defining Free Will

1.4.1 Defining what free will is has proved to be a problem. The approach adopted in the present work is to link free will to the ability of a person, or more generally a psychological agent, to "make their own fate", and, as shall be outlined at the end of this section, to do so in a self-directed and creatively originative way. But first it is appropriate to briefly consider some of the things the free-will community has had to say.

1.4.2 Traditionally, free will has been a topic confined to philosophy. Although belief in free will is widespread this is a belief that during most of the twentieth century received almost no attention from psychologists. Indeed, in the introduction to the book *Are We Free: Psychology and Free Will* the editors' note that 'the term *free will* didn't even merit an entry in a recent eight-volume *Encyclopedia of Psychology* [Oxford University Press]; in fact, it didn't even appear in the index.' (Baer, Kaufman, and Baumeister 2008, p. 3)

1.4.3 Perhaps one of the reasons why scientific psychology has ignored free will – or rather "had" since in recent years things have changed – is that it is difficult to define what it is. In everyday life the term free will is often used to underline the fact that a choice is truly a person's own. And among other things, this usually means that it is expected that the person take responsibility for a choice so made – as is clear, for example, when, after people have tried to dissuade someone from taking a particular course of action, they are told "Well, just appreciate that you're doing this of your own free will."

1.4.4 The notion that by exercising your free will you are responsible for what follows has long been one way of defining what it is. Michael McKenna (2015), in his entry on 'compatibilism' in the authoritative on-line *Stanford Encyclopedia of Philosophy*, adopts this approach when he writes: 'It would be misleading to specify a strict definition of free will since in the philosophical work devoted to this notion there is probably no single concept of it. [...] [A]s a theory neutral point of departure, free will can be defined as *the unique ability of persons to exercise control over their conduct in the fullest manner necessary for moral responsibility.*'

1.4.5 Note that this characterisation makes no mention of self-directed origination, nor anything similar, and that because of this it

17

may be seen as a compatibilist-friendly definition. On the other hand, dictionary definitions do tend to emphasise that free will entails some sort of originative power. According to the *Oxford English Dictionary* **free will** is: '1 Spontaneous will, unconstrained choice (to do or act). 2 The power of directing one's own actions without constraint by necessity or fate.' *Webster's Dictionary* (1998) gives the following definition of **free will**: '1 The power of self-determination regarded as a special faculty. 2 *Philosophical*. The doctrine that man is entirely unrestricted in his ability to choose between good and evil: opposed to *determinism*.' And it defines the philosophical term **determinism** as: 'The doctrine that man's choices, decisions, and actions are decided by antecedent causes, inherited or environmental, acting upon his character: opposed to *free will*.'

1.4.6   These dictionary definitions indicate that there are two separate notions embodied in the concept of free will: that of "voluntariness", and that of "non-necessitated self-determination". The hard determinist, Ted Honderich (Honderich 1993, p. 5), has argued that much of the disagreement about what free will is rests on an unwillingness of most participants in the debate to accept that our everyday use of this term encompasses both of these concepts.

1.4.7   The idea of voluntariness is not particularly problematic and most participants in the debate accept that to exercise *free* will means the agent must be operating voluntarily: that is, operating while not under undue "constraint, coercion, compulsion, or control" – to use a shorthand phrase for conditions that are difficult to define precisely. However, the idea of non-necessitated self-determination *is* problematic since it seems to be incompatible with the natural order: an order in which it is commonly believed everything either has a cause; or otherwise is a product of undirected indeterministically arising quantum events. The philosopher Alfred Mele, who has written extensively on free will, makes clear what is required.

> Sometimes you would have made an alternative decision if things had been a bit different. [...] But this isn't enough for the kind of openness at issue: call it *deep openness*. What's needed is that more than one option was open to you, given everything as it was at the time – your mood, all your thoughts and feelings, your brain, your environment, and indeed the entire universe and its entire history. Having been

18

able to have made a different decision if things had been a bit different is one thing; having been able to have made a different decision in the absence of any prior difference is another. (Mele 2014, p. 2)

Note that Mele is tacitly assuming that the universe has an entirely definite state at the instant in time in which someone exercises their free will, something which process philosophies and independence indeterminism does not accept. Put in the terms Mele uses — which are in line with the traditional view of the free-will problem — non-necessitated self-determination is problematic. Indeed, the Scholastics attacked this problem head-on and argued that humans possess a very special power which is known as the Liberty of Indifference: a liberty in which the Will, seen as a special faculty, is taken to operate in complete isolation from any influences external to itself, including other parts of a person's mind-brain.

1.4.8   Here it is necessary to break the flow of the discussion to say something about the term "mind-brain" that has just been introduced — a term that will be used frequently in this book. The dictionary (*Webster's* 1998) tells us that the **mind** is 'The aggregate of all conscious and unconscious processes originating in and associated with the brain [...]', and that the **brain** is 'The enlarged and greatly modified portion of the central nervous system contained within the cranium of vertebrates [...].' These definitions suggest that the mind is a processual entity whereas the brain is a structural/material one. Yet both of these entities jointly realise the mental life of a psychological agent and in recognition of this use of the term mind-brain seems appropriate. With this usage established, discussion of the Liberty of Indifference may be resumed.

1.4.9   Writing in the 17th century Philip van Limborch, a friend of the British empiricist philosopher John Locke, described the Will as a special faculty as follows.

The true identity therefore of the Will consists in an active Indifference, whereby, having all things requisite for Action, it may act or not act, and do this rather than that. And this Liberty is so far essential to the Will, that Man has it not only in a State of Innocence; but has it in every State or Condition whatsoever, the State of Sin not excepted. (Limborch 1713, p.141)

19

The "Indifferent Will" is the term that shall be adopted for such a will – a will such that 'having all things requisite for Action, it may act or not act, and do this rather than that.' The key point about an Indifferent Will, if it exits at all, is that it is a part of a person that operates in a way uninfluenced and unconstrained by their history and present circumstances, and by their self. Here it is appropriate to say something about what, in the present work, the self is taken to be.

1.4.10   A self is understood to be something that is only possessed by a psychological agent – indeed, the notions of a psychological agent and of a self are, in this work, considered to be inseparable. Whether or not all psychological agents must be biological beings is an open question, but anything that is to qualify must have functionally distinguishable and relatively independently operating parts – parts that collectively may be identified as constituting the entity's self – and must include what in human terms may be referred to as motivational, emotional (affective), and executive parts. According to the conception adopted here there is no place for an Indifferent Will – rather, the phenomena that lead some people to infer the existence of such a thing are taken to be features of the way a psychological agent's self operates. More discussion of this conception of the self may be found in sections 1.6 and 10.3.

1.4.11   As many commentators have noted, the Indifferent Will is something that perhaps we don't want: something we can know only through its actions *after the event*; something whose internal workings cannot be represented in consciousness; and something rather alien that our self can never influence or control. R. E. Hobart, in a well-known paper – 'Free Will as Involving Determination and Inconceivable Without It' – puts the matter as follows.

> Indeterminism maintains that we need not be impelled to action by our wishes, that our active will need not be determined by them. Motives "incline without necessitating." We choose amongst the ideas of action before us, but we need not choose solely according to the attraction of desire, in however wide a sense that word be used. Our inmost self may rise up in its autonomy and moral dignity, independently of motives, and register its sovereign decree.
>
> Now, *in so far* as this "interposition of the self" is undetermined, the act is not *its* act, it does not issue from any con-

tinuing self; it is born at the moment, of nothing, hence it expresses no quality; it bursts into being from no source. The self does not register *its* decree, for the decree is not the product of just that "*it*". The self does not rise up in *its* moral dignity, for dignity is the quality of enduring being, influencing its actions, and therefore expressed by them, and that would be determination. *In proportion* as an act of volition starts of itself without cause it is exactly, so far as the freedom of the individual is concerned, as if it had been thrown into his mind from without – "suggested" to him – by a freakish demon (Hobart 1934).

1.4.12   Free will defined in terms of an Indifferent Will makes an easy target for ridicule by scientists and others. For example, Patricia Churchland, a well-known eliminative-materialist philosopher, in a *New Scientist* special issue on the 'Big questions in Science', writes as follows on the question, 'Do we have free will?'.

> A rigid philosophical tradition claims that no choice is free unless it is uncaused; that is, unless the "will" is exercised independently of all causal influences – in a causal vacuum. In some unexplained fashion, the will – a thing that allegedly stands aloof from brain-based causality – makes an unconstrained choice. The problem is that choices are made by brains, and brains operate causally; that is, they go from one state to the next as a function of antecedent conditions. Moreover, though brains make decisions, there is no discrete brain structure or neural network which qualifies as "the will" let alone a neural structure operating in a causal vacuum. The unavoidable conclusion is that a philosophy dedicated to uncaused choice is as unrealistic as a philosophy dedicated to a flat Earth. (Churchland 2006)

1.4.13   This is a rather unfair attack on many present-day naturalistically inclined libertarians since they do not seek to explain the existence of an Indifferent Will. Rather, they seek to explain the existence of processes of self-directed origination that reflect the influence of such factors as the agent's motivations, emotions, background, abilities, values, character, and the circumstances within which they currently find themselves. In the present work, in order to make the difference between these two views of originative free will

21

clear, the former type shall be referred to as "indifferently originative free will" and the latter as "self-originative free will". It is this latter kind of free will that is the concern of this book. And while the main focus of the book is on human free will, some of what will be said applies to the less complex, and also less free, form of free will enjoyed by higher animals.

1.4.14   These various points provide context for the view taken in this book of what free will is: namely, that it is the ability of a person (or more generally a psychological agent) to "make their own fate" in a way that requires that they be able to self-directively originate things in their world. Although instinctive, habitual, and other well-established forms of more or less automatic behaviour are, under independence indeterminism, seen to involve self-directed origination, these sorts of behaviour involve only type-determined origination – that is, they only involve types of origination that are *prefigured* relative to the agent and their circumstances at the time. And this means that many participants in the free-will debate, while accepting that such self-directed behaviour may satisfy the needs and wants of the agent, would not accept that what was going on entailed *non-necessitated* self-determination in any strong sense. Free will is often taken to mean that an agent "could have done otherwise", and it is generally *not* meant that the agent could have done otherwise in only minor ways – that is, in ways consistent with the agent's behaviour involving only type-determined self-directed originations. Rather, what is meant is that the agent could have done something distinctly different, such as choosing to do something quite different, or deciding to carry out a chosen task in a distinctly different way. This suggests (and it is assumed to be so in the view of free will adopted here) that the decision process involved in such cases – what shall be called the "free-will process" – is special in that it entails a strong form of non-necessitated self-determination. Under independence indeterminism this strong form of non-necessitated self-determination is assumed to involve a special kind of originative process – one involving what is referred to as "creative origination" – and is such that it does not follow a pre-established or prefigured type of course and is capable of producing novel (i.e. non-prefigured) outcomes relative to the agent and domain concerned.

1.4.15   Additionally, the assumption being adopted in the book is that free-will processing only arises and continues if two conditions hold. Firstly, that the psychological agent concerned is currently actively engaged (consciously, subconsciously, or unconsciously) in trying to resolve some internal conflict and/or indecision regarding some matter. And secondly, that the agent does not have available, or does not wish to use, automatic, pre-established or prefigured ways of achieving a resolution of the conflict and/or indecision. If, for any reason, either of these conditions ceases to hold then it is assumed that free-will processing – i.e. non-necessitated self-determination – concerning the matter in question will cease. However, if the cessation is not a result of the conflict being finally resolved then it is understood that at some point in the future the agent may resume free-will processing on the same matter. And it is accepted that in some cases repeated attempts to resolve conflict and/or indecision within the self may continue for an extended period, perhaps even for many years.

1.4.16   In assuming that free-will processing only occurs when an agent is actively trying to resolve conflict and/or indecision about some matter, it follows that it will not take place if the agent's mind-brain is occupied with something else (e.g. busy with some activity, being 'lost' in a movie or a book, or socialising with friends), or is in some condition (e.g. intoxicated, drugged) that prevents or blocks the conflict/indecision from arousing activity within the agent's mind-brain to resolve it. With human persons it seems that one of the reasons why they engage in such blocking behaviour is to escape from or avoid having to face up to conflicts within themselves that they cannot readily resolve.

1.4.17   The existence of creative origination is a key assumption of the approach to explaining free will adopted in this book. Independence indeterminism provides a naturalistic basis for the possible existence of creative origination but further evidence is needed to make a good case for it actually existing in the universe. Such evidence is provided in several places throughout the book (section 2.4 and Chapter 8, in particular), but the matter needs to be further discussed at this early stage.

1.5 Introducing Creative Origination

1.5.1 Consider first what non-creative origination is taken to be. Under independence indeterminism non-creative origination is assumed to be very widespread – the mundane example given of a raindrop falling on your head is a case in point. Any origination (e.g. an independence interaction, or a quantum indeterministic event) which is of a type that is prefigured or immanent within a domain is taken to be a non-creative origination relative to that domain, and the term type-determined has been introduced to refer to such originations. An independence interaction is taken to be of a prefigured type when it occurs between types of things that commonly exist within the domain concerned and when it is a result of these types of things behaving according to their well-established natures and ways of interacting given the conditions that obtain at the time. For instance, under independence indeterminism, chemical reactions may be understood to involve various types of independence interactions taking place among the types of participants involved (e.g. the types of atoms, molecules, and ions), with the types of interaction that arise being an almost invariable consequence of the particular physical circumstances (of, for example, temperature, pressure, and the relative concentrations of the reactants and products) that exist. It is because the independence interactions involved and the products produced are of prefigured types that what is going on is *not* considered to involve *creatively* originative processes. Nevertheless, because, under independence indeterminism, chemical reactions are understood to be processes involving innumerable interactions between specific things that are changing (e.g. thermally vibrating and moving around) largely independently of one another prior to their interaction, it is accepted that they involve independence interactions and hence are taken to be originative processes, albeit type-determined originative processes.

1.5.2 Consider creative origination. Under independence indeterminism and according to present knowledge, this form of origination seems to be almost entirely confined to the living and human realms (however the relatively recent appearance of artificial intelligence (AI) may lead to the emergence of a third realm in which creative origination exists). In these realms many processes run in a non-creatively originative way, as for example do most biological processes and much animal and human behaviour. Nevertheless, it seems that creative origination does play a key role in these realms. For instance, under independence indeterminism, evolution by natural selection is taken to be a creatively originative process because the specific species that it gives rise to are considered not to be prefigured. Also, almost all learning is understood to be a creatively originative process because what is learnt is (usually) not prefigured relative to the learner (although it may be prefigured from a more general point of view).

1.5.3 In the human realm, creative origination has become very highly developed and particularly so with the advent of human civilisation, culture, and technology – all of which are developments that seem to have depended upon creative origination for their emergence, as well as themselves being sources of continuing creative origination. Apart from learning (but intimately connected and intertwined with it) is another general kind of creative origination – "inventiveness" – that plays a major part in human life. Inventiveness takes various forms, but to illustrate it consider just one form: problem-solving. The human capacity for problem-solving (both individual and collective) is very great compared to animals (and any AI systems that at present exist). The key feature that makes problem-solving a *creatively* originative process (rather than solely a type-determined one) is that at its commencement its course, and whether the problem-solver achieves a solution or resolution of the problem, is not prefigured. To take a simple example: a person may come across a crossword clue that they cannot readily solve, but by continuing to work on it, and perhaps by leaving it alone for a while or sleeping on it, they may eventually be able to get the solution. There may well be many things in the person's mind-brain and environment that may help them achieve a solution, but for creative origination to occur there must not exist any pre-established or prefigured means by which they may obtain a solution (or if there is, they must have decided to avoid making any use of it). At present, how inventiveness works is poorly understood. In future a better general understanding of how this and other forms of creative origination take place may be obtained, but however complete knowledge and understanding of the overall processes involved may become, the nature of creatively originative processes as they are defined here means that such knowledge will never enable reliable predictions to be made of the specific ways of running and the specific outcomes that particular instances of creatively originative processing produce. This means, for example, that however complete knowledge and understanding of the process of biological evolution may become this will never allow reliable prediction of the specific future species that it will give rise to. And it means also that no matter how well processes of human creative origination may come to be understood this understanding will never allow reliable prediction of the specific products of human creativity: for instance, the future specific works of literature and the arts, the future specific businesses that will be formed, and the future specific scientific and other theories that will emerge.

1.5.4 Human free-will processing typically involves creatively originative activity in four areas. Firstly, a person may carry out creative activity in order to produce (or modify) the alternatives that figure in the conflict/indecision situation they are confronting. Secondly, they may work to creatively originate, explore, elaborate, or modify the reasons (emotional, motivational, rational, etc.) they have for and against the various alternatives. Thirdly, the various parts of their self may engage in creatively originative conflictual, competitive, cooperative interactions with these interactions often being centred on the alternatives and reasons that are currently in play. And fourthly, a person's self and its various parts may undergo creatively originative change in such a way that the conflict is removed or becomes resolvable. Collectively, these four interacting areas of creatively originative activity and change may be seen as constituting the "ARCS" of human free-will processing, with the capital letters of the acronym standing for Alternatives, Reasons, Conflict, and Self-change respectively.

1.5.5 With difficult and prolonged cases of human free-will processing significant creative origination in all these four areas may take place. For example, in trying to decide whether of not to make a major career change a person may be involved in many episodes of internal conflict and interaction among the various parts of their self and this may involve creative change in all of these four areas. For instance, under the Alternatives area of their creative free-will processing activity, a person will likely explore and research the various alternatives that they consider as possibilities, and in so doing, and in response to other changes taking place within them and around them, they may uncover new alternatives, and perhaps also find themselves rejecting some they previously considered as possibilities. As the person considers and deliberates about alternatives, and in other ways, they may come to create a better understanding of what factors are important in a new career and in making such a big change to their life, and this activity will constitute the Reasons part of their creative free-will processing. Throughout such free-will processing there is likely to be continuing conflictual, competitive, cooperative and other interaction among the various parts of the person's self. For example, conflicting motivations may arise – such as the need to provide for the family, and the need for sufficient income to maintain one's status and desired standard of living conflicting with the need for a more fulfilling life. And together with these motivational conflicts there are likely to be a mix of emotions such as being elated by what the future may be able to offer on the one hand, and being fearful about not being able to cope with all the uncertainty and disruption on the other hand. And together with these sources of conflict the executive self may raise rational objections to certain courses of action. This Conflict within the self, and the non-prefigured way in which it proceeds, will have continuing influence on the other sorts of creative changes occurring within the individual. Finally, in addition to the above three forms of creative free-will processing it may be the case that the person finds that creatively originated changes are taking place within their self. For example, it may be that the strength of some of their motivations change over the period of time they struggle with their conflict and indecision, and that this change proceeds in a non-prefigured way. For example, they may find that as time goes by they have downgraded the value they put on their financial status and have upgraded the importance of having a fulfilling job. This then is creatively originative change involving the person's Self. Although deep, difficult, and usually prolonged free-will processing does occur most free-will processing involves only weak creative origination with a resolution of the conflict or indecision often being fairly rapidly achieved. Nevertheless, providing the originative process by which the conflict/indecision was resolved was not wholly type-determined then it is still taken to be a free-will process. For example, not much creative origination usually takes place when a person is deciding what menu items to have when they are out for a meal, but if they are not succumbing to pure habit and have some genuine conflict or in-decision over what to choose then creative origination is seen to play some part in the person making their choice.

1.5.6 Creatively originative processes are often influenced by randomly occurring or non-directed originations. According to the mainstream view of science today, de novo origination is very largely confined to the atomic and sub-atomic levels and is a consequence of quantum indeterministic events such as the disintegration of an atomic nucleus. But under independence indeterminism, de novo ori-ginations are assumed to be very common at all levels of existence because independence interactions are assumed to be very common at all levels. This means, for instance, that chance independence inter-actions may result in the random association of ideas within the mind-brain of psychological agents – ideas which may influence pro-cesses of creative origination, such as problem-solving. However, if free-will processes were creatively originative solely because of such chance events then only a weak claim could be made that it was the mind-brain that was the principle source of the creative origination involved. Fortunately, one of the great strengths of independence in-determinism is that under this metaphysics, humans (and more gener-ally psychological agents) may be understood to operate in a creat-ively originative way that not only makes use of chance originations but also of originations resulting from the directive influences and directive activities of the various parts of the agent's mind-brain and self – including, for example, such directed *creative* activity as is in-volved in searching for and researching alternatives.

1.5.7 Another point that needs to be addressed in this brief in-troduction to creative origination is why conflictual, competitive, co-operative interaction is taken to be a creatively originative process. This sort of activity is common in the living and human realms and quite often the *types* of outcome that it may produce are prefigured. For example, with predator/prey interactions the types of outcome that may arise are usually prefigured – for instance, that the predator catches its prey, or the prey escapes. However, as long as the overall course (rather than merely the detailed course) of the interaction on any particular occasion does not consist of a prefigured sequence of well-established types of move and counter-move as, for example, may be the case with early moves in a game of chess, or with animals in a mating ritual, then what is going on may be taken to be a creatively originative process. And this is so even if, in the type of situation considered, there are fairly well-established probabilities attached to the possible types of outcome.

1.5.8   It might be thought that in assuming that creatively originative processes exist under independence indeterminism inadequate justification has been given for why the course such processes follow, and the outcomes they produce, are not prefigured. After all, macroscopic-scale things don't just pop into existence out of nothing but always seem to be the result of interaction among pre-existing things. And if this is the case, and considering a process to be made up of a succession of interactions among pre-existing things, then it would seem to be true that the course and outcome of all such macroscopic processes should be prefigured. This argument not only relies on a tacit assumption (that independence indeterminism does not accept) that a process may legitimately be thought of as a succession of well-defined states, but it also assumes that what exists in a creative domain are well-defined types of things with well-defined ways of interacting. However, in creative domains this is not always true. For instance, many of the *specific* thoughts, perceptions, memories, imaginings, feelings, motivations, etc. that enter into independence interaction within the mind-brain of a person engaged in a *particular* episode of free-will processing are likely to have features that effectively make them unique types of things with respect to how they may interact and influence one another within the specific process concerned. For instance, think of all the unique factors associated with the specific alternatives, reasons, and conflicts that may be involved in a person's free-will processing as they struggle to decide whether or not to take up a particular job-offer.

1.6   The Human Self

1.6.1   In everyday life the concept of the human self is rarely subjected to analysis. However, because of its importance in the free-will debate – and in particular because of the approach that is being adopted in this book – it is something that should be discussed. Unfortunately, after millennia of theorising about "the self" there is little agreement about just what it is. A fundamental assumption made in the present work is that the human self is something that only fully develops as part of an individual human being's socialisation, and in recognition of this assumption the term "human person" (or "human", or "person"), rather than "human being", is generally used. According to this view it is human persons that are significantly different from animals, not human beings.

1.6.2   A further fundamental assumption that is made – one widely but not universally held – is that the self is not a single unitary entity but rather a collective, or loose coalition of somewhat independently operating but nevertheless frequently interacting subsystems and sub-selves. There are several theories of the self based on this view, but here it will suffice to mention just two. In the classical tradition, Plato saw the Soul (roughly equivalent to the self as the term is being used in this book) as being composed of three parts: Reason, Spirit, and Appetite. He saw these as relatively independent sources of influence on the doings of a person with the proper condition of the Soul consisting of Reason being in control of Spirit and Appetite – although he recognized that people did not always achieve rational control over these other aspects of their Soul. An example from a much later period is Freud's tripartite functional division of the psyche (or self) into the id, ego, and super-ego. According to this view the id is understood to be a wholly unconscious part of the psyche – 'a chaos, a cauldron full of seething excitations [...] it has no organization, produces no collective will, but only a striving to bring about the satisfaction of the instinctual needs [...]' (Freud 1933). The ego, which among other things, draws strongly upon the cognitive and executive functions of a person, is seen as the most organized and rational part of the psyche, with much of its activity involving consciousness. The super-ego harbours the standards, values, ideals, and conscience of a person, with much of its content being derived from parental and social sources and influences. The super-ego is more organized than the id, to which it stands in opposition. The ego may be understood as striving to successfully serve (and control) the demands of the id and the super-ego while at the same time taking into account the realities of the external world and the person's actual powers and resources. The ego of a mature person is usually (but not always) able to override the demands of the id and the super-ego.

1.6.3   In the present work a view of the human self is adopted that follows roughly the same pattern as the above two accounts. Again, a tripartite division is adopted, namely into "the motivational self" (see section 10.5 for more discussion), "the emotional self" (see section 10.6), and "the executive self" (see section 10.7). Unlike in Freud's account, the motivational self is taken to be not only harbouring primitive biological drives, instincts, and urges but also many other motivations that have been acquired by a person through the course of their life. These acquired motivations include some from their socialisation, some from the various groups they have belonged to (and those they currently belong to), some from emotionally charged and other experiences they have had, and some they have adopted through their own creative processes of thought and free-will processing. It is also assumed that the motivational self includes many more or less specific ends and purposes constructed or acquired by a person's executive self. A person's constructed or acquired motivations are taken to include such things as their values and standards; the duties and obligations they have accepted; their aversions and inclinations; and their life-hopes, projects, goals, and intentions. The emotional self is taken to be the source of many of the emotions (or affective states) that humans experience and it is understood that these may directly influence the person's behaviour. It is also accepted that the emotional self may have an indirect influence on behaviour through installing within a person's motivational self aversions to some types of things and attractions to others. The executive self is taken to be similar to Plato's Reason and Freud's ego and is understood as being, most of the time, in charge of a person's purposive activity.

1.6.4   It is assumed that a person's executive self has a major influence on how a person shapes their life. It is assumed that most people live their life within their own unique 'world' – a world that shall be referred to as their "lifestructure" (see section 10.4). It is accepted, because the evidence supports this, that much of a person's executive activity is concerned with attending to, maintaining, extending, modifying, abandoning, and creating aspects of their lifestructure. And, again because the evidence seems to support this, the view is taken that many of the conflicts and states of indecision (and therefore occasions for free-will processing) that a human person experiences are related to their attempts to manage and shape their life-structure in order to satisfy their motivations in an emotionally acceptable way. But, as alluded to earlier (1.4.16), as well as accepting that human persons make positive efforts to improve their life – improve it relative to their own criteria of what they think counts as success – it is also accepted that people engage in various activities to block or blank out negative self-evaluations and escape from, or relieve themselves from, conflicts and negative emotions. For example, people indulge in alcohol, drugs, and comfort eating; they engage in a great range of escapist activities; and some people try to keep themselves so fully occupied that they don't have the time or energy to acknowledge and consider the perceived failures and dissatisfactions of their life. However, as well as being drawn to blocking and blanking activities, it seems people often search for and engage in pursuits (e.g. projects, hobbies, sports, community work) in order to have parts of their lifestructure that can provide satisfactions that they cannot find in other parts – for example, in their job or in their home life. Finally, it is assumed that human persons engage in wide-ranging self-evaluation – more strongly and frequently at some times, and less strongly and frequently at other times in their lives.

1.6.5 It is apparent from the above that a rather eclectic and idiosyncratic view of the self is being adopted in the present work. It has been constructed to try to make sense of the unique nature of human free will and of many of the peculiarities of human life – peculiarities that make the way humans live their lives, and many of their preoccupations, very different from those of any animal.

1.7   Outline of the Book

1.7.1 Chapter 2 further develops the notion of independence indeterminism – the central novel idea of the book, and one which is returned to and developed in various ways in later chapters.

1.7.2 Chapter 3 first looks in more detail at determinism and it is then argued that the law of cause and effect does not provide a sound basis for claiming that determinism rules in the universe. This leads into a discussion of the contemporary way philosophers think about determinism. The chapter ends by considering how well inde-

pendence indeterminism competes with determinism as a fundamental metaphysical thesis.

1.7.3   Chapter 4 returns again to independence indeterminism
and considers how it relates to science and current mainstream scientific thinking. In Chapter 5 the other main theme of the book is
taken up with a discussion of some of the important ideas about free
will that have emerged in the last fifty years or so.

1.7.4   The next four chapters are mainly devoted to further discussion of independence indeterminism, starting (in Chapter 6) with
a more detailed look at the assumption of independence of change.
Chapter 7 goes into more detail about directed origination – discussing both conceptual and implementation issues. Chapter 8 focuses
further on creative origination. Chapter 9 broadens the discussion
and considers the wider significance of independence indeterminism,
including how it provides a new perspective on the mind-body problem, how it accounts for the existence of non-reducible emergence,
and why it supports naturalism as a metaphysical position but rejects
physicalism.

1.7.5   Chapter 10 attempts to identify the main factors involved
in human free will. Finally (in Chapter 11), in the light of the preceding chapters and the approach to explaining free will developed in the
book, the question "How free are We?" is considered from various
perspectives.

2 Independence Indeterminism

2.1 Independence of Change

2.1.1   As was stated right at the beginning of this book, the single primary assumption of independence indeterminism is that **true independence of change is extremely common in our universe**. Put slightly differently this assumption asserts that "stretches of change" that to some extent run, or proceed, truly independently of one another are extremely common. *True* independence of running among stretches of change means how any one of them runs is not tied or related in any definite way to how any of the others run. This key point deserves further discussion.

2.1.2   To keep things simple only two stretches of change will usually be considered. This does not affect the generality of the conclusions reached. Consider the following example. One stretch of change is that involved in me typing this sentence, and the other is that involved in what our cat, Purdy, is doing while I do this. Both of these are complex stretches of change that, at least theoretically, could be decomposed into a network of shorter stretches of change. As mainstream physicists currently understand the world, this decomposition does not end in a succession of instantaneously existing and unchanging states of the universe, or even in a succession of instantaneous states of a set of irreducible fundamental entities. Rather, the mainstream view sees what is going on as a continuous flux of interaction and change among elementary particles and fields. According to this view, even things that appear to our senses not to be changing – rocks, say – are only unchanging at an overall level and not deep down at the molecular, atomic, and sub-atomic levels. At the top level of the two stretches of change there are the movements of me and the cat. At the next level down, there is the activity of our limbs and organs; and down further, the activity of the cells of which these are composed. Still further down, there is the activity of the molecules and atoms that constitute the cells. And going down still further mainstream physicists believe that the nucleus of each atom consists of continual interaction among the protons and neutrons that constitute it. Further down still, theories and experiments lead physicists to believe that the existence of each proton and neutron is realised by continual interaction among elementary particles known as quarks – an interaction that is mediated by other elementary particles known as gluons.

2.1.3 Why should it be necessary to *assume* that some true independence of change exists between my typing activity and the activity of our cat? Surely this is obviously the case? After all, don't people live their lives believing without question that some independence exists between the way most stretches of change run? If they didn't believe this how on earth could they go about their daily business without questioning whether or not the world and all its other goings-on would allow them to do what they wanted to do? If there really was no independence then both I and Purdy would be living our lives in complete lockstep: we would each be playing out wholly necessary and unalterable roles in the fully pre-determined and completely definite history of the universe. And this would be true of the networks of subsidiary activity that are believed to contribute to the realisation of these two high-level stretches of change. This alternative picture – of everything that happens occurring in fixed, definite, and fully predetermined lockstep – is the picture "absolute determinism" paints of the universe. Note: the term absolute determinism is introduced to denote the operation of determinism throughout all and every part and level of existence.

2.1.4 No matter how obvious true independence of change may seem to be there are no empirical or logical means for determining whether or not such true independence actually exists. But equally, there are no empirical or logical means for determining whether absolute determinism is true or false. Both must therefore be regarded as wholly metaphysical beliefs (see 1.2.1). The reason why there are no empirical means for determining whether two or more stretches of change are running truly independently is because they involve one-off happenings that cannot be re-run to see if how they run may vary with respect to one another. The best that can be done is to see whether the *types* of change each represents may vary with respect to one another. For instance, to continue with the example, a reasonably large set of pairs of video recordings could be gathered, with each pair consisting of a recording of me typing a sentence, and a recording of what our cat Purdy was doing at the same time. This set of

35

pairs could then be examined to see if complete correlation existed between my activity and Purdy's activity. For example, it might be found that for every different word I typed Purdy had a specific kind of movement. But even without actually performing such an investigation our knowledge of typing and cats tells us that we would not find such complete correlation. Nor, indeed, would even very complex relations be found that established the existence of full correlation. All the evidence is that there is no complete correlation between the typing of sentences and the activity of cats, which of course indicates that some independence exists between these *types* of change. However, this does not prove that when I type a *particular* sentence, and Purdy carries out some *particular* activity that these two uniquely dated and located stretches of change run independently of one another. It does not prove this because, in considering the history of the universe as a whole, it may be – as indeed absolute determinists argue – that it was determined at the creation of the universe (or for eternity if the universe has no beginning) that these two specific stretches of change would arise together and run in complete lockstep. And if this is in fact the case then the stretches of change do not run *truly* independently even if they appear to do so.

2.1.5   Given that there are no empirical means by which to definitely establish whether two or more specific stretches of change are, to some extent, running truly independently of one another, it is nevertheless very commonly assumed that true independence of change does exists. And generally this is assumed to be the case when it is believed that three conditions are met:

> (i) that stretches of change of the types concerned are not completely causally linked;
>
> (ii) that no third party is fully determining how such types of stretches of change jointly run; and
>
> (iii) that such types of change do not run in a perfectly synchronised way.

2.1.6   To clarify, consider the application of these three conditions to a specific example – one involving what seems to be an independence interaction, and is similar to the raindrop-landing-on-your-head example introduced in 1.1.6. The example concerns a particular leaf floating down a particular stream at a particular time and a particular raindrop falling through the air nearby which later collides with the leaf. Even if they have never consciously observed such an occurrence, it is easy for most people to imagine what is involved. Accepting that most people would not usually consciously carry out any of the following reasoning it is worth trying to spell out why they would tacitly accept that the above three conditions are met in the case being considered. As far as the first condition is concerned, most people's past experience tells them that the changes that leaves experience in such situations – for example, flowing more or less steadily downstream, swirling around for a moment in an eddy, or being caught in a branch that has fallen into the stream – do not seem to be reflected in correlated changes occurring to falling raindrops (whether they are nearby or not) and this therefore leads them to think no significant causal linkages exist. Furthermore, science knows of no causal linkage between these types of stretches of change other than an extremely weak and negligible gravitational attraction. As regards the second condition, people's knowledge and experience of the world generally leads them to believe that there is no third party that is fully determining the way these two types of stretches of change run. (Some religious people think otherwise since they see God as fully determining everything that happens.) Nevertheless, most people do accept that in many situations there are third party influences at work that do affect the running of the various stretches of change involved. For instance, it is generally accepted that both gravity and the wind affect the falling of raindrops and the movement of leaves down streams. However, there seems to be little evidence that these third-party influences produce *full* correlation between the two motions. Regarding the third condition, there is no evidence that leaves floating down streams and raindrops falling through the air change in a perfectly synchronised manner (even though for short periods they may roughly do so). This means that people generally believe the third condition is upheld as well. Because these three conditions are, usually tacitly, understood to be satisfied most people would accept that the raindrop and the leaf were, prior to their collision, changing truly independently of one another.

2.1.7   Given what has just been said it appears there are good grounds for thinking that the raindrop striking the leaf was an independence interaction and therefore an originated event. Nevertheless, it is worth spelling out in some detail how his conclusion may be reached. According to the above reasoning, there is sufficient evidence to believe that the raindrop and the leaf, prior to their collision, were not in causal interaction and that there was no third party determining how each was changing. It cannot be known for sure whether or not these two stretches of change were running in hidden lockstep, but there is no evidence for this. Hence, since it appears the three conditions given above have been met, it is reasonable to assume that the raindrop and the leaf were undergoing change *truly* independently of one another prior to their collision. This means that no determinate relationship existed that fully tied together, linked, governed, or described how these stretches of change were running relative to one another. Which in turn means that their future interaction was indeterminate since how a raindrop and a leaf are changing relative to one another affects whether or not they will interact.

2.1.8   At this point it is helpful to introduce an idea and terminology that shall be used throughout the book. Rather than talking of how one stretch of change runs relative to another it is often more accurate to use the general concept of "joint-change". Joint-change is change composed of several relatively separate changes taking place together but considered as a single kind of change distinct from the component changes of which it is constituted. For example, a person striding briskly along manifests joint-change composed of the relatively separate movements of their arms and hands, their legs and feet, and their torso and head – with perhaps their hair waving about in response to these movements (and perhaps also the wind). Although these relatively separate changes may be apparent as such to an observer, what is also apparent is the joint-change they produce – namely, the change representing a person striding briskly along. Of course, with a person striding along most of the component changes of the joint-change are not running wholly and truly independently of one another – for instance, the person's legs and arms generally move in a more or less coordinated way; and the movements of their torso and their head are mainly related to the motion of their legs and arms. Nevertheless, at least at a detailed level, there is a good deal of independence of movement among these various parts of the person's body. There are many instances of joint-change of this sort that we recognise by its having an identifiable holistic character. For example, the joint-change composed of the sounds produced by the separate instruments and voices of an orchestra or band is perceived by us as a coherent whole. However not all joint-change is composed of related or connected changes. For instance, recall the example in 1.1.3 of three (assumed to be) truly independently running changes – namely, gusts of wind around my house, what an earthworm was doing under the lawn at the same time, and what an engine in a car passing by in the road was doing. We can just about imagine (but not actually directly perceive) the joint-change composed of these three independently running changes, and it seems reasonable to assume that this particular joint-change did actually exist – at least in some sense of exist. But although this may be so, this sort of joint-change doesn't seem to have any role or presence in existence. Rather its presence seems to be entirely passive. That is, it doesn't seem to influence or affect anything, or contribute to a system's behaviour, and so it seems to be something of a non-entity, or a "no-thing", or what shall be referred to as a "passive existent". And for the same reasons, the joint-change composed of a raindrop falling and a leaf moving down a stream also seems to be a passive existent. What adds to the ephemeral and almost non-real nature of such joint-change is that, in being composed of truly independently running changes, such joint-change runs indeterminately, and to acknowledge this it shall be referred to as "indeterminately changing joint-change".

2.1.9 Some interactions that appear to be independence interactions turn out, upon closer examination, not to be. For example, consider two billiard balls moving on an apparent collision course on a billiard table. It might be thought that their motions are independent because there is no significant causal interaction between them, and no third party is governing their ongoing joint motion. However as long as each ball is moving in a time-determinate manner (i.e. as a determinate function of time – see 3.3.3) in all ways relevant to whether or not they interact, then in these respects the two balls will be moving in synchrony and the third condition for believing independence of change exists – i.e. non-synchronicity of change – will not be met. Hence, such interactions do not qualify as independence interactions.

2.1.10 However, although all factors that affect whether two or more things interact may be varying in a time-determinate way, if other factors involving the things are varying independently then this may introduce indeterminacy in how change in the things develops *after* interaction actually occurs. To continue with the example, the thermal motion of the molecules in the two billiard balls will be changing independently (according to the above criteria and line with what mainstream physicists believe) and although this will not (significantly) affect the time-determinacy and therefore the synchrony of the translational motion of the balls it might, in some ways, influence the exact course of change that occurs within the balls during and immediately after their actual collision and make the details of what follows at the microscopic level more or less indeterminate. What is being highlighted here is a general point: determinacy of the occurrence of an interaction does not necessarily mean determinacy in what follows. Nevertheless, as already noted (see 1.1.7), many independence interactions, once they occur, often do produce change that follows a fairly deterministic course. For example, the way billiard balls respond to a collision at the macroscopic level is (very largely) deterministic – it is only at the microscopic level that the response may be somewhat indeterministic.

2.1.11   Stretches of change that run in a time-determinate relationship to one another are usually open to independence interactions occurring that can disrupt their synchrony of change. So, to go further with the billiard ball example, the two balls may be heading for a predictable collision but while they are moving towards one another a light bulb above the billiard table may shatter (apparently independently of what the balls are doing) and produce debris that participates in independence interactions with the balls so destroying the time-determinacy and synchrony of their change. This illustrates a general principle: namely that no guarantee exists that disruptive independence interactions will not occur during time-determinate change.

2.2   Undirected Independence Interactions

2.2.1   The vast majority of independence interactions are undirected and so may be taken to be a matter of chance. The independence interaction considered earlier of a particular raindrop colliding with a particular leaf floating down a particular stream on a particular occasion is taken to be an undirected, or chance, independence interaction. However, the landing of raindrops on leaves is an entirely expected *type* of independence interaction in the circumstances concerned. That is, under independence indeterminism, it is not regarded as a matter of chance that in a rainstorm taking place over a stream with leaves floating down it that some raindrops will fall on some of the floating leaves. Indeed, some types of independence interaction are so common within specific kinds of domain that they are almost certain to happen, and to indicate that this is so the term "type-determined independence interactions" will be used. For instance, the interaction of a particular photon of light from the sun with a particular chlorophyll molecules in a particular leaf of a particular plant will, according to independence indeterminism, be an originated event. But such *types* of event are certain to occur in domains where sunlight is falling on the leaves of plants so they are taken to be type-determined independence interactions, and since they are originated events they are type-determined originations (see 1.2.10).

2.2.2 According to independence indeterminism, undirected independence interactions are occurring all the time, with the vast majority – but certainly not all of them – having little significance. For example, electromagnetic radiation of all forms (e.g. radio waves, microwaves, infra-red light, visible light, ultra violet light, x-rays, and gamma rays) are constantly entering into (mostly) chance independence interactions with matter. The consequences of these chance independence interactions vary greatly. Most entail only local effects but some may produce effects that have wider significance as, for instance, do the photons of visible light that fall upon the retina of a person's eye and contribute to their visual perception of the world around them. A great many chance independence interactions are between material objects. For instance, air molecules are in constant independence interaction not only with one another but with atoms and molecules belonging to objects of all sorts. And when people walk about they are, at the molecular-level, entering into chance independence interactions with the surfaces upon which they tread – and of course the same is true of the molecular-level independence interactions between the feet of animals and the ground upon which they move, and the tyres of vehicles and the road or surface they travel over. However this does not mean that people, animals, and vehicles move around in an undirected way – only that the particular molecular-level interactions taking place are chance independence interactions. Turning again to chemistry, under independence indeterminism, this may be understood to be the field of science concerned with what molecular formations and transformations are likely to occur when certain types of atoms and molecules interact under certain types of conditions. Many chemical couplings and de-couplings are initiated by independence interactions between atoms, molecules, and ions and therefore must (under independence indeterminism) be considered to be originations. However, because these interactions arise in a statistically regular way, chemists are often able to establish statistically valid deterministic laws to describe chemical behaviour. Many biological chemical processes – and some human produced ones – are carefully orchestrated and regulated to ensure that certain types of independence interaction, and therefore certain types of chemical couplings and de-couplings, occur in specific sequences. But this control and regulation does not operate at the level of individual independence interactions, which remain chance originations.

2.2.3 Human life is full of undirected, or chance, independence interactions. Many of these – as, for example, with photons of light interacting with cells in our retinas, molecules of air interacting with our ear drums, and aromatic chemicals interacting with certain tissues in our noses – provide the raw input for our perception of the world. For example, as we walk through a busy shopping mall we perceive, with the aid of our various senses, the presence of all sorts of different things and happenings within the mall. Most of these perceptions are fleeting and do not trigger action or conscious thought, but some perceptions do lead to significant consequences, such as those involved in facilitating our safe (and polite) movement through the mall, those that allow us to identify shops and items of interest to us, and those that help us recognise friends and acquaintances. However, although we may be moving more or less purposively through the mall, much of what we perceive from moment to moment will largely be a matter of chance independence interactions. For example, what particular people we happen to pass is largely a consequence of a great number of chance independence interactions: chance interactions that affected precisely when each of these people (and we ourselves) set out for the mall, chance interactions that occurred on our journeys to it, and chance interactions that influenced how each of us worked our ways through the mall so that we happened to pass one another just when, where, and how we did.

2.2.4 Although the vast majority of chance independence interactions that humans experience have no long-term significance, some do. Indeed, the lives of many people have been affected in major ways by chance independence interactions. For example, some people have met their partner largely as a consequence of a chance independence interaction, or a series of such interactions. And some chance independence interactions – such as being struck by lightning, or being involved in a bad accident – may have very significant consequences. An example of a rather extraordinary case of a chance independence interaction of this sort is described by Mark Twain in his book *Life on the Mississippi*. He writes about a resident's report of life in Vicksburg during its siege and bombardment in the American Civil War. This is what the resident told Twain:

> 'Coming out of church, one morning, we had an accident – the only one that happened around me on a Sunday. I was just having a hearty handshake with a friend I hadn't seen for a while, and saying "Drop into our cave tonight after bombardment [the residents had dug caves to protect themselves]; we've got hold of a pint of prime wh– ." Whisky, I was going to say, you know, but a shell interrupted. A chunk of it cut the man's arm off, and left it dangling in my hand (Twain, 1883).

In human history also, quite extraordinary sequences of chance independence interactions have sometimes had considerable significance – one of the most famous cases being the series of chance events that led to the assassination of Archduke Franz Ferdinand, an event that some historians suggest triggered a series of other events that led to the start of the First World War.

2.3 Directed Origination

2.3.1 Although the vast majority of independence interactions are a matter of chance not all of them are. For example, when a dog catches a rabbit this event is an independence interaction since prior to the catch the dog and the rabbit are moving and operating partly independently of one another (at least according to the criteria of in-

43

dependence of change outlined above – see 2.1.5), but it is generally not thought that the catch is a chance interaction. Similarly, when a tennis player's racquet makes contact with the ball this is rarely thought of as a chance independence interaction. Here are a few more examples. When a bird lands on the branch of a tree it does not do so by chance. When an animal treks to a waterhole to quench its thirst its arrival is not a matter of chance. And when an automobile is assembled the parts that constitute it do not come together by chance.

2.3.2   In the cases just mentioned the non-chance independence interactions are produced by the directive activity of a directive system (see 1.1.9). Very often the non-chance independence interactions involved in such activity are of a familiar type relative to the domain concerned and to this extent they are type-determined independence interactions. And in being type-determined it is easy to think that the associated directive activity must run in a type-deterministic way. This does frequently occur but it is not necessarily the case as creative origination may be used by some directive systems.

2.3.3   To develop the way the production of non-chance independence interactions, directed origination, directive activity, and related concepts are understood according to independence indeterminism it is worthwhile further discussing the examples just mentioned. When a dog catches a rabbit after chasing it, it is generally assumed that during the chase both the dog and the rabbit had their own particular goal: for the dog, the capture of the rabbit, and for the rabbit avoidance of such capture. In other words, it is usually believed that the dog was trying to bring about a certain type of independence interaction, and the rabbit was trying to prevent such a type of independence interaction occurring. Each animal may be understood to be operating as a particular type of directive system during the chase – the dog as a prey-chasing directive system, and the rabbit as a predator-escaping directive system. Of course, dogs and rabbits, like all purposive higher animals, are capable of many different forms of directive activity, and are able to choose among these. Whether higher animals make such choices by exercising their free will – that is, by not only doing so voluntarily but also in a non-necessitated self-determined way – is an open question, but it is assumed in the present work that in some situations some animals may resolve internal con-

44

flict and indecision in a weakly creative way involving a struggle between competing or conflicting motivations as, for example, may occur when an animal is torn between continuing to pursue some goal or abandoning its pursuit.

2.3.4 A defining feature of a directive system is that the actions produced by it tend to be so matched to the varied and varying conditions of the situation within which the actions take place that a particular type of directed outcome tends to be produced. The directed outcomes that directive system work to produce are usually referred to as "objectives" or "goals", however in the present work use of the term goal shall be restricted to refer to the directed outcomes that purposive agents such as higher animals and humans seek to bring about. According to independence indeterminism, a directed outcome will be an originated event if the varied and varying conditions arise and change independently of the directive system's actions. This is assumed to be so in the dog/rabbit chase, which means the capture of the rabbit by the dog is an originated event. However, because this outcome was not solely a matter of chance but a consequence of directive activity it was a *directed* origination. Although the rabbit failed to achieve its goal – avoidance of capture – this does not mean no evidence exists for believing it was carrying out goal-directed activity. However, the evidence that does exist only makes sense when related to knowledge of what goal-directed activity in a such a kind of chase generally looks like. Whether all directive activity has objective features that distinguish it from other forms of activity is not clear. However, some interesting work (Weir and Wale, 2011) suggests that at least in some cases there are such objective features.

2.3.5 The second example is similar to the situation just discussed in that there are two opposing purposive agents (tennis players) with incompatible goals: each wants to win, but both can't. The independence interaction consisting of a tennis player's racquet striking a tennis ball is not generally considered to be a chance event because it is recognised that the motion of the racquet has usually been guided by the directive activity of the player concerned – activity controlled by the player in an effort to strike the ball in such a manner that it is likely to be sent to the other side of the court so that it is not "out", and that if it is "in" that it lands in such a way that the opposing player is unable to make a valid return of play, or is only able to make a weak return. To achieve this objective, it is necessary for the player to carry out activity (e.g. involving coordinated movements such as running, twisting their body, moving their arm and wrist) that takes account of their current position, the independent motion of the ball, and the objective they have in mind. Again, this is a case of directed origination.

2.3.6   When a bird lands on a branch it is producing a directed independence interaction, usually one brought about while the bird is carrying out some other larger-scale directive activity – for example, searching for food, or surveying and checking its territory, or seeking material to build a nest. It is a directed outcome because the bird must appropriately adjust its flight and orientation to the particular independently arising and changing circumstances it is operating under – circumstances that include its current motion, the (possibly slightly changing) position of the branch on which it is aiming to land, the position of branches and foliage that may block its passage to its target landing site, and the wind conditions.

2.3.7   With the fourth example knowledge is being used by an animal to guide its actions so that it may get to a location where it believes it should be able to enter into directive activity (drinking) to satisfy a more or less pressing need (for water) that the animal believes it cannot adequately satisfy in its present location. Again, this is an example of goal-directed behaviour. Typically, the animal uses its (usually learned) knowledge of where the waterhole is relative to its present location, and its knowledge of what the terrain is like between where it currently is and the waterhole, to set a rough course to follow. However, the animal cannot expect to achieve its objective by following its planned course blindly: it must be able to deal appropriately with unexpected circumstances – such as when encountering a predator, or when finding its route blocked in some way. Again, the activity of the animal is such that it is appropriately adjusted to independently arising and changing circumstances in such a way that its directed outcome, or goal in this case, tends to be achieved. And because this is so its behaviour is goal-directed.

2.3.8   The final example concerns the directed independence interactions involved in the assembly of an automobile. Almost all of these are type-determined independence interactions since they are the product either of machine-based directive systems operating according to pre-set rules, or the result of human operators behaving in more or less routine ways. That is, in both cases, the independence interactions are of a prefigured type in the domain concerned. However, although some operations involved in the assembly process may be carried out by blindly executing a sequence of actions most require actions that must be matched to the particular circumstances that obtain so that slight variations (e.g. in the position or orientation of things) may be taken into account to ensure that the desired assembly sub-objective is met. This means that automobile assembly must, under independence indeterminism, be viewed as a process involving directed origination. If a human person is the directive system doing the assembly then they will be operating in a purposive manner because they have awareness of what they are doing and what they are trying to achieve, and are capable of deciding to stop what they are currently doing, or of deciding to vary their activity. If a fully automated system is doing the assembly it is debatable whether it is operating purposively because purposiveness is not attributed to most machines. But if the whole assembly process taking place in the plant is being monitored and controlled by an artificially intelligent executive system then such a system will almost certainly have something akin to an awareness of what it is doing and trying to achieve overall, and what the various assembly and other processes taking place in the plant should be doing and are actually doing. In which case it may be appropriate to say that such an "executive directive system" is acting in a purposive manner, and therefore may be regarded as a purposive system. (The issue of what makes an entity purposive, or purposeful, is a large one and will not be pursued fully in the present work. Ackoff and Emery in their book *On Purposeful Systems* define a purposeful system as: '[O]ne that can change its goals in constant environmental conditions; it selects goals as well as the means by which to pursue them. It thus displays *will*. Human beings are the most familiar examples of such systems.' (Ackoff and Emery 1972, p. 31).)

2.3.9   Generalising from these examples it may be said that directive activity is such that it tends to bring about and/or maintain a particular type of condition (a directed outcome, objective, or goal) by appropriately matching its actions to independently arising and changing circumstance – circumstances that are not in themselves

47

conducive to the occurrence of the directed outcome and may in some cases be such as to positively oppose or disrupt its occurrence.

2.3.10 The examples of directed origination just discussed all concern the *achievement* of some condition, but there is an important and large class of directive systems whose objective is to *maintain* some condition relatively constant. Homeostasis, as such condition-keeping directive activity is referred to within biology, plays a vital role in enabling living organisms to remain alive and function effectively. For example, mammals have a thermo-regulative system – a directive system – for maintaining their core body temperature at a fairly constant level in spite of variations in such things as the degree to which they are exerting themselves, and the external temperature. And, considering condition-keeping directive activity more generally, as people grow up and during their lives, they usually acquire various condition-keeping abilities and skills – such as being able to keep their balance when walking, or when riding a bike or a horse. They also acquire, with a greater or lesser degree of success, other less obvious condition-keeping skills, such as being able to keep on the roadway when driving and being able to maintain a safe relationship with other vehicles; such as being able to maintain generally good relations with neighbours, colleagues, etc.; such as being able to maintain a desired weight and level of fitness; and such as being able to maintain their financial position in good order.

2.3.11 Turning to the world of engineered artefacts, there are many examples of condition-keeping directive systems. For instance, speed governors for engines have long existed and are used to maintain a fairly constant output-speed in spite of varying demands on the engine. Another similar case is automatic gain (amplification) control which is built into radios, cellphones, etc. to maintain a constant volume of sound output in spite of variations in the strength of the received signal. More complex artificial directive systems designed to maintain a given condition exist – for example, auto-pilots have the objective of keeping an aircraft or a boat on a pre-set course in spite of independently varying wind, weather, and other conditions.

2.3.12 According to independence indeterminism all directed outcomes are originations. They are understood to be originations because they are seen to be the result of a directive system taking appropriate action in the face of independently arising and changing circumstances, disruptions and disturbances. However, in some cases, a directed outcome will be an originated event because two or more directive systems work directively, but largely independently, to bring it about. As an example, consider a situation in which two friends have agreed to meet up at a specific place at a particular time on a given future date. Suppose, as would usually be the case, that the friends act fairly independently of one another in their efforts to make the meeting. If they do actually manage to meet as agreed, most people would not think this event was solely a matter of chance be-cause they would recognise that both of the friends were acting directively to be at the agreed place at the time in question. But in such a case there is no *single* directive system coordinating and controlling the meeting-up. Rather, the directed outcome is the result of two independently operating directive systems each with their own objective, which, if their individual objectives are met, will result in the overall directed outcome being achieved. Many directed outcomes involve directed origination of this cooperatively produced sort.

2.4   Directive Systems and Creative Origination

2.4.1   Some introductory remarks about creative origination have already been made (see section 1.5), and the topic will be treated more widely in Chapter 8. In this section the five examples that have just been discussed will be further considered to provide an overview of the sort of role creative origination typically plays in the emergence and operation of directive systems.

2.4.2   The first example was of a dog chasing and catching a rabbit. This is a case of conflictual and/or competitive interaction involving two relatively independently acting purposive agents. Because the chase involves independence interactions and therefore origina-tion, there can be (under independence indeterminism) nothing in existence at the commencement of the chase that fully determines the particular details of how the chase will play out. However, given that such chases usually involve familiar moves and interactions on the part of the dog and the rabbit it seems there isn't much *creative* origination involved. Certainly, a good case may be made for creative origination being involved in the biological evolution of the dog's and the rabbit's innate skills, but this creative origination occurred in the past. Similarly, although the animals' directive activity during the chase may depend to some extent upon what they have learned, it is not generally believed that this learning was all creatively originated during the actual chase itself; rather it is generally thought that most of it was creatively originated in the past. However, both the dog and the rabbit are likely to have some capacity to invent novel moves and tactics as the chase is taking place, in which case on some occasions some creative origination would be involved. Additionally, the dog may experience some motivational conflict between continuing with the chase or abandoning it, and some (weak) creative origination may be involved in its resolving this conflict.

2.4.3   It may be helpful at this point to consider a form of competitive interaction that does not involve any origination. Imagine a game of noughts and crosses (tic-tac-toe) played by two computers each using an algorithm certain to produce either a win or a draw. Let us suppose that the computer that starts a game is selected randomly and its mark is placed at random on one of the blank squares in the 3x3 grid. Once this has happened the game would proceed entirely deterministically as each program in turn executed its algorithm to determine where to place its mark. This is a (marginally) competitive situation involving two opposing directive systems but with the setup being such that any game follows a course that is predetermined once the initial random selection of first-player and first-move has occurred. And because the course of the game is predetermined once these initial conditions are set, it would be correct to say that the run of the game is not originated, and certainly not *creatively* originated. How does this situation differ from that of a dog chasing a rabbit? Firstly, the computers executing their algorithms are not purposive systems: they have no awareness of what they are doing, and they cannot choose between a range of different directive activities. Secondly, the game takes place in a closed and very limited 'world' in which no external events or conditions, other than the state of the nine-square grid, need be taken into account. This is not the case in a dog/rabbit chase: the chase may take place in a variety of different environments most of which are open to various events arising during the chase (such as the intervention of other animals or humans) that may influence how the dog and the rabbit behave. And thirdly, whereas the noughts-and-crosses game runs deterministically (at least

50

from a functional point of view) the dog/rabbit chase does not since it involves many independence interactions, including those occurring within the mind-brains of the dog and the rabbit.

2.4.4 The second example concerned a tennis player hitting a ball with their racquet. A tennis match is an example of a competitive struggle and, for the reasons that apply to dog/rabbit chases but more so, it involves some creative origination. However, only a particular small part of a tennis match is being considered: that of a tennis player striking a tennis ball with their racquet. The question of where the player's ability to do this comes from is generally answered by saying that biological evolution has played a major part; but it is usually accepted that learning has also played an important part. However, is any creative origination involved in the actual performance of a stroke? A lot of the time there probably isn't because the player is exercising well-honed skills in a more or less automatic way. But looked at in detail this may not always be the case. Even in a match a player may show some inventiveness in at least a few of their strokes. That is, rather than relying solely upon well-ingrained types of responses a player may sometimes creatively construct their stroke. However, more usually it is in training and practice that a player may purposively set out to be creative; perhaps with such goals in mind as aiming to correct a weakness in a certain type of stroke, or to enhance the effectiveness of a stroke, or to learn a new stroke.

2.4.5 Tennis, to be played well, requires a good deal of disciplined and thoughtful learning – self-directed learning, in other words – and much practice. The learning is thoughtful because the player must analyse their play and attempt to identify what features of it need to be changed (possibly even eradicated), or improved, and what new skills need to be acquired. This is a process whose success is often greatly enhanced with the assistance of a coach. The sort of learning required for high-performance play does not happen automatically, or simply through uncritical playing of tennis. An expert tennis player not only has to learn how to play the game better, but they also need to learn how to organise themselves in such a way that they are able to carry out this learning in an effective manner. This "learning to learn" how to become a highly skilled tennis player involves many things, including learning how to sustain motivation, learning how to overcome problems and difficulties, learning how to maintain a sufficient level of disciplined and focused practice, learn-ing how to recover psychologically from setbacks during play, and learning how to analyse their play in order to identify reasons for their successes, mistakes and failures. What is going on with this learning is a creative process of some significance. It entails the player bringing into existence and appropriately integrating structures, procedures, and processes within themselves which were not pre-figured to arise when they started. This lack of inbuilt or instinctive guidance, or prefigurement, is one reason why a good coach may be so helpful. And it also illustrates why certain kinds of creative origin-ation cannot be carried out with much success by an agent on their own but requires the cooperative directive activity of other agents. The theory and practice of what has been called "self-organised learning" and "leaning conversations" has been developed by Laurie Thomas and Sheila Harri-Augstein over many years and their work makes clear the creatively originative nature of what is involved – see, for example, (Thomas and Harrie-Augstein 1985), and (Harrie-Aug-stein and Thomas 1991).

2.4.6   The third example concerned the directive activity in-volved in a bird landing on a branch. The ability of a bird to carry out this sort of activity seems to be largely innate and therefore it may be assumed it was creatively developed through biological evolu-tion. Nevertheless, probably a little practice in the use of this innate ability is also required before a bird becomes fully competent in exer-cising it. However, it appears that no creative origination is involved in executing this directive activity once the bird has become fully skilled in its use. But this might not always be so because under cer-tain tricky conditions a bird may not have readily available all that it needs to be able to deal with the situation and so it may have to be in-ventive to some extent. In this case some creative origination would be involved.

2.4.7   The fourth example concerned the use of knowledge by an animal to get to a waterhole. Providing the journey to the water-hole does not present unfamiliar problems, not much creative origin-ation would need to be involved. But if an unfamiliar problem was encountered, such as the animal's chosen route being blocked by a major landslide that required a large detour, then some creative ori-gination might be needed: for instance in the animal's search for an alternative route, or in overcoming conflict within its self about whether to continue with its plan or completely abandon it and try some different approach to obtaining water.

2.4.8 However, there is a wider question: Does the acquisition of knowledge involve creative origination? To be able to answer in the affirmative, the acquisition of the knowledge should not be prefigured within the agent prior to its coming to possess it. This is very often the case because what knowledge an agent acquires is situation-specific – for example, knowledge about how to get to a particular waterhole depends upon the specifics of the terrain concerned. But there is another related question: Do agents have a genetic (or designed-in) predisposition to acquire certain types of knowledge? If they do then there seems to be some degree of prefigurement involved. Human persons tend to differ greatly from animals in this respect since although, like animals, humans are predisposed to acquire certain types of knowledge – e.g. about their surroundings, about members of their social group, and about their mother tongue – there is a great deal of knowledge that humans have which they had no innate predisposition to acquire. For example, humans have no innate predisposition to acquire the particular factual knowledge they learn at school, or the particular job-specific knowledge they learn as part of their employment, or the vast range of the particular social, economic, political, religious, and cultural knowledge that is related to their specific lifestructure. Although much human knowledge is absorbed in an almost unconscious way in a process that seems to involve only weak creative origination, there are other kinds of human knowledge acquisition that involve a stronger more purposefully directed kind of creative origination. For example, the knowledge acquisition processes involved in academic and professional learning, or the learning of a craft or trade, or the learning of difficult new skills.

2.4.9 The final example concerned the directed independence interactions associated with the assembly of an automobile. Not much creative origination is involved in the bringing together of specific parts since almost all such assembly operations are either automated or carried out by a human using well-established procedures. Of course, the automatic processes and the machinery that realises them, and the associated human-based assembly procedures, have to be designed and design almost always involves creative origination.

Furthermore, the operatives need to learn the assembly procedures they carry out and this will involve some degree of creative origination. And sometimes a human operative will need to solve problems – for example, the non-arrival of needed parts, mis-assembly at a preceding stage, or breakdown of a power-tool – and this may require some creative origination.

2.4.10 Looking at the production of motor cars more generally, it is apparent that a vast web of directive activities is involved – a web that is deeply embedded within and supported by modern technological civilisation. An automobile assembly plant with its supporting facilities is a creatively originated entity. Nowadays it is not created from scratch since automobile assembly plants currently exist quite widely and knowledge of these helps guide and inform much of the design, planning, and construction of new ones. Nevertheless, some decisions specific to the construction of any particular automobile plant have to be made in a creative rather than in a routine way.

2.5 Independence Indeterminism Helps With Other Problems

2.5.1 A central concern of the present work is with how independence indeterminism helps resolve the problem of free will. However it is not surprising that such a radically new naturalistic metaphysics may also help resolve some other long-standing philosophical disputes since it provides a very different interpretation of the nature of our universe than that which is currently generally held. In this section it is indicated how independence indeterminism may be able to do this in a couple of cases. In Chapter 9 the significance of independence indeterminism is discussed more fully.

2.5.2 Closely linked to the problem of free will is what is known as the mind-body problem. On one side of this dispute are those who believe that the mind is no more than the activity of biological matter (mainly neurological matter). On the other side are those who believe mind is something more than this.

2.5.3 As already noted (1.4.8), the mind is generally understood to be a processual entity and the brain a material/structural one. In line with what is commonly accepted, "mind-processes" (i.e. the processes that constitute mind) will be taken to require a brain for their

54

realisation, but with the proviso that many of these processes also require that the brain be in appropriate interaction with a suitable environment. Such "input/output dependent mind-processes" (IOD mind-processes) as they shall be referred to, typically consist of a "process core" interacting with a set of "process peripherals" which are themselves interacting with an environment. For example, the mind-processes associated with reading a book, watching a movie, or having a conversation require that the brain (the process core) be in appropriate interaction with the agent's sensory/motor systems (the process peripherals) and that these systems be in interaction with a suitable environment – one that contains a book, movie, and co-conversant respectively. The is an obvious point but it is an important one – and it is one that is not emphasised in many discussions of the mind-body problem.

2.5.4 The next point is a direct consequence of adopting independence indeterminism. Quite apart from whether or not independence interactions occur within the brain during mind-processes, they certainly occur between a psychological agent and their environment during input/output dependent mind-processes. And in this case such mind-processes must follow an originated course – that is, a course that cannot be wholly reduced to the properties of an agent's body and its environment because some of the changes involved arise through independence interactions, which are interactions whose occurrence is not wholly reducible to anything pre-existing prior to their occurrence.

2.5.5 Another important point that follows from adopting independence indeterminism is that it makes no sense to talk of the brain as a whole as operating as a deterministic system because there is general agreement that the activity of the mind-brain is composed of many interacting, but also partly independently operating, parts, sub-systems, and sub-processes, which implies that independence interactions are common within the mind-brain meaning its activity follows an originated course. This goes against what many scientists and others assume to be the case – for example, recall Patricia Churchland's words quoted above (see 1.4.12): 'brains operate causally; that is, they go from one state to the next as a function of antecedent conditions'. Note that under independence indeterminism there can be no determinate relationships governing the joint-change that the independently running parts, subsystems, and sub-processes of the mind-brain undergo.

2.5.6 Although the above points are valid according to independence indeterminism, it might be that even though mind-brain processes follow an originated course they always run in a fully type-determined way. In which case it would be true that the *general* way in which all *particular* instances of mind-brain activity ran would be fixed – i.e. type-determined or prefigured. However, given the assumption that psychological agents are, to a greater or lesser extent, capable of creative origination, and that when so operating their mind-brain processes do not follow a wholly prefigured or type-determined course, then this conclusion would not be true. That is, such agents when operating in a creatively originative manner would produce originations that transcend what was prefigured in their bodies and their environments.

2.5.7 What has just been said does not resolve the mind-body problem since there are important matters that have not been touched upon, such as the existence in humans (and possibly some animals) of conscious subjective experience (see 10.2.4). But the fact that independence indeterminism has a place for directed origination, creative origination, and self-directed origination (including self-directed *creative* origination) does bring an important new dimension to the debate.

2.5.8 The second long-standing dispute that independence indeterminism helps resolve is that between reductionists and emergentists. Reductionists hold that the world consists of nothing but fundamental simple entities and the activities and interactions these engage in. An entity may be taken to be fundamental if it has irreducible properties and behaviours; and it may be taken it to be simple if it possesses no parts. Reductionists deny fundamental existence to all complex entities (i.e. entities composed of parts). This means, for instance, that they deny *fundamental* existence to entities such as protons and neutrons, atomic nuclei, atoms, molecules, stars and planets, biological cells and living organisms, and all artefacts, since they see all the properties and behaviours of such entities as wholly reducible (in principle) to interaction among fundamental simple entities such as the elementary particles and fields that physics currently identifies. Furthermore, some reductionists are also absolute determinists so they see the emergence of all complex entities to be wholly pre-figured and to be the result of what fundamental simple entities actually exist, how these are distributed and arranged, and how they interact and how they come and go from existence. However, those reductionists who accept that quantum indeterminacy exists do have a place for origination, but not for creative origination because all quantum indeterministic events are understood to be type-determined occurrences which arise with definite probabilities.

2.5.9 In opposition to reductionists, emergentists do not believe that existence consists solely of the distribution and activity of fundamental simple entities. They believe that some complex entities have properties and behaviours that cannot be reduced and so must be taken to be fundamental in their own right. But the difficulty that emergentists have faced is in finding a convincing naturalistic explanation for why the properties of a complex entity cannot, in principle, be reduced to the properties of its parts and how these interact. However, by using independence indeterminism, emergentists are able to provide such an explanation. To see this, consider those entities whose identities are realised (in part at least) by independence interactions taking place among their parts. Many such entities – e.g. neutrons and protons, atomic nuclei, atoms, and molecules – realise their continuing existence and identity through wholly type-determined independence interactions among their parts and so to this extent have a continuing existence that is reducible at the type level. But there are other complex entities that do not run internally in a wholly type-determined way because their continuing existence involves some creative origination. The realm of life – if it may be considered to be an entity – is perhaps the most striking example of this. Within this realm, and particularly within the human realm, there are many entities whose continuing existence (and identity) depends to some extent on the entity carrying out creative origination. For example, higher animals (and to a much greater extent, humans) rely for their continuing existence on learning and inventiveness. And entities such as ecosystems depend for their continuing existence not only upon numerous independence interactions among many different organisms and physical entities but also on the creative capacity of organisms to adapt to changing circumstances. Human social entities – e.g. business firms, clubs and societies, schools and universities, and political parties – also depend for their continuing existence upon being able to creatively respond to changing circumstance. Under independence indeterminism it is accepted that all of these entities are irreducible – and irreducible in a very strong sense because of the non-prefigurement of some aspects of what they do and what they may become.

2.5.10   Only two long-standing philosophical disputes have been discussed here, but it should be clear from what has been said that it is origination (chance origination, directed origination, and creative origination) that provides the vital new ingredient. Once origination takes centre stage, it must be accepted that the future can never be fully accounted for by the past and the present, even though in certain respects it may be possible to become fairly sure about some of the general features the future will possess.

3   Determinism

3.1   Introduction

3.1.1   The idea of determinism takes several forms, but "naturalistic absolute determinism" is our main concern. Often however, the term absolute determinism will be used, or sometimes just "determinism" on its own when no confusion is likely to arise. Non-naturalistic forms of absolute determinism, such as theistic determinism, will not be considered. However, what is known as logical determinism occupies a middle ground and something should be said about it before going further.

3.1.2   Aristotle drew attention to the key logical principle that every proposition is either true or false, and that no third value, such as "indeterminate", is possible. Although this bivalence view of the truth-value of propositions presents no obvious problem when the truth-value is determined by past or present existence this is not the case for propositions referring to future existence, as Aristotle realised. In discussing the issue, Aristotle asks us to consider the proposition: "There will be a sea battle in the bay tomorrow." According to the principle of the excluded middle, this proposition must be either true or false. And since one view of logic is that the truth-value of a proposition (considered as a Platonic entity, rather than a potentially fallible human construction) is a timeless property, it must today be either true or false that there will be a sea battle in the bay tomorrow. And since, arguably, all future events may be described by propositions, there must be a true proposition already existing for every future event – which means the future must be fixed.

3.1.3   Logical determinism seems to have a strong hold on people once they understand the argument. However, under independence indeterminism many aspects of the future are not yet determined because they depend upon what will get originated. And if this is the case then it doesn't make sense to say of something that has no certainty of either existing or not existing that it's existence must now be either true or false. Under a metaphysics that supports absolute determinism it *does* make sense to say this because everything that has existence (whether in the past, present, or future) is fixed once an absolutely deterministic universe has come into existence. Hence logical determinism is compatible with absolute determinism. But arguing for absolute determinism on the basis of the validity of logical determinism only works if every aspect of existence can be expressed in terms of propositions, and if the Platonic view of propositions is accepted, and these are both contentious matters – indeed, they are at least as contentious as the arguments in support of absolute determinism itself.

3.1.4 The idea of absolute determinism has become formally clarified only in the last fifty years or so. Prior to this, two other ideas that seemed to imply absolute determinism were (and to a great extent still are) used instead of this more formal account. These two ideas are the principle of sufficient reason, and the law of cause and effect. With regard to the first idea, Leibniz wrote: 'There can be found no fact that is true or existent, or any true proposition, without there being a sufficient reason for its being so and not otherwise, although we cannot know these reasons in most cases.' (Honderich, 1995, entry on 'Sufficient reason, principle of'.) The second idea – one that has been elevated to the status of law – is that every effect has a cause. While the principle of sufficient reason and the law of cause and effect do seem to provide an informal basis for absolute determinism, it has proved difficult to state these ideas rigourously. This has meant that libertarians have not been able to fully drive home the point that under absolute determinism every detail of everyone's life is completely fixed and predetermined, and has been so fixed and predetermined for ever. However, relatively recent work on formalising what absolute determinism is and what it implies has given libertarians a new confidence as it has forced compatibilists to acknowledge just how much this form of determinism limits what free will may be taken to be. But before discussing this newish work it will be helpful to consider some earlier ideas about determinism, and also make an argument for rejecting cause and effect as an adequate basis for absolute determinism.

3.2   Ideas about Determinism

3.2.1   The idea of absolute determinism has ancient roots. Plutarch (c 46-120) writing about the pre-Socratic philosophers noted that:

> Thales says that necessity is omnipotent, and that it exerciseth an empire over every thing. Pythagoras, that the world is invested by necessity. Parmenides and Democritus, that there is nothing in the world but what is necessary, and that this same necessity is otherwise called fate, justice, providence, and the architect of the world (Plutarch).

3.2.2   The ancients were greatly concerned that Fate had an iron rule over our lives and that no matter what we did, including self-directively originating and executing plans and actions, Fate would always manage to so arrange events that our fated future was sure to occur. Later, with the advent of the ancient Greek atomists – Leucippus and Democritus (5th Century BCE) in particular – a naturalistic cosmological theory was proposed that was thoroughly deterministic. For example, Leucippus, in the sole surviving piece of text attributable to him, states that 'Nothing happens at random, but everything from a rational principal and of necessity.' Epicurus (c341-270 BCE) adopted, extended, and systematised the work of the atomists and was the first thinker to fully appreciate the consequences of absolute determinism for free will. Only fragments of Epicurus's writing exist, but his ideas were taken up and described in *De rerum natura* (On the Nature of Things) by the Roman poet Lucretius (c.95-52 BCE). Lucretius writes on Epicurus's ideas as follows.

> When the atoms are travelling straight down through empty space by their own weight, at quite indeterminate times and places they swerve ever so little from their course, just so much that you can call it a change of direction. If it were not for this swerve, everything would fall downwards like raindrops through the abyss of space. No collision would take place and no impact of atom on atom would be created. Thus nature would never have created anything.

3.2.3   Lucretius goes on to explain how these causeless swerves offer an escape from the all-pervasive and unbroken chains of cause and effect that Greek atomism otherwise entails, and he sees this as providing a basis for free will.

Again, if all movement is always interconnected, the new arising from the old in a determinate order – if the atoms never swerve so as to originate some new movement that will snap the bonds of fate, the everlasting sequence of cause and effect – what is the source of free will possessed by living things throughout the earth? What, I repeat, is the source of the will-power snatched from the fates, whereby we follow the path alone which we are severally led by pleasure, swerving from our course at no time or place but at the bidding of our own hearts? There is no doubt that on these occasions the will of the individual originates the movements that trickle through his limbs. [...] So you may see the beginning of movement is generated by the heart; starting from voluntary action of the mind, it is then transmitted throughout the body and the limbs. (Lucretius, pp. 67-68)

Unfortunately, Lucretius does not say how 'voluntary actions of the mind' are produced. If they are produced by random swerves then this does not help. And it doesn't help if they are produced deterministically. What is required is non-necessitated self-directed determination and Lucretius does not say how, or if at all, Epicurus explained this.

3.2.4   The idea of absolute determinism finds expression in literature. For example in the *Rubaiyat of Omar Khayyam* (Fitzgerald 1936) we find the following stanzas:

> For let Philosopher and Doctor preach
> Of what they will, and what they will not – each
>   Is but one Link in an eternal Chain
> That none can slip, nor break, nor over-reach.

> And that inverted bowl we call The Sky,
> Whereunder crawling coop'd we live and die,
>   Lift not your hands to It for help – for It
> As impotently rolls on as you or I.

> With Earth's first Clay They did the Last Man knead,
> And there of the Last Harvest sow'd the Seed:

And the first Morning of Creation wrote
What the Last Dawn of Reckoning shall read.

3.2.5   William James, in a well-known passage, has described absolute determinism in the following way.

> Those parts of the universe already laid down, appoint and decree what other parts shall be. The future has no ambiguous possibilities hidden in its womb: the part we call the present is compatible with only one totality. Any other future complement than the one fixed from eternity is impossible. The whole is in each and every part, and welds it with the rest into an absolute unity, an iron block, in which there can be no equivocation or shadow of turning. (James 1923, p. 150)

3.2.6   Writing somewhat earlier than James – in another well-known passage – the mathematician, scientist and philosopher Pierre-Simon Laplace states the idea of absolute determinism from a scientific point of view as follows.

> We ought then to regard the present state of the universe as the effect of its antecedent state and as the cause of the state that is to follow. An intelligence knowing all the forces acting in nature at a given instant, as well as the momentary positions of all things in the universe, would be able to comprehend in one single formula the motions of the largest bodies as well as the lightest atoms in the world, provided that its intellect were sufficiently powerful to subject all data to analysis; to it nothing would be uncertain, the future as well as the past would be present to its eyes. (Laplace 1820)

In this passage, Laplace uses a formulation of absolute determinism – one that has gained favour among philosophers in recent times – in which he sees the instantaneous total state of the universe together with the laws of nature as fully determining the next instantaneous total state of the universe, and so on for ever. Note that Laplace is apparently entirely comfortable with the idea of there being a wholly definite instantaneous total state of the universe – an idea that makes no sense from the point of view of process metaphysics and independence indeterminism (see 1.1.8).

3.2.7   Those who believe in the truth of absolute determinism must also believe (or at least accept as a necessary logical consequence of that belief) that each person's life – including their own – follows a course that was fully determined prior to their birth. Lamont highlights just what this means as follows.

In *A Mummer's Tale* by Anatole France, Dr Socrates upholds the determinist viewpoint when he urges that M. Chevalier was not to be blamed for his suicide, because it was preordained from eternity. Says the eloquent Dr. Socrates: "To call upon a poor wretch to answer for his actions! Why, even when the solar system was still no more that a pale nebula, forming, in the ether, a fragile halo, whose circumference was a thousand times greater than the orbit of Neptune, we had all of us, for ages past, been fully conditioned, determined and irrevocably destined, and your responsibility, my responsibility, Chevalier's and that of all men, had been, not mitigated, but abolished beforehand. All our movements, the result of previous movements of matter, are subject to laws which govern the cosmic forces, and human mechanism is merely a particular instance of the universal mechanism." (Lamont 1967, pp. 23-24)

3.2.8   The principle of sufficient reason and the law of cause and effect lack solid backing, even though they both have strong intuitive appeal. The law of cause and effect has most often been put forward as the main reason for believing in absolute determinism. But, as will now be argued, it does not provide an adequate basis for such a belief.

3.3   Cause and Effect is Not a Basis For Absolute Determinism

3.3.1   Cause and effect applied universally has often been taken to imply absolute determinism. For example, Karl Popper writes that:

One of the simplest and most plausible arguments in favour of determinism is this: we can *always* ask, of *every* event, why it happened; and to every such why-question we can always obtain, in principle, a reply which enlightens us. Thus every event is 'caused'; and this seems to mean that it must be determined, in advance, by the events which constitute its cause. (Popper 1982, p. 9)

64

This informal statement may be slightly tightened as follows.

(1)   Every event (past, present, and future) has a cause which precedes it and necessitates its occurrence.

(2)   Every cause is an event.

(3)   Therefore every event is the necessary outcome of an unbroken chain of causes stretching back forever, or to some special non-caused creation-event that brought the universe into being.

3.3.2   This argument has attracted a lot of criticism. Mainstream practice takes an event to be: 'roughly, a happening, occurrence, or episode' (Honderich 1995, entry on 'event'). This way of characterising an event excludes unchanging states from being events. However, even though events are currently the leading candidate for what causes and effects are, their ontological basis cannot be regarded as wholly settled. Jaegwon Kim comments as follows.

> Any discussion of causation must presuppose an ontological framework of entities among which causal relations are to hold, and also an accompanying logical and semantic framework in which these entities can be talked about. We often take *events* as causes and also as effects; but entities of other sorts (if indeed they are 'other sorts'), such as *conditionals*, *states*, *phenomena*, *processes* and sometimes *facts*, are also pressed into service when we engage in causal talk, although with these there is some controversy as to their suitability as terms of causal relations. (Kim 1971).

3.3.3   In ordinary thinking about cause and effect, states or conditions are often thought of as causes (as they are often thought of as effects). For example, we say things such as "Of course, it was the state of his mind at the time that caused him to take his own life"; or, "The condition of the engine was sure to cause a breakdown sooner or later." The idea of states or conditions being causes is supported by our knowledge that many processes proceed from one state or condition to the next in an orderly manner, and it is easy to think of each present state or condition as being the cause of the next one in the process. Some machines run in this way, and many biological processes pass through a regular sequence of states or conditions. Also, many social processes – such as applying for a job or obtaining a professional qualification – pass through a succession of fairly well-

65

defined states. What is characteristic of such processes is that they all seem to run in a condition-determinate way – that is, they manifest "condition-determinate change". However, it seems no natural process manifests perfect "time-determinate change" although there are many that do so approximately and some processes (e.g. atomic clocks, see 6.6.3) do so very closely. These two important concepts shall be defined as follows.

Condition-determinate Change

> A thing or situation is changing in a condition-determinate way if its next condition, or state, is fixed by its present con-dition together with any input it receives while in this condi-tion.

Time-determinate Change

> A thing or situation is changing in a time-determinate way over a period if its condition at any stage is a determinate function of the time that has passed since the commence-ment of the period.

3.3.4   To clarify these ideas, consider a few examples. The life-cycle of an annual flowering plant is condition-determinate but it is not time-determinate. The cycle is condition-determinate because it goes through a definite sequence of conditions: germination of the seed, growth of the plant, flowering, pollination, seed dispersal, death. But it is not time-determinate because these conditions do not occur at predetermined times relative to when the seed was planted. Rather they occur at times that vary from one year to the next de-pending upon factors such as the weather and the particular location of the plant. An ordinary wind-up clock changes in a condition-de-terminate way but, unlike a plant, it also changes in a (nearly) time-de-terminate way. Similarly, the motions of the planets in our solar sys-tem are both condition-determinate and (nearly) time-determinate. A dog chasing a rabbit is an example of a process that runs in neither a condition-determinate nor time-determinate way. It does not run in a condition-determinate way because how the chase evolves (the partic-ular sequence of conditions it goes through) is not predetermined, and it is not time-determinate because the times of occurrence of the various conditions or states that arise are not fixed at its outset. Most open human social interactions (e.g. conversations, competitive sports, wars, and market-based commerce) generally run in neither a condition-determinate nor time-determinate manner.

3.3.5 All instances of cause and effect are instances of condition-determinate change because each particular cause determines a particular effect. However, because the time between a cause and its effect is rarely mentioned, it cannot be presumed that all instances of cause and effect are instances of time-determinate change. And without cause and effect being able to guarantee time determinacy of change it cannot provide a basis for absolute determinism. This follows because there can be no guarantee of future synchrony between separate chains of cause and effect that are not running in a time-determinate fashion, which means that any future interaction between such chains will, in general, not arise in a determinate way.

3.3.6 Consider now the notion of a cause and its effect. There seem to be two conceptions of what a cause and an effect may be, quite apart from whether they are events or something else. On the one hand, these two terms might be referring to what shall be called a "full cause" and a "full effect". But, on the other hand, they might be referring to what shall be called a "conspicuous cause" and a "conspicuous effect." In everyday talk the latter sense is generally meant, as for example with statements such as: "It was the ice on the road that caused the crash", or "It was the spark that caused the explosion." When talking in this way it is usually tacitly accepted that the conspicuous cause alone – "the ice on the road", "the spark", in the examples – was *insufficient* for the effect to occur, and yet rarely is any attention paid to the other factors comprising the full cause. Similarly, when talking of the effect "the crash", or the effect "the explosion" generally what is meant are only those events that are significant and more or less conspicuous, and not those events produced by the cause-and-effect happening that are not obvious or are considered insignificant. For example, the full effect of a crash between two cars not only consists of damage to the cars, people involved, etc. but also includes a change in the spatial relationship between these things and *everything* else in the universe. It seems, therefore, that adequate sense cannot be made of the notions of cause and effect without using the ideas of full causes and full effects, but these are very difficult things to pin down since it seems possible that they may include very substantial parts of existence. Little attention seems to have been given

67

to trying to rigorously define what constitutes a conspicuous effect, but some work has been done on clarifying what is meant by a conspicuous cause.

3.3.7   J. L. Mackie refers to conspicuous causes as INUS conditions. That is, something that is an *insufficient* but *necessary* part of a condition which is itself *unnecessary* but *sufficient* for the effect. He introduces the idea as follows: 'Suppose that a fire has broken out in a certain house, but has been extinguished before the house has been completely destroyed. Experts investigate the cause of the fire, and they conclude that it was caused by an electrical short-circuit at a certain place.' (Mackie 1965, (1975, p.15)). Mackie points out that the experts are not saying that the short-circuit was a necessary condition for the house catching fire at this time (other events, such as the overturning of a lighted oil-stove, could have produced the same outcome). And the experts are not saying the short-circuit was a sufficient condition for the fire since other conditions were also required to be present (for instance, flammable material in the close vicinity of where the short-circuit occurred, and the presence of oxygen to support combustion). Furthermore, for the fire to take hold there had to be an absence of certain conditions (such as an efficient automatic sprinkler system, or a person in the vicinity of the short-circuit who would have quickly put the fire out). Mackie writes: 'Far from being a condition both necessary and sufficient for the fire, the short-circuit was, and is known to the experts to have been, neither necessary nor sufficient for it' (Mackie 1965 (1975 pp. 15-16)). And it is also known that the full cause involving the specific short-circuit while being sufficient for the house catching fire was not necessary for the occurrence of this outcome because it could have been produced in other ways by some other full cause. Hence the short-circuit was an insufficient but necessary part of a condition which was itself unnecessary but sufficient for the house catching fire – an INUS condition.

3.3.8   It is not INUS conditions but full causes that are referred to in the causality formulation of absolute determinism given above. But even with this clarification the formulation has several further weaknesses. One of these follows from the Eighteenth century philosopher David Hume's criticism of the idea of causality. Hume convincingly argued that there is no empirical justification for asserting that a cause *necessitates* its effect, since it is just past experience that

68

leads people to believe that, in the future, a particular type of cause will produce a particular type of effect. Hume argued that observed *constant conjunction* does not imply *necessity of conjunction*: things might happen differently in the future to how they happened in the past. Of course, it may simply be asserted that a full cause is such that it does *necessitate* its full effect, but then a metaphysical rather than an empirical assertion is being made. And furthermore, there still remains the difficult problem of being able to specify what constitutes the full-cause and the full effect that are necessarily linked together when these are likely to involve large parts of existence.

3.3.9 The point noted earlier (3.3.5) about the law of cause and effect not specifying the time-determinacy of the change involved – that is, in not specifying what the temporal gap is between cause and effect – needs further consideration because it undermines the case for this law being adequate to ensure absolute determinism. In discussing the short-circuit example it was noted that the house would not have caught fire had, for instance, an effective sprinkler system been able to put the fire out before it spread. The action of the sprinkler comes within the temporal gap between the occurrence of the full cause involving the short-circuit, and the conspicuous effect, which is the house catching fire. In general, if there is any finite temporal gap between a cause and its effect then there is the possibility of something happening within the gap that breaks the cause-effect link. And that the concept of cause and effect requires there to be a temporal gap has been argued forcefully by some philosophers. For example, Bertrand Russell, writes as follows.

> [...] if the cause is a process involving change within itself, we shall require (if causality is universal) causal relations between its earlier and later parts; moreover, it would seem that only the later parts can be relevant to the effect, since the earlier parts are not contiguous to the effect, and therefore (by the definition) cannot influence the effect. Thus we shall be led to diminish the duration of the cause without limit, and however much we may diminish it, there will still remain an earlier part which might be altered without altering the effect, so that the true cause, as defined, will not have been reached, for it will be observed that the definition excludes plurality of causes. If, on the other hand, the cause is purely static, in-

69

volving no change within itself, then, in the first place, no such cause is to be found in Nature, and in the second place, it seems strange – too strange to be accepted, in spite of bare logical possibility – that the cause, after existing placidly for some time, should suddenly explode into the effect, which might just as well have done so at any earlier time, or have gone on unchanged without producing its effect. This dilemma, therefore, is fatal to the view that cause and effect can be contiguous in time; if there are causes and effects, they must be separated by a finite time-interval [...]. (Russell 1918, p. 175)

3.3.10   If there must be some temporal gap between a cause and its effect, then an effect cannot be a *necessary* consequence of a cause because, in principle, some effect-destroying intervention may arise within the temporal gap. One way to avoid this problem is to take the complete state of the universe at one instantaneous moment to be the full cause of its total state at the next instantaneous moment, with instantaneous moments being so closely packed that there is no gap between any adjacent pair of them. But this is a Laplacian-like total-state formulation of determinism and not a cause-and-effect one.

3.3.11   Consider finally the conclusion to the causality argument for absolute determinism given above – namely, that: 'every event is the necessary outcome of an unbroken chain of causes stretching back forever, or to some special non-caused "creation-event" that brought the universe into being.' This is perhaps the most disturbing aspect of the cause-and-effect argument for absolute determinism because if there is a need to accept the occurrence of a special non-caused creation-event that originates the universe, why not allow many origination events to occur? If it is maintained that no creation-event has ever occurred then it must be concluded that the universe has existed for eternity. This is a perfectly acceptable metaphysical proposition, but not one that seems to gain much support from current mainstream scientific thinking.

3.3.12   Given the above arguments it seems that cause and effect is not an adequate basis for absolute determinism, and without an adequate basis the metaphysical thesis of absolute determinism will have little force. Hence, if the age-old problem of free will and determinism is to retain its hold on people then what is needed is a stronger basis for determinism than what reasoning from cause and effect can provide.

3.4 Absolute Determinism Defined Without Cause and Effect

3.4.1   Many English-speaking philosophers during the early and middle decades of the twentieth century accepted that compatibilism had resolved the problem of free will and determinism. Then, in the 1970s, a number of philosophers began to develop a robust and formal view of absolute determinism that did not make use of the notion of cause and effect. This work came to be known as the "The Consequence Argument" because it established the full force of the consequences of absolute determinism. According to Tomis Kapitan (2002, p. 128) the Consequence Argument (also known as the Incompatibility Argument, and the Unavoidability Argument) was 'independently developed in the 1970s by David Wiggings, Peter van Inwagen, James Lamb, and Carl Ginet.' These writers were not the first to point out the severe consequences of absolute determinism – William James's writing (see 3.2.5), for instance, had made quite clear what it implies. However, many philosophers seemed to have been able to avoid facing the full force of these consequences because, as argued in the previous section, the idea of cause and effect could not provide a solid argument for absolute determinism, which is the form of determinism that has such unwelcome consequence for any sort of free will really worth wanting.

3.4.2   The Consequence Argument makes use of two key ideas. The first idea is to express the thesis of absolute determinism in logical terms without making use of the notion of cause and effect. The second idea is to propose, justify, and then make use of some version of the very general principle of inference that if something is unavoidable – that is, cannot be changed by any natural being or process – then so are its consequences unavoidable. Not only does this principle seem to be intuitively valid, but it is also very similar to the widely accepted rule of modal logic that whatever is a consequence of a necessity is itself a necessity.

3.4.3   The incompatibilist philosopher, Peter van Inwagen, has been a consistent and strong advocate of the Consequence Argument, and it is his work, as reported in his book *An Essay on Free Will* that shall be considered here. In this book, van Inwagen presents three closely-argued formal versions of the Consequence Argument, and although it is recognised that none of these arguments may be wholly sound (see Kapitan 2002) they are nevertheless presented sufficiently rigorously to require that they be taken seriously by those, such as compatibilists, who seem to wish to deny the full consequences of absolute determinism. It is not within the scope of the present work to discuss Van Inwagen's formal versions of the Consequence Argument, or the detailed technical discussion in the literature about them, but it is worth summarising some of the key points he makes. He states the argument informally as follows.

> If determinism is true, then our acts are the consequences of the laws of nature and events in the remote past. But it is neither up to us what went on before we were born, and neither is it up to us what the laws of nature are. Therefore, the consequences of these things (including our present acts) are not up to us. (Inwagen 1983, p. 16)

3.4.4   In developing his formal versions van Inwagen enters into a full and careful discussion of the various concepts and issues that must be considered if a convincing case is to be made. One of his most important contributions is to give a definition of (absolute) determinism in terms of propositional logic. He writes:

> We may now define 'determinism'. We shall apply this term to the conjunction of these two theses:
>
>> For every instant of time, there is a proposition that expresses the state of the world at that instant;
>>
>> If p and q are any propositions that express the state of the world at some instants, then the conjunction of p and the laws of nature entails q.
>
> This definition seems to me to capture at least one thesis that could properly be called 'determinism'. Determinism is, intuitively, the thesis that, given the past and the laws of nature, there is only one possible future. And this definition certainly has that consequence. (p. 65)

van Inwagen recognises that his definition means that the future determines a unique past. This aspect of the definition does not disturb van Inwagen, but he accepts that it may not be acceptable to others (e.g. those who believe in the "arrow of time" – see section 9.8). He points out that by including a suitable "later than" clause determinism of the past may be excluded, and that this change will not affect the Consequence Argument. He is particularly pleased that 'the horrible little word "cause" does not appear in this definition.'

3.4.5   Van Inwagen is clear that 'Determinism is about propositions, but the free-will thesis is a thesis about agents', and that this mean the free-will thesis needs to be restated in appropriate terms. Van Inwagen does this by arguing that an agent with free will is such that it is 'able to render false' some propositions. He recognizes that there are many propositions that no natural agent can render false – for example, no natural agent can render false the proposition "Magnets attract iron." But he argues that there are other propositions that many people would assume could be rendered false if an agent had free will and the desire to do so. Van Inwagen gives as an example the proposition "I have never read *The Teachings of Don Juan*." It is generally assumed that providing he has originative free will then it is within van Inwagen's power to render this proposition false by actually reading the *The Teachings of Don Juan*. However, if van Inwagen does not have originative free will then it will not actually be up to him whether or not *he* renders the proposition false but entirely a matter of what the state of the world in the distant past and the laws of nature have determined will be the case.

3.4.6   The Consequence Argument achieved a new status of philosophical respectability for just how incompatible absolute determinism is with originative free will. And this considerably unsettled many compatibilists. However they have responded strongly, doing so in two main ways. Firstly, by seeking to find logical flaws in the argument – an approach that is highly technical but which remains a live topic in the specialist literature. And secondly, by continuing to challenge libertarians to find a natural form of self-directed origination when only the existence of purely chance origination seems to have any scientifically acceptable basis.

3.4.7   It is important to understand that the Consequence Argument rests on metaphysical assumptions and that as such these cannot be empirically confirmed or denied. Nevertheless science is seriously at odds with the assumptions of the Consequence Argument on two major counts. Firstly, the mainstream interpretation of quantum theory asserts that indeterminism is a real feature of the microscopic world and this means that absolute determinism cannot be true because the present instantaneous total state of the universe together with the laws of nature does *not* fully determine all atomic/sub-atomic happenings. However, it cannot be said that science definitely rejects the Consequence Argument because in recent years new deterministic interpretations of quantum physics have gained ground so it would be incorrect to say that there is no doubt among physicists that indeterminism is real. (The article 'No Dice' by Mark Buchanan – *New Scientist*, 22 March 2008 – describes some attempts to establish a fully deterministic account of the quantum world.)

3.4.8 The second major way in which the assumptions of the Consequence Argument are at odds with mainstream science concerns the concept of the universe having an instantaneous state at each moment of time. There are two serious problems with this as far as mainstream science is concerned. The first is that Einstein's special theory of relativity establishes that no empirical meaning can be given to there being a universe-wide "now", which means this idea must be taken to be a metaphysical one. The second problem is that most statements of absolute determinism – van Inwagen's for example – are based on the idea of the state of the world at an instant. But a truly instantaneous state cannot be identified empirically. One reason for this, according to mainstream thinking, is that time is understood to change continuously – indeed, many of the current mathematical formulations of the key theories of physics are based on this assumption. But just as there is always a real number between any two real numbers, there is always an instantaneous state between any two instantaneous states. However some physicists suggest that time may be quantised at an incredibly small scale – the so-called Planck time scale, which is of the order of 10^{-43} seconds – which would mean that no change is continuous. However even if this were the case, it seems highly unlikely that all quantised change throughout the universe would take place in lockstep, which is what would be required if there is to be a definite immediate predecessor and successor state for every discrete total state of the universe. A further reason why truly instantaneous states cannot be identified empirically is that all observations and measurements require that something (e.g.

a sense organ, or an instrument) changes its condition, and since no change can take place in a true instant, no instantaneous measurement of anything is possible. These reasons mean that the idea of the universe proceeding through a series of instantaneous total states must also be regarded as a purely metaphysical one.

3.4.9   The points just made suggest that science can offer little support for absolute determinism as long as it is formulated in the way van Inwagen outlines. Alternative formulations are possible. For example, one that some cosmologists favour is based on the view that the big bang initiated a quantum state encompassing the entire universe and that the time evolution of this state is completely described by a single time-determinate wave function – a wave function that never "collapses" (or perhaps only collapses when our universe ceases to be). At present there are two main problems with this idea. Firstly, there is no widely accepted theory of quantum gravity – that is, a quantum theory that encompasses gravity. And secondly, there is no evidence that such a single time-determinate quantum wave function exists.

3.4.10   Although absolute determinism as formulated by van Inwagen and others in expounding the Consequences Argument is able to gain little support from mainstream science this does not mean that it is necessarily a false concept, merely that it is a metaphysical one.

3.5   Quantum Entanglement and Absolute Determinism

3.5.1   Although, as just discussed, there is little evidence from science that absolute determinism is true there is a feature of quantum mechanics – known as entanglement – that might possibly support the truth of absolute determinism. Quantum mechanics under the Copenhagen interpretation is an indeterministic theory in two ways. Firstly, it takes the quantum properties (e.g. position, momentum, spin, and polarisation) of a particle (e.g. an electron or a photon) as not having a determinate value until some interaction with the particle – known as a "measurement" – produces a single definite value. Secondly, the theory is only able to specify the probability with which a measurement will produce a particular value, which means individual measurements produce their results indeterministically.

75

Quantum entanglement, says that certain processes of generation or interaction involving quantum particles result in one or more of the properties of the particles becoming dependent upon one another so that a measurement, and therefore the fixing, of such a property for one particle instantly results in a correlated fixing of this property for the other entangled particles, no matter how widely separated the particles may be when the measurement is made.

3.5.2   Quantum entanglement seems to imply what Einstein referred to as "spooky action at a distance" – that is, the transfer of influence or information between particles taking place faster than the speed of light, which, according to the theory of relativity, cannot happen. Einstein was not prepared to accept this implication of quantum mechanics as understood by the Copenhagen school, and he argued that there must be hidden variables of which quantum mechanics was not taking account. However, this difference of opinion – which came to a head in the 1930s – remained a matter of competing thought experiments and theoretical arguments because physicists could not see a way of performing experiments that would resolve the issue.

3.5.3   This impasse remained until 1964 when John Stewart Bell devised a way by which experiments might be performed that would be capable of deciding the issue. It is not appropriate here to go into the details of his argument, but what he established was an experimental method capable of showing that no theory based on hidden variables that are only able to influence one another at or below the speed of light can ever produce all the experimentally confirmable predictions of quantum mechanics formulated according to the Copenhagen interpretation. Or put another way, Bell's method is able to determine whether or not there are quantum phenomena that imply the existence of "spooky action at a distance".

3.5.4   Since the publication of Bell's work several experiments have been performed based on his method. Although these experiments tended to confirm that no sub-luminal hidden-variable theory can account for the results produced, none of these experiments was entirely free of loopholes. However, in August 2015 the results of experiments – performed by Ronald Henson and colleagues at Delft University of Technology, The Netherlands – were reported that seemed to show that all loopholes had been closed and that spooky action at a distance is real (Henson 2015).

3.5.5 Loophole-free empirical confirmation of apparent spooky action at a distance together with solid empirical evidence that no influence or information can be transmitted faster than the speed of light points to a clear inconsistency among empirical findings. Interestingly, this inconsistency would not exist if absolute determinism were true of our universe. Bell himself recognised this and spoke of it in a 1985 BBC Radio interview when he said:

> There is a way to escape the inference of superluminal speeds and spooky action at a distance. But it involves absolute determinism in the universe, the complete absence of free will. [If we] [s]uppose the world is super-deterministic, with not just inanimate nature running on behind-the-scenes clockwork, but with our behavior, including our belief that we are free to do one experiment rather than another, absolutely predetermined, including the 'decision' by the experimenter to carry out one set of measurements rather than another, [then] the difficulty disappears. There is no need for a faster-than-light signal to tell particle A what measurement has been carried out on particle B, because the universe including particle A, already 'knows' what that measurement, and its outcome will be (Bell, 1985).

3.5.6 However, present-day mainstream thinking in physics does not support the existence of absolute determinism because it has a place for quantum indeterminacy. Nevertheless, there is a non-mainstream view of quantum physics that does away with this indeterminacy – a view that when Bell came across it stimulated him to develop his 1964 theorem.

3.5.7 In 1927 De Broglie – who had earlier postulated that material particles have a wave-like quality, something that is now an empirically established feature of quantum physics – developed a completely deterministic theory to account for quantum phenomena. He introduced the idea of "pilot waves" which fully determine the position and trajectory of particles, and which in conjunction with the Schrodinger wave equation, allowed most of the empirical findings of quantum physics to be explained. For reasons that are not altogether clear (for further information see Turner, M.) few physicists took up pilot wave theory until David Bohm did so in 1952. Pilot wave theory remains highly contentious. Possibly one reason for this is that pilot waves, and the definite positions and trajectories of the particles that pilot waves determine, are not observable. Another possible reason is that the variables that define a pilot wave's influence on the position and trajectory of a particle have values that, in the limit, may depend upon the condition of the entire universe. For these, and other reasons, pilot wave theory has not attracted much mainstream attention or support. However, analogues involving small oil drops being moved about on the surface of water by ripples, and theoretical work that supports non-localism within the quantum realm, have led to a recent upsurge in interest in such theories.

3.6 Independence Indeterminism v Absolute Determinism

3.6.1 Given that absolute determinism is a naturalistic metaphysical thesis, it is open to being replaced, without prejudice, by another naturalistic metaphysical thesis. But up to now no alternative has managed to gain anything like as much support. Perhaps one reason why determinism (as a loosely understood notion rather than as a formally stated metaphysical concept) is so readily accepted is because the macroscopic world seems to most people, and to scientists who investigate it, to behave deterministically almost all of the time. Independence indeterminism does not accept this common view and asserts instead that the macroscopic world is constantly undergoing indeterministically occurring change because of independence interactions. However, if independence indeterminism is to gain widespread acceptance then there must be a sea-change in the way most people understand how the world behaves, and although this may be difficult to achieve it does not seem to be impossible, as shall now be indicated.

3.6.2 Perhaps the first question that needs to be considered is why macroscopic determinism seems to be so widely accepted. Humans, and many animals, can often visually track the change that independently changing things are undergoing, and with this information (and experience and knowledge) often anticipate the likely occurrence of near-future independence interactions. These anticipations are not always correct – particularly when something unexpected intervenes – but much of the time they are, or at least they are correct enough for practical purposes. This capacity to anticipate the likely occurrence of near-future independence interactions is vital to the success of carrying out many forms of directive activity. Driving a car safely is an obvious example, but there are many other more mundane examples such as being able to catch a ball, and being able to walk around without bumping into other moving things. But there are further reasons for the widespread belief in macroscopic determinism. One of these is that many independence interactions are type-determined and so seem to be a deterministic consequence of the nature of the domain in which they occur. However, when people think like this, what they tend to forget is that each independence interaction is a uniquely dated and located event for which they can almost never predict all the details – for instance, details such as the *precise* time and location of the interaction, and the *precise* and complete condition of the things involved when the interaction occurs. Once it is accepted that all this detail must necessarily be fully pre-determined under absolute determinism it can be seen that the ability to predict independence interactions is not perfect. Furthermore, Leibniz's principle – that everything has a reason for being – seems to have a strong grip on the thinking of many people and this also supports belief in absolute determinism. And even though the law of cause and effect does not provide a sound basis for absolute determinism (see section 3.3), it is easy for people to think that it does.

3.6.3   In order to see how independence indeterminism might be able to undermine the commonly held belief in determinism it is useful to consider *independence* interactions only, and not examine what may be referred as "dependence interactions" – interactions between things that are in a relationship of *dependence* or *interdependence* as, for example, are the bodies of the solar system. Consider again the earlier example of a raindrop striking a leaf floating down a stream (see 2.1.6). Very shortly before the raindrop hits the leaf (well less than a second) it may be fairly certain to an observer that the interaction will occur. Human sensory and mind-brain processes operate insufficiently fast for a person to actually make such a prediction in real-time but a high-speed film played back in slow-motion may allow a prediction to be made. It is very unlikely that a prediction of all the details of the interaction could be made, for instance *precisely* where and how the raindrop strikes the leaf and the *precise* condition of the raindrop and the leaf when this occurs. But fairly good and fairly reliable predictions might possibly be made in this way. However, what about making successful predictions of independence interactions that are in the far-future and not the near-future? Sticking with the raindrop and leaf example, five minutes before the particular raindrop and leaf entered into independence interaction there will be no chance of predicting this event. Indeed, it wouldn't be known where to point the camera. Could reliable predictions be made five seconds before a collision? Even this seems unlikely. What about predicting the occurrence of the collision before the solar system was formed? This seems to be a ridiculous question to ask. But why? If absolute determinism is correct then the raindrop/leaf interaction was just as fixed then as when its occurrence was, say, a tenth of a second away.

3.6.4   What is being highlighted here is that the belief that determinism applies to independence interactions is based on an ability to anticipate near-future independence interactions, not far-future ones. The truth is humans (scientists included) have no reliable success in predicting *particular* far-future independence interactions, although they might do quite well predicting the far-future occurrence of certain *types* of independence interactions. However, it is evidence of successful and reliable prediction of *particular far-future* independence interactions that is required if absolute determinism is to be supported by empirical findings rather than being a bald metaphysical assumption. Of course, the argument is made by absolute determinists that this failure is a result of not being able to obtain the vast amount of information about the world that would be needed to make successful far-future predictions and is not a result of an inherent indeterminacy of joint-change among apparently independently running stretches of change. But this is not the point. Independence indeterminism does not deny that far-future independence interactions are a product of very complex sequences of dependence and *independence* interactions. What it denies is that these sequences are fully predetermined because it concludes — based on its single primary assumption that true independence of change is extremely common in the universe — that *independence* interactions arise indeterministically, which is something absolute determinism denies. The key difference between the two metaphysical views is that absolute determinists believe that independently changing things change in lockstep whereas independence indeterminists (i.e. those people who accept independence indeterminism) do not believe this because they believe there is no determinate relationship that fully governs or describes how independently changing things jointly change.

3.6.5   What has just been said may be summarised in the following way. Just prior to the occurrence of an independence interaction, determinism often seems to be true, and independence indeterminism often seems to be false. However, when an independence interaction is in the far-future it is, in practice, impossible to identify exactly what exists in the present that necessitates its later occurrence and so determinism seems to be false, and independence indeterminism seems to be true.

3.6.6   Belief in independence indeterminism does not demand a change to most people's everyday understanding of how the world works. For instance, they may go on making more or less accurate and useful near-future predictions of some types of independence interactions and have good reason to believe that these will be successful most of the time. People already know they are not successful all of the time, and most people explain these failures not by doubting that determinism rules in the world but by believing that interfering causes intervened which they were unable to observe or predict and take into account. The fact that people are often able to make successful near-future predictions of independence interactions is a consequence of two conditions holding. Firstly, that no interfering influences arise that disrupt the change the things are undergoing during the short period before their interaction. And secondly, that the things are changing (in ways that affect whether interaction occurs between them) in a roughly time-determinate manner over this same short period. The first condition is often met – but not always. The second condition is also often met (at least sufficiently not to affect anything but the details of the interaction), and when it is met independence is lost because the things are changing in lockstep and so their future interaction ceases to be an *independence* interaction. Science is often able to deal with *dependence* interactions by using deterministic descriptions and laws, and with type-determined *independence* interactions by using statistical descriptions and laws. This means that independence indeterminism does not contradict the empirical findings of science. However, it does contradict some of the fundamental metaphysical, and often tacitly held, beliefs of scientists.

3.6.7   Finally, mention must be made of another reason for preferring independence indeterminism to determinism: namely, that belief in independence indeterminism is compatible with two commonly held beliefs while belief in determinism is not. One of these beliefs is that humans possess free will, and the other belief is that change take place truly independently of almost everything in existence except for the (usually) few things that are involved. This means that those people who believe in determinism yet operate as if they accepted these two beliefs must be living some sort of lie, or at least be operating under some sort of illusion. Hence, because independence indeterminism avoids this, it seems it should to be preferred to absolute determinism.

3.6.8   Although widespread acceptance of independence indeterminism is not going to happen overnight there seem to be no obvious reasons why it should not be accepted over the longer term. Its picture of the world is not of a unity (the picture that absolute determinism presents) but of a non-unity – of a world of separated and more or less independent happenings and doings. And it is also a picture of a world with an irreducible indefiniteness or looseness to the way it proceeds or runs – a world with many gaps within and between the causal networks of existence. To some people this may seem to be a deeply dispiriting picture, but independence indeterminism does have the great virtue of presenting a world that allows new things to come into being through new connectivities and causal networks becoming originated, and through some of these becoming originated not along prefigured lines but in a truly creative way – and in some cases in a directively creative way.

3.6.9   Humans have an immense creative potential, a potential which less capable agents lack and which has enabled the emergence and continuing development of the "realm of civilization" – a realm that, for example, has brought into existence things such as the computer being used to write this, and the economic and regulatory systems that have been created that enable and govern its manufacture, distribution, and sale. And perhaps when people more widely recognise the extraordinary powers of true creative origination that humans individually and collectively possess they shall come to accept independence indeterminism because it has a place for such powers, whereas determinism does not.

4 Science and Independence Indeterminism

4.1 Introduction

4.1.1 Independence indeterminism takes independence interactions to be indeterministically arising events. It might be thought that scientists would have no objection to this view because the laws of science are either about things engaged in dependence interactions – that is, in relationships of *dependence* and not *independence* – or about the statistical properties of type-determined independence interactions occurring among certain types of things in certain kinds of do-main. However this is not the case because scientists currently have a strong attachment to a macroscopic deterministic view of the world. This is a deeply held view, as shall be illustrated by considering two pieces of writing. Further examples need not be given since the views expressed are widely held and commonly encountered in science, and indeed elsewhere in the modern world. The first piece is by James Peterson, a scientist who is much concerned with the modelling of independence interactions but who feels that such events are in fact fully determined even though, for pragmatic reasons, he accepts that it makes sense to assume that they arise indeterministically, or non-deterministically to use his term – a term used mainly in computer science. The second piece is by Earnest Nagel, a respected philo-sopher of science, and it represents his view on chance and inde-pendence interactions – a view that is thoroughly in line with main-stream scientific thinking. It will become clear how dependent on purely metaphysical assumptions the views presented are.

4.1.2 Following this discussion are four further sections. The first of these considers whether two well-established areas of science – quantum theory and deterministic chaos theory – can together show that macroscopic indeterminacy is common, and the conclu-sion is reached that they can't. The next section discusses two ways in which science accepts determinism: in its deterministic sub-state laws, and in system determinism. This is followed by introducing a new way of understanding what a system is that works well for systems composed of loosely coupled components which may be realised in multiple ways. The final section continues the discussion on how compatible independence indeterminism is with science.

4.2 Peterson on the Modelling of Independence Interactions

4.2.1 The first piece of writing to be discussed comes from James Peterson's book *Petri Net Theory and the Modeling of Systems*. Petri nets were invented in 1939 by thirteen-year-old Carl Adam Petri, and later developed in his PhD thesis. Petri nets, which are formal mathematical structures, have found many applications – for example, in concurrent programming and software design, in workflow management, and in discrete process control. Peterson writes: 'Petri nets were designed for and are used mainly for *modeling*. Many systems, especially those with independent components, can be modeled by a Petri net. The systems may be of many different kinds: computer hardware, computer software, physical systems, social systems, and so on.' (Peterson 1981, p. 31) Peterson goes on to give some examples, and then writes 'These examples illustrate several points about Petri nets and the systems which they can model. One is the inherent *parallelism* or *concurrency*.' (p. 35) He explains that a Petri net "execution" – any particular run of events that a particular Petri net allows – exhibits nondeterminism when more than one transition is possible at a given moment, and he suggests this is like what seems to happen in the real-world when things are happening concurrently (and, by tacit assumption, often independently). After making these points he says:

> The questions involved with these concepts can get quite philosophical in nature. For example, I, personally tend towards a deterministic view of the universe, and there is no randomness. Randomness is merely a result of incomplete knowledge of the state of the universe and its individual transitions. In this sense, the selection of one of a set of enabled transitions to fire is determined in the modeled system [i.e. in the real world], [but] not in the model simply because the model does not represent the complete information about the system. (p. 37)

4.2.2 The reason why this latter comment is such an interesting example of a scientist's belief in macroscopic determinism is that it comes from a specialist who is actually working with an important method for modelling and investigating the behaviour of systems involving independently changing things – systems of a sort that Peterson himself recognizes are common in the world. Nevertheless, it would seem Peterson cannot bring himself to accept that independence interactions might be indeterministically arising events.

4.2.3   Peterson's metaphysical predilection for macroscopic determinism is widely shared among scientists and many other people. It is very widely believed that were it possible to identify all the factors at work in any given macroscopic situation – that is, were it possible to access the "complete picture" – then, in principle, it would be possible to predict the future course of all that was to happen in the situation. And this would be so even though some of the happenings involved interactions among things that were prior to their interaction apparently changing independently of one another. Most scientists subscribe to this view so they believe, for example, that although the outcome of flipping a coin may appear to be a matter of chance this is not actually so since if all the factors influencing the coin's motion were known it would be possible – given a complete understanding of physics – to predict the coin's course in the minutest detail and know beforehand which side would be showing when the coin came to rest. Similarly, most scientists believe that exactly where a steel ball launched into a spinning roulette wheel will come to rest is fully determined by the initial conditions of the situation and the laws of nature. In other words, although scientists accept that what appear to be independence interactions are involved in the change going on in such situations, most scientists do not see these interactions as arising indeterministically. Rather, they see them as fully determined, and fully determined in a way that would be obvious if knowledge of all the factors involved and the relevant laws of nature were available. This is just the view of independence interactions for which Nagel argues.

4.3   Nagel on the Determinacy of Independence Interactions

4.3.1   Ernest Nagel in his book *The Structure of Science* has a section entitled 'Chance and Indeterminism' in which he seeks to establish that the idea of a chance event is compatible with its being caused or determined (Nagel 1961, pp. 324-335). He distinguishes between and discusses several meanings of the word chance but here it is only the meaning that is associated with the interaction of independent causal chains that shall be discussed.

4.3.2   In considering this meaning of chance, Nagel introduces a familiar kind of example. 'Suppose [...] that a man leaves his home in order to purchase some tobacco, but that on the way he is felled by a brick displaced from the roof of a building.' Nagel goes on to say: 'The man's misfortune is then said to be a chance occurrence not because it is "uncaused" (indeed, the description of the event indicates the cause), but because it occurs at the "juncture" of two independent causal sequences, one that terminates in the man's being beside the building at a given time, and the other that terminates in the brick's motion at that time.' He then adds: 'These causal series are said to be "independent" in the sense that the events in one do not determine the events in the other: had the brick not fallen the man would have proceeded on his journey to the tobacconist, and had the man not been at a particular spot the brick would have struck the ground. Accordingly, the man's injury is alleged to be fortuitous or accidental, since however complete may be our knowledge of the circumstances leading to the man's journey or of the conditions making for the brick's passage, neither body of knowledge by itself suffices to foretell the accident.' What is needed in order to predict the accident is full knowledge of the time-determinate *joint-change* of the man and the brick. But according to independence indeterminism no such knowledge is possible because no determinate relationship exists between stretches of change that are running truly independently. In believing that such a determinate relationship does actually exist (even if it can never be known what it is), Nagel is tacitly assuming that determinism holds for the situation – that is, he is adopting a particular metaphysical view.

4.3.3   Nagel appreciates that an appeal to common sense is not sufficient to establish that what are apparently independence interactions are actually fully caused or determined events. Nagel writes: 'The notion needing special attention is that associated with the phrase "independent causal chains"'. He acknowledges that the image of each causal line being 'determined by the "inherent" character of

87

the line' is a common one. But he rejects this image as naive, saying 'there are an indefinite number of distinct causal determinants for the occurrence of any specific event. Accordingly, if the image of a line or chain is adopted for describing the causal relations of events, an event is more appropriately described as being the common intersection of an indefinite (if not infinite) number of lines. But if this more complex image is employed, it no longer is even apparently clear just what we are to understand by "independent causal lines", since now every event is the node of very many causal influences.' However, it seems that Nagel does not feel this is a wholly adequate way of dealing with the issue. He goes on to write: 'Greater clarity concerning the sense of "chance" under discussion can be obtained if we reformulate the distinction in terms of relations between *statements* rather than events or happenings.' Interestingly, this approach is akin to that of van Inwagen's who argued for his thesis of determinism in terms of propositions about such things as the total state of the universe and the laws of nature rather than in terms of these things directly (see 3.4.4).

4.3.4 The statements Nagel uses to describe what is going on are expressed in the standard propositional and mathematical language of macroscopic physics, and draw upon the deterministic assumptions that are part of that field. By proceeding in this way – i.e. with an inbuilt assumption of fully time-determinate change involving the two independent causal sequences – it comes as no surprise that Nagel is able to show that apparent independence interactions of the sort being considered are fully determined and are therefore not instances of true chance. Nagel feels no need to justify why it should be possible, at least in principle, to produce a complete time-determinate prediction of such a complex sequence of happenings as is involved in a man going out to buy tobacco: he simply takes it for granted, as many physicists do, that it must be possible to do this even though this has never been achieved in practice. What he is revealing here, but not explicitly acknowledging, is his attachment to a deterministic view of nature, and one that is based on metaphysical assumptions rather than empirical findings.

4.3.5 It is apparent that Nagel, in common with many others, rejects what independence indeterminism assumes – namely that an interaction between independently running causal chains is an originated event and, when there is no directive activity involved, a purely chance originated event. It appears that few people have thoroughly explored the conceptual consequences of assuming that apparently independent causal chain do in fact run truly independently and not in time-determinate lockstep. Some thinkers get close to doing so. For instance, the nineteenth century French mathematician, philosopher, and early contributor to mathematical economics, Antoine Augustin Cournot, in his book *Exposition of the Theory of Chance and Probabilities* asserted that: 'Events caused by combinations of encounters of phenomena belonging to independent series, are those which we call fortuitous or resulting from randomness.' (Cournot 1835 (2013), §40). But rather than developing the wide-ranging conceptual consequence of this assertion, Cournot mainly turned his attention to the mathematics of probability and its various applications.

4.3.6   In the 1960s, when Nagel published his book, his discussion of chance would satisfy most scientists because it was thought that the intrusion of quantum indeterminacy into the macroscopic realm could very largely be ignored. However, this view has now changed.

4.4   From Quantum Indeterminacy to Macro-Indeterminacy ?

4.4.1   Scientists' belief in macroscopic determinism has been undermined in recent decades by the rise of deterministic chaos theory and the study of complex systems. The idea is that certain indeterministically arising quantum events might produce macro-level indeterminacy by seeding systems which possess chaotic dynamics with tiny variations in initial conditions. It has been established that many systems whose behaviour is non-linear have modes of operation in which vanishingly small differences in initial conditions lead to large and non-systematically (i.e. chaotically) varying differences in long-term behaviour. (A non-linear system is one in which equal increments or decrements in the input do not lead to equal increments or decrements in the output.)

4.4.2   Fields of study in which chaotic behaviour is known to occur include the dynamics of the solar system (e.g. irregular motion of Saturn's moon Hyperion); fluid flow (e.g. turbulence); chemical reactions (e.g. catalytic processes); ecological systems (e.g. population dynamics); weather systems (e.g. their long-term dynamics); physiological systems (e.g. neurons, the dynamics of the heart); and engineered systems (e.g. electrical circuits, mechanical systems, feedback systems).

4.4.3   Deterministic chaos theory has its roots in classical dynamics and even in Newton's time it was realised that dynamical systems involving many interacting bodies (the solar system, for example) could show very unstable behaviour. Much later (at the end of the nineteenth century) Henri Poincare investigated the inherent instabilities of celestial mechanics and he is considered to be the father of modern deterministic chaos theory. However for several decades his work was largely regarded as a curiosity and it was not until the 1940s with mathematical investigation into the stability of systems, and other work, that deterministic chaos theory began to take off. One major breakthrough came in the early 1960s when Edward Lorenz, in developing highly simplified models of the dynamics of global weather systems, produced computer simulations which showed chaotic behaviour under certain parameter settings. He noticed that when restarting a certain computer simulation part-way through using rounded numerical values (obtained from a printout and not from the greater-precision values stored in the registers and memory of the running simulation program) that the re-started simulation produced a trajectory and outcome significantly different from what was produced when the simulation was left to run uninterrupted. Further investigation revealed that the long-run behaviour of the simulation was sensitive to vanishingly small variations in initial conditions – which meant that when rounded values were entered on restarting rather than full-precision values, the slight variations made a big difference. And this was true even though the simulation was running entirely deterministically. Lorenz's mathematical model was extremely simple but it seemed to be capturing the main qualitative features of the global weather system, and this seemed to suggest that the real weather system was also sensitive to vanishingly small variations in initial conditions. To emphasise the possible chaotic nature of weather systems and the limits to weather forecasting this might impose, Lorenz wrote a paper in 1972 for the American Association for the Advancement of Science with the rather provocative title:

'Predictability: Does the Flap of a Butterfly's Wings in Brazil set off a Tornado in Texas?' (Lorenz 1972). This was where the popular term for deterministic chaos – the "butterfly effect" – comes from.

4.4.4 Although there is little doubt that chaotic behaviour is common within the macroscopic realm, it is not clear whether quantum indeterministic events (such as the decay of radioactive nuclei) are able to provide variations in initial conditions sufficient to make a difference in the long-run behaviour of macroscopic systems. Robert Bishop writes: '[...] although the abstract sensitivity arguments do correctly lead to the conclusion that the smallest of effects can be amplified, applying such arguments to concrete physical systems shows that the amplification process may be severely constrained. For example, investigating the role of quantum effects in the process of friction in sliding surfaces indicates quantum effects can be amplified by chaos to produce a difference in macroscopic behaviour, provided that the effects are large enough to break molecular bonds and are amplified quickly enough.' (Bishop 2002, p. 120) It seems that on present evidence indeterministically produced quantum events rarely trigger macroscopic chaos. However, recall (1.2.9) that by using a device such as a Geiger counter, quantum indeterministic events can be arranged to give rise to indeterministically arising macroscopic events.

4.5   On Sub-state and System Determinism

4.5.1 Given that mainstream science is able to offer little support for the existence of absolute determinism, are there forms of determinism that it can support? The answer is a clear yes in that science has no problem with the existence of what shall be referred to as "sub-state determinism". Indeed, most of the classical equations of physics are deterministic in this sense since they assert either that certain definite relationships hold between particular types of quantities, or that certain quantities change in a time-determinate way. For example, Einstein's famous equation $E=mc^2$ asserts that a determinate relationship exists between the total energy, E, associated with a mass, m, (with c being the velocity of light in a vacuum, which is taken to be a constant of nature). However, this law of physics – like all laws of science as we have them at present – deals only with aspects, or sub-states, of existence, not with everything. An example of a sub-state *time-determinate* equation is Newton's law of motion which says that the rate of change of the momentum of a body is proportional to the net force applied to it. And once again this is a statement about certain sub-states of existence, not about the whole of existence.

4.5.2   Quantum physics also has its sub-state determinate equations. In this realm matter appears to have both wave and particle properties. The Schrodinger wave function – which is an entirely time-determinate equation – describes how the wave (rather than the particle) properties of a quantum system change in time. This equation does not specify when or where a quantum system will lose its wave properties and assume a particle identity, but the square of the amplitude of the Schrodinger wave at each point in space at each moment of time is proportional to the probability of a particle arising at that point should what is known as "the collapse of the wave function" (i.e. transition of the system from having a wave identity to a particle identity) occur at that moment.

4.5.3   These examples are of laws concerning sub-states, or aspects, of existence – not the whole of existence. This means that such laws are based on the tacit assumption that true independence of change exists between the set of sub-states that a law ties together and other sub-states of existence that are not mentioned in the law. And it is also tacitly assumed that investigators (e.g. scientists) are free to manipulate a particular set of such sub-states to examine the validity/invalidity of such a law without being constrained in what they do (and when and where they do it) by exactly what else is going on in existence. That these beliefs are held – albeit usually tacitly – gives strong support to the assumption of independence of change. However, in real-life situations, rather than experimental ones, the specific sub-states or aspects of existence that are referred to in a law are often influenced in complex ways so making it difficult to discover the laws in the first place. For example, while Newton's laws of motion and gravitational attraction assert that a feather and a stone fall at the same rate in the same gravitational field, their motion only manifests this if they fall in a vacuum – if they fall in air, then the force of air resistance on the feather (as a fraction of the gravitational force on it) is much greater than the corresponding fraction of the force of air resistance on the stone and this imbalance destroys their equal rate of fall.

4.5.4 Another form of determinism that is compatible with independence indeterminism is what shall be referred to as "system determinism". Certain systems, from a functional point of view, operate entirely deterministically. The operation of some such systems may be represented by adopting what is known as the finite state machine approach. A finite state machine is a form of abstract model. Three "alphabets" are defined: the set of *inputs* (e.g. symbols, signals, or events) to which the system is responsive; the set of *outputs* that the system produces that may affect its environment or other systems to which it is connected; and the set of *internal states* that the system may assume. A bathroom pull-switch for operating an electric light is, functionally, a very simple system which may be described in these terms. It has one input: a pull on the cord; two outputs: electric power available on its output terminals, no electric power available on its output terminals; and two internal states: switch closed, switch open. The possible transitions, or changes, the system may undergo are given by listing, for every combination of input and internal state, the effect this combination has on the internal state of the system, and on the output. So, for a properly operating pull-switch, we have:

Input to System	Present Internal State	New State	Output
Pull cord	Switch open	Switch closed	Power on output terminals
Pull cord	Switched closed	Switch open	No power on output terminals

The simplifying assumption has been made that power is constantly available to the switch, but this could be treated as another aspect of the input to the system rather than treating it as a constant feature, in which case a more complex finite state machine model would be required.

4.5.5 Once systems with many inputs, outputs, and internal states are considered, things can get very complex. Fortunately it is sometimes possible to decompose a complex system into a set of interactions between simpler sub-systems so making description of the overall system's operation more straightforward than would otherwise be the case.

4.5.6 Although, according to the mainstream scientific view, deterministic physical systems do exist, care must be taken to spell out what is meant by this. There are two main ways of considering a physical system: from a material perspective, and from a functional perspective. So far, a pull-switch system has been considered from a functional perspective, but if a material perspective were taken then much larger alphabets of inputs, outputs, and internal states would need to be specified and a vastly more complex transition table would need to be given. For instance, from a material perspective pull-cord inputs will vary considerably both in strength and direction of pull; the switch will go through a whole series of changes in internal state as its parts move and interact to make or break the circuit; and the output power will not instantly change but will take a short, but measurable, time to settle to its new condition. As the level of phys-ical detail taken into account is increased, so an increasingly complex system description will be needed to accommodate this added information. Indeed, once the level is reached where quantum effects become important, quantum indeterminacies will destroy the determinism apparent when the system is considered in less detailed terms. Hence, from a material perspective, and assuming quantum indeterminacy is a real feature of the microscopic world, it is not possible to give a completely deterministic account of the behaviour of a material system. However from a functional perspective this can sometimes be done because much of the material detail (including microscopic detail) that realises the system's functionality doesn't matter much. For example, from a functional point of view, one pull switch is much like another even though they may be constructed according to somewhat different designs, and be made of somewhat different materials. Indeed, many of the material properties of a system are not relevant at all to the existence of its functional properties – for example, the colours of the components of a pull-switch are generally irrelevant to its functionality.

4.5.7 A general conclusion that may be drawn is that functional determinacy (functional *condition*-determinacy rather than functional *time*-determinacy) is quite common but that material determinacy, once the full details are considered, is not. However, much that happens in the world depends upon functional behaviour and how such behaviours connect together into networks of functionally significant happenings – networks that usually have a constancy of function that is not necessarily reflected in a corresponding constancy of their material realisation. For example, what is important to a person about a pull-switch in a bathroom is that they can pull it and get the room illuminated, and with this functional condition achieved, can then carry out various functionally significant behaviours that are important to them. Exactly what sort of pull switch there is in the bathroom, and exactly what sort of light-source it switches electrical power to, and exactly what provides the electrical power are matters that are irrelevant to the person as long as the switch does what they want.

4.6 Beyond Systems to RENOIRs

4.6.1 As just noted, many functional systems may be materially realised in a variety of different ways – that is, their functionality is what is known as "multiply realisable". Furthermore, some functional systems may have their functionality realised by a varying 'cast' of 'actors' or participants. Many human systems – e.g. businesses, schools, sports teams, committees, political parties – are like this. Social processes – human and animal – typically involve conflictual, competitive, and cooperative interaction among the participants. While such forms of interaction sometimes run in a creatively originative way, very often they run in a fairly type-determined way. For instance, many social behaviours of animals are like this – see, for example, Tinbergen's work on the courting ritual of the three-spined stickleback (1953, p. 10). But so also are many human social processes: think of how many of the processes within and between businesses may be understood as interactions between functionally defined roles which allow little room for creative origination. But human social processes are certainly not devoid of creative origination – indeed, they often provide the context within which creative origination arises and thrives. And even with functionally defined roles and interactions within businesses and human organisations, the individuality of the particular persons filling such roles cannot necessarily be ignored – think of how important the individuality of the leader of an organisation may be, or how a personality clash may disrupt the smooth-running of a work-place.

4.6.2 As soon as functionality and process are emphasised rather than materiality and static structure the vocabulary commonly available is found wanting. The trouble is that although some entities (e.g businesses, organisations, ecosystems) have a more or less definite and continuing functional identity it is often not possible to link this identity to a specific single continuing material presence. In adopting naturalism, it is not doubted that the identity of such entities is always realised in some non-spooky way, nevertheless it is generally accepted that their continuing identity is realised by a changing cast of participants and hence a changing materiality, which means that accounting for them in terms of a fixed material structure is not appropriate. What seems to persist with the continuing existence of such entities is a network of influence relations: a network that may be realised by a changing set of material components or participants. To mark this different point of view the acronym RENOIR – Relatively Enduring Network Of Influence Relations – shall be introduced.

4.6.3 To get a firmer idea about RENOIRs, consider a few examples. An extended family is usually something with a relatively enduring existence. However, its membership changes over time as babies are born, and as members die. A family also changes because its members age, form (and dissolve) partnerships with other people, and move their location of residence. But in spite of all this change something tends to endure, and what this seems to be is a network of relationships – relationships of actual and potential influence existing among the members of the family. These relationships may change, but they still remain relationships belonging to the entity that is the family in question. A living cell may also be understood to be realised and sustained by relatively enduring networks of influence relations, with the specific things (e.g. the particular molecules, and physical structures) that realise these influence relations constantly changing. Similarly, an ecosystem may be understood to be realised and sustained by relatively enduring networks of influence relations among living things and the physical structures and processes of the environment concerned, with the particular living things involved undergoing constant turnover.

4.6.4 One important feature of some RENOIRs is their ability to maintain their continuing existence even when some aspects of their functionality are temporarily absent through lacking an appropriate current material realisation – for example, think of an organisation temporarily without a CEO, or a firm that has lost a manufacturing facility through fire. Such RENOIRs – or complex adaptive systems as they are sometimes referred to – are resilient, adaptable, and capable of learning and invention and it is these capabilities that generally allows them to produce appropriate material replacements for missing functionality. It is these and other creative capabilities, coupled with the many non-creative but directively originative capabilities that such entities possess, that generally allows them to survive in the face of major changes to their environment, and major disruptions to their functioning.

4.6.5 A RENOIR may be realised in an entirely structurally determined way, and in this case it is usually appropriate to think of the entity in terms of its physical structure. For example, although a wind-up clock may be understood functionally as a relatively enduring network of influence relations it is often more meaningful to relate the network of influence relations to the physical nature and structure of the parts of the clock and how they interact and affect one another. Similarly with a radio, an automobile engine, a computer, or a mobile phone. All of these functionally deterministic systems have their influence relations realised by a relatively fixed set of structurally related physical parts and interactions among them. But entities such as a living cell or a human organisation cannot be so characterised because there is a constant turnover of the specific material realising the entity, and also no fixed physical structure of spatio-temporal relationships among the more or less freely moving material participants (e.g. biomolecules, or persons respectively) that realise the network. Furthermore, while the participants of such RENOIRs are not actually taking part in the influence relations that realise a particular RENOIR they are generally free to operate independently – including interacting in other ways such as participating in other RENOIRs. For example, a particular molecule in a cell may participate in different chemical pathways at different times, or may participate in a chemical reaction that has nothing to do with the functional operation of the cell. Similarly, in a human organisation, the people involved in realising and sustaining its operation generally do not spend all their time doing so – they have many other activities that they get involved in (e.g. chatting to their colleagues about non-work matters), and they participate in many other RENOIRs that, for instance, are associated with other aspects of their lifestructure such as their families, their clubs, and the religious groups they belong to.

4.6.6 The large degree of independence or looseness that often exists among the participants of a RENOIR means that many of the interactions that give rise to the network of influences relations that define and realise it are independence interactions. For instance, independence interactions arise whenever a participant stops whatever activity they are involved in and enters into an interaction relevant to realising the RENOIR – as, for example, happens when an employee starts work. Also, many of the influence relations that define a RENOIR are realised through independence interactions between participants rather than through permanent structural relationships. For example, in a cell chemical reactions that realise relevant influence relations in the life of the cell arise because of independence interactions among the relatively freely moving reactants, and not, as for instance is the case with a piece of clockwork, because the participants are in a relatively fixed structural relationship. And nowadays in many human organisations the influence relations important for its functioning are realised by means of remote communication – e.g. by mobile phone, or email – in which the spatial relationship between the communicants is relatively unimportant. According to independence indeterminism, when the influence relations of a RENOIR are realised through independence interactions, the behaviour of the RENOIR is intrinsically indeterministic (although in many cases it will be strongly type-determined). By "intrinsically indeterministic" is meant that the indeterminism comes from within the RENOIR rather than solely from independence interactions between the RENOIR and its environment.

4.6.7 The reason for introducing the concept of a RENOIR is that the operation and behaviour of psychological agents, and humans in particular, is much more readily understood using this idea than the idea of a system as being a material/structural entity. And this is particularly true when independence indeterminism is adopted as the naturalistic metaphysics of choice rather than determinism. The concept of a RENOIR is implicitly understood by many people but it is rarely given the sort of explicit attention that it has been given here. And, to the author's knowledge, this concept does not have a single word by which it may be referred to, hence the introduction of the acronym RENOIR. Note that the concept of a REN-OIR is simply one way of thinking about what a system is, and because the word system is much more widely understood than REN-OIR (which is as yet unknown outside this book), it is this word that shall most frequently be used even when it would perhaps be more useful to think of the entity as a RENOIR.

4.7 Independence Indeterminism is Compatible With Science

4.7.1 As has already been discussed there are forms of determinism that are an established part of science (specifically, sub-state determinism and system determinism) which are compatible with independence indeterminism. Are there forms of determinism recognised by scientists that are *incompatible* with independence indeterminism? Absolute determinism is not, but then mainstream scientists who accept the existence of quantum indeterminism do not accept absolute determinism. What about macroscopic determinism? The generally accepted view within science is that because quantum indeterminacy plays a minor role in the macroscopic realm, this realm operates almost wholly deterministically which means that macroscopic determinism is incompatible with independence indeterminism which assumes that true independence of change is extremely common within the macroscopic ream and that indeterminately arising independence interactions are very common. This means that independence indeterminism is seriously at odds with current mainstream thinking in science. However, were independence indeterminism to become generally accepted by scientists (and its primary assumption already is *implicitly* accepted), then would this actually make much difference to science? It is likely that it would not because science is, on the one hand, mainly concerned with *dependence* interactions – which it is often able to deal with using its deterministic methods – and on the other hand with *type-determined* independence interactions, which it is often able to deal with using statistical and probabilistic methods.

4.7.2 Nevertheless, the metaphysical position of most present-day scientists has no place for the existence of indeterminately arising independence interactions. Indeed, most scientists would accept Nagel's view that independence interactions (or, in Nagel's terms, interaction among previously independently running causal chains) are deterministically arising occurrences, and that this would be obvious if access to the "complete picture" were available. However this view is not backed up by what science is able to establish empirically, as may be appreciated by further consideration of Nagel's example of a falling brick striking a man as he walks to the tobacconist.

4.7.3 Presently available expertise might just about allow a deterministic simulation model to be constructed capable of predicting some aspects of the motion of a man as he walked down a street towards a tobacconist. But walking is a voluntary activity that may be interrupted, or changed, by the mind-brain activity of the person doing the walking. For instance, a man, while walking towards a tobacconist, may suddenly remember that he has forgotten to bring any money with him and may turn about and head back home. Or, as another example, he may meet a friend on the way and decide to stop and have a brief chat. Given that many influences may affect the walking-behaviour of a person, it is quite beyond present-day science to provide a consistently reliable time-determinate model capable of predicting specific instances of non-constrained human walking behaviour. However, science *is* capable of producing a model for making (nearly) time-determinate predictions of the motion of a brick while it falls from a building once the conditions of its dislodgement are known. But science seems quite incapable of developing a model for predicting exactly when a particular brick will become dislodged and fall from a particular building.

4.7.4 What is needed for a correct prediction of the independence interaction of the brick striking the man is information about everything relevant that is going on in the universe at the time of making the prediction, coupled with knowledge of a set of time-determinate laws of nature that would allow a correct prediction to be made. Suppose that the prediction is made when the man leaves his house and that his walk to the tobacconist takes five minutes. According to a fundamental assumption of the theory of relativity – which states that no influence can travel faster than the speed of light in vacuum – a sphere must be considered that is centred on the street in question and which has a radius equal to the distance light travels during five minutes. This would be a sphere with a radius of about 90 million kilometres (light travelling at about 300,000 kilometres a second for 300 seconds), and the state of everything in it relevant to the possible future interaction of the brick and the man would have to be known. However, science is incapable of obtaining a truly in - stantaneous description of anything (see 3.4.8), and even if it could it is nowhere near having knowledge of a set of time-determinate laws sufficient to allow a correct prediction to be made. Indeed, it may be that quantum indeterminacies mean that no set of strictly time-determinate laws can do the job.

4.7.5   It seems, therefore, that Nagel's view that macroscopic independence interactions are never indeterministic occurrences simply cannot be verified by what science can do. Hence, without damaging the empirical findings of science, nothing would be lost by scientists abandoning the belief that macroscopic independence interactions are deterministically produced events and accepting the belief that they arise indeterministically. Of course, this latter belief can no more be empirically confirmed or denied than can the former. Nevertheless, abandoning belief in macroscopic determinism would be a big change to the way scientists thought about the *metaphysical* basis of existence and would take some getting used to.

5 More on Free Will

5.1 Introduction

5.1.1 This chapter considers some of the significant contributions to the free-will debate made over the last fifty years or so. The treatment is by no means comprehensive, but it does address some of the ideas that represent relatively new and significant approaches to old problems.

5.1.2 The first piece of work considered concerns findings and views that suggest that the conscious sense people have of having freely willed an action is an illusion. Following discussion of this work, which seems to assume a deterministic view of mind-brain functioning, consideration is give to some recent approaches to developing scientifically credible accounts of self-originative free will – approaches, however, that all suffer from the weakness of relying solely on quantum indeterminacy as the source of the de novo origination in the free-will process. Next, a paper by Peter Strawson is discussed in which he argues that the possession of reactive attitudes by humans (such as resentment and gratitude) undermines the importance of the free-will dispute because whichever way it turns out it is unlikely to have much bearing on how people actually react to one another. Following this, the work of Harry Frankfurt on higher-order desires is considered – work in which he argues that one important thing that makes humans different from animals is that people care about the desires they actually have and that they sometimes desire to alter these desires. The issue of free will has long been closely associated with whether or not humans are full moral agents and so relatively recent work on this matter is considered next. This then leads on to a discussion of a question central to the free-will debate: Could we have done otherwise than what we actually did?

5.2 Conscious Free Will

5.2.1 In recent years, the term conscious free will has been used to label the conscious feeling people usually have that they have freely willed what they do. It has long been argued that this feeling gives us evidence that humans do in fact possess free will, but it has also long been argued that it does no such thing. In the last few decades a good deal of experimental research seems to support this latter view. And some participants in this research, and others, have drawn the conclusion that if the conscious sense of having freely willed an action is an illusion then it must be that people don't have free will at all. However this conclusion does not necessarily follow since it is reasonable to assume that subconsciously and unconsciously running parts of a person's self play an important role in the self-directed origination of their decisions and doings, and just because they may not be conscious of how these parts operate, run, and interact this does not mean they don't belong to the person's self. Nevertheless, these recent findings and ideas about conscious free will make some important points.

5.2.2   Among several contemporary workers, Daniel Wegner in his book *The Illusion of Conscious Free Will* stands out as someone who has made a particularly strong case against conscious free will, so it is this book that shall be used as the basis of the discussion.

5.2.3   Wegner adopts a scientific approach to whether belief in conscious free will is an illusion. The experimental work he has done and the various scientific findings he draws upon in making his case lead him to the conclusion that by the time a person is consciously aware of making a choice, unconscious processes have already made it for them. He therefore reasons that the belief that humans have free will is an illusion. He argues that while people have a "self-explanation mechanism" that, normally, makes them feel that it is their conscious thinking that determines what they do, it is actually other neurophysiological processes that are responsible.

5.2.4   Wegner draws upon a good deal of psychological and neuroscientific evidence to establish a number of facts. He notes well-known neurophysiological conditions such as alien hand syndrome (in which a person experiences one of their hands operating as if it had a mind of its own); automatism (in which a person has no conscious awareness of performing an action); illusions of control (when a person feels they are controlling something which in fact they are not controlling); and phantom limb syndrome (sensing the presence of, and consciously willed movement of, an amputated limb). He also mentions work on direct stimulation of the brain's motor centres which enables an experimenter to produce, say, smooth

103

hand movements in a conscious subject independently of the subject willing such movement to happen. When this is done the subject will disown the movement, recognizing it as something they did not consciously will. However, stimulation of other areas of the brain may result in movement accompanied by a conscious experience of ownership of the action, leading the subject to construct some more or less rational explanation for why the movement occurred as it did.

5.2.5 In support of his argument, Wegner uses experimental work that establishes two important results. First, that voluntary movements are regularly preceded by unconscious brain activity (indicated by a "readiness potential" that may be detected by using an EEG – an electroencephalograph machine). And second, that conscious awareness of wanting, choosing, or willing such a movement occurs a significant time *after* the occurrence of the readiness potential. The former finding was established in the 1960s and the latter by Benjamin Libet and his colleagues in the 1980s.

5.2.6 In the Libet experiments – the results and implications of which have come to have an important place in the free-will debate – subjects were asked to make voluntary wrist flexions at some moment of their own choosing and without prior planning. The researchers found that the following sequence of events occurred. First, about 0.55 seconds before muscle movement actually begins, a readiness potential is detected in the subjects. Next, at about 0.2 seconds before actual movement, the subjects report conscious awareness of wanting or choosing to flex their wrist. This means that "conscious will" arises about 0.35 seconds *after* the readiness potential indicates that subjects are going to move their wrist. Finally, at about 0.08 seconds *before* the subjects actually begins to move their wrist they report conscious awareness of the wrist starting to move. With planned movements the readiness potential is detected much earlier – perhaps two or more seconds before the actual movement. (Wegner 2002, pp. 50-55)

5.2.7 Libet's results suggest that when a person makes a voluntary movement the decision to make the movement is not something that belongs to their consciousness but rather is done unconsciously, and that only after it has been so done does it become expressed in consciousness in such a way that it feels to the person that they consciously willed the action. Wegner points out that since readiness potentials are prior to and regularly associated with the performance of voluntary movement, it may reasonably be assumed that the unconscious processes producing the readiness potentials are also involved in determining the conscious experience of choosing, or wanting, or willing to do the act. He says: 'It seems that conscious wanting is not the beginning of the process of making voluntary movement. The position of conscious will in the time line suggests perhaps that the experience of will is a link in a causal chain leading to action, but in fact it might not even be that. It might be a loose end – one of those things, like action, that is caused by prior brain and mental events.' (p. 55)

5.2.8   Although Libet's experiments, and other investigations, seem to establish beyond scientific doubt that non-conscious processes determine a person's actions prior to them becoming consciously aware of deciding to perform them, this is a conclusion that has not gone unchallenged. For instance, Alfred Mele has been a strong critic of this view and has written a short book entitled *Free – why science hasn't disproved free will* in which he exposes several weaknesses and loopholes in Libet's work (Mele 2014).

5.2.9   Nowhere in his book does Wegner consider that the processes whereby an action is produced may be originative, and might indeed be self-directively originative – indeed, "indeterminism" is not included in the index. He seems simply to tacitly accept, as do most scientists, that everything involved in producing choice and action must be fully determined. Further, his work is based on the tacit assumption that people don't possess free will, and since he recognises that typically people consciously believe that they do possess it, he sees his task as that of providing a scientifically supported case for showing that this belief is illusory. In spite of this being his position, many libertarians would accept the importance of much of what Wegner says about the nature of conscious will. For instance, towards the end of the book he writes:

> [...] Conscious will can be understood as part of an accounting system. Its regular appearance in actions of all kinds serves as an aid to remembering what we are doing and what we have done. This in turn allows us to deserve things. [...] We must remember what we have done if we are going to want to claim that our actions have earned us anything (or

prevented us from deserving something nasty). [...] The authorship emotion is one of the things people intuitively believe that they would miss if it were gone. It would not be particularly satisfying to go through life causing things – say, making scientific discoveries, winning sports, creating social harmony, helping people, or even digging nice big holes in the yard – if we had no personal recognition of these achievements. (pp. 327-329)

And in the same vein he later writes:

Illusory or not, conscious will is the person's guide to his or her own moral responsibility for action. If you think you willed an act, your ownership of the act is established in your own mind. You will feel guilty if the act is bad, and worthy if the act is good. The function of conscious will is not to be absolutely correct but to be a compass. It tells us where we are and prompts us to feel the emotions appropriate to the morality of the actions we find ourselves doing. Guilt, pride, and other moral emotions would not grip us at all if we didn't feel we had willed our actions. (Wegner, p. 341)

5.2.10 For Wegner, it seems that consciousness plays a minor role in the actual *production* of human choices and actions; for him, its major function is to make people *aware* of what it is they have chosen or willed to do. However, he supports this conclusion by largely considering experiments in which the subjects are explicitly requested to try not to *consciously* decide to act, but to do so spontaneously and unconsciously. And the experimental setups that are used generally do not introduce any significant conflict within the subjects about what to do. This means that the findings of such experiments have little to say about the nature of the prolonged and difficult decision-making that faces most people from time to time, and in which self-originative free will of the sort explored in this book is understood to have a significant role. Furthermore, like many neuroscientists and others, Wegner has all too readily identified free will as necessarily being a conscious process and not one in which unconscious and subconscious influences and processes play fundamental roles. Nevertheless, Wegner has made a significant contribution to the free-will debate.

5.3   Bob Doyle's Cogito Model of the Free-Will Process

5.3.1   Wegner does not see indeterminacy as playing a significant role in the production of human actions since, like most scientists, he believes macroscopic determinism dominates throughout all stages of the processes involved. However, as the work of Bob Doyle illus‐ trates, a scientifically plausible case for origination being involved in the free-will process may be made.

5.3.2   Bob Doyle has devoted much of his time to developing what he refers to as "The new information philosophy", a major part of which is deeply concerned with the problem of free will – see his book *Free Will: The Scandal in Philosophy*. His website, www.informa‐ tionphilosopher.com, offers ready access to much of his work.

5.3.3   In common with several writers on free will, Doyle offers a two-stage model of the free-will process. In the first stage, which involves the production and modification of alternative possibilities for choice or action, indeterminism may play a significant role. How‐ ever, the second stage – which is concerned with evaluating and choosing among these alternatives – Doyle sees as being adequately determined: that is, sufficiently determined for a person to be re‐ sponsible for what they choose to do. Daniel Dennett has suggested that indeterminism may also play a role in producing the reasons for and against the alternatives being considered in a decision situation (Dennett 1978, pp. 286-299). Doyle writes about his two-stage Cogito model (from the Latin *co-agitare*, to shake together) by saying it 'loc‐ ates randomness (either ancient chance or modern quantum inde‐ terminacy) in the mind, in a way that breaks the causal chain of phys‐ ical determinism, while doing no harm to responsibility.' (Doyle 2011, p. 187) He notes (p. 66) that elements of the model have been pro‐ posed by various philosophers – see his 'Two-Stage Models of Free Will' (Doyle 2011, Chapter 12), for a detailed account. Doyle rejects the idea of the indeterminacy inherent in a decision process being such that it occurs at the point of final decision. In other words, he rejects the traditional idea that a decision remains entirely open right up until the instant it is finally decided by an act of free will. Rather, he argues that the indeterminacy exists – as noise – during the pro‐ cess by which alternative possibilities are formed and modified. He writes: 'The mind, like all biological systems, has evolved in the presence of constant noise and is able to ignore that noise, unless the noise provides a significant competitive advantage, which it clearly does as the basis for freedom and creativity.' (Doyle 2011, p. 188)

5.3.4   Doyle sees the origination of alternative possibilities through noise as being based on a person's perceptions of the external world, their communicative interactions with others, and by their "Micro Mind" generating associations between thoughts. Doyle writes:

> Imagine a Micro Mind with a randomly assembled "agenda" of possible things to say or do. These are drawn from our memory of past thoughts and actions, but randomly varied by unpredictable negations, associations of a part of one idea with a part or all of another, and by substitutions of words, images, feelings, actions drawn from our experience. In information communication terms there is cross-talk and noise in neural circuitry. [...] [N]ew experience is likely to be stored in neural pathways alongside closely related past experiences. And a fresh experience, or active thinking about an experience that presents a decision problem, is likely to activate nearby brain circuits, ones that have strong associations with our current circumstances. These are likely to begin firing randomly, to provide unpredictable raw material for actionable possibilities. [...] [T]he randomness of the Micro Mind is simply the result of ever-present noise, both thermal and quantum noise, that is inherent in any information storage and communication system. [...] The Cogito model is not a mechanism. It is a process, and information philosophy is a process philosophy. (pp. 190-192)

5.3.5   Doyle contrasts the indeterminacy of the Micro Mind with the determinacy of the Macro Mind: that part of the mind-brain responsible for evaluating alternatives and determining what the agent's choices and doings shall be, and a system that in its operation generally succeeds in suppressing the ever-present indeterminacy due to noise that exists within the neural circuitry that realises it. However Doyle rejects the idea of a clear separation between indeterministic and deterministic parts of the free-will process because he sees decision-making as a complex re-entrant process involving generating and modifying possibilities, evaluating them, and tentatively deciding

108

before a firm or actioned decision arises. In his view this is an origin-ative process but one with an overall determinism adequate to ensure that the final decision is something for which the agent, rather than random indeterminacy, is responsible.

5.3.6 One major weakness of Doyle's account of the free-will process is that the only de novo sources of origination are noise and quantum indeterminacy, and these sorts of indeterminacies are not open to control or influence. Given this, it may be argued that all that is really required is randomness, not true origination. On this view, a deterministic source of randomness (such as a deterministic al-gorithm for generating pseudo-random numbers) is capable of pro-ducing all that an indeterministic source can produce. However this is not an altogether fair criticism because the problem of free will and determinism is not that determinism cannot, in principle, explain the manifest behaviours associated with what are believed to be instances of the exercise of free will, because it can. Indeed, if it couldn't then compatibilism would fail as a viable thesis. Rather, the weakness of determinism is that it must deny that any sort of self-directively *ori-ginative* activity is possible, including that involved in resolving con-flicts and indecisions within the self and the mind-brain of a psycho-logical agent, which in the present work is taken to be what the free-will process entails.

5.3.7 A second major weakness of Doyle's model – one that follows from all de novo origination being a result of noise and quantum indeterminacy – is that there is no place for the processes of the self as such to be de novo originative and creative. This is pos-sible under independence indeterminism which means it is able to provide a richer basis for explaining human free will than can ac-counts based on random and uncontrollable indeterminism alone.

5.4 Criterial Causation – Peter Tse's Account of Free Will

5.4.1 Although Bob Doyle's model of the micro-mind has a sci-entifically plausible basis it lacks detail and does not identify specific neural-level structures and processes that would provide randomly originated yet contextually appropriate alternative possibilities. Peter Ulric Tse in his book *The Neural Basis of Free Will: Criterial Causation* overcomes this weakness by providing a detailed research-backed account of just how such contextually appropriate origination, and other mind-brain activity supporting free will, may be produced by neural processes. Tse is a cognitive neuroscientist who has carried our detailed laboratory research into vision, attention and consciousness. However, he also has a deep interest in the neural bases of human creativity, free will, and symbolic processing. At the centre of his approach is the idea of "criterial causation". This is not a new idea – although the term seems to be new – but Tse has refined the concept and given a precise account of how it may operate within the mind-brain.

5.4.2   Criterial causation occurs when a system sets up the criteria, and the corresponding decoders, for what patterns of information it will respond to. Typically, these are patterns that in the absence of such a system have no causal effect. With most patterns, although the events and structures that instantiate the various parts of the pattern individually may have causal effect, the spatial, temporal and other *relationships* among them that define the pattern or criteria often do not: rather, it takes the presence of a system (or decoder in a system) that is responsive to these pattern-relationships to provide such an effect. A couple of further points are important. Firstly, a pattern may be realised in many physically different ways, and may be quite loosely defined in terms of the events and relationships that constitute an instantiation of it – for example, think of the very many possible hand-written instantiations that may be made of a given word. Secondly, a pattern exists within a field – or a context, ground, or environment – in which many events, structures, and spatio-temporal relationships may exist other than those that are part of the pattern. This means a pattern-responsive system needs to be able to discriminate between events and relationships that belong to the pattern and those that do not. For example, to recognise a particular face in a crowd a person must filter out all the non-face features of the scene and also apply criteria relevant to the face they seek to recognise in order to identify it. However, concentrating on patterns is actually starting at the wrong end since many patterns – specifically those that have no causal effect in the absence of systems responsive to their presence – don't properly exist in their own right. Rather, in the absence of systems capable of giving them causal effect, such patterns

110

are passive existents (see 2.1.8). Mind-brains possess an extraordinarily large number and range of highly interconnected and dynamically alterable criteria-responsive subsystems and it is through the construction, use, and dynamic combining and re-combining of these that animals (and humans) are able to carry out complex forms of criteria-sensitive directive activity. For example, think of a squirrel rapidly traversing branches and jumping between trees and the complex and continual pattern-responsive processing that this entails. Or, as another example, think of the patterns that a player in a football game needs to be sensitive to in order to play well. And it should be noted, although this is not the main focus of Tse's book, that just as there are pattern-responsive systems there are also pattern-producing systems. For example, a person who hand-writes a message is producing a spatial pattern of marks; and in speaking they are producing a temporal pattern of sounds. Pattern-producing and pattern-responsive systems are the basis of information processing systems, and a mind-brain contains a great many of them.

5.4.3   There is nothing particularly contentious about what has just been said because determinists don't find anything in it that is incompatible with their world view. Nevertheless, determinists would not accept that criterial causation could ever be an originative process, whereas independence indeterminists, and others like Peter Tse, would argue that it can be, and indeed often is. To develop this point and see how criterial causation might figure in everyday decision-making consider an example: the directive activity involved in a car safely crossing a busy road junction. A directive system able to drive a car safely through traffic must be appropriately sensitive to its situation – i.e. responsive to happenings in its environment while taking into account the car's present state. In order to safely cross a busy road junction such a directive system will need to have criterial decoders able to identify "safe-to-cross" patterns of road-junction activity so that it is able to carry out "junction-crossing" behaviour when it detects it is safe to do so. The safe-to-cross pattern may be instantiated in a great many different ways and the criterial decoders for identifying the presence of this pattern should be able to correctly recognise these varied instantiations.

5.4.4   In order to highlight the possible place of free will in this junction-crossing example consider two distinctly different sorts of

111

directive system that are (generally) able to drive a car safely across busy road junctions: namely, a skilled human driver, and a fully-automated system as found in self-driving cars. It shall be assumed that a human driver possesses self-originative free will but that a self-driving car does not. This assumption is made on the basis of two beliefs. Firstly, that a human person, even when operating to realise a particular sort of familiar directive activity such as driving a car, does not have to follow pre-established procedures. This does not mean that humans never operate in pre-established and habitual ways because they very often do, rather it means that it is not necessary that they do so. In contrast to this a fully automated car-driving system, whilst it may have some capacity to improve its performance through learning, does operate by necessarily following pre-established procedures and rules which it cannot override. Secondly, it is assumed that a normal human has many motivations other than those concerned with driving a car, and that these may give rise to conflict within the person of a sort that they sometimes cannot resolve by pre-established means and which may then arouse free-will processing within them. For instance, conflict about what to do may arise within a driver who is rushing to get to a hospital with their seriously sick child but who finds themselves held up from being able to safely cross a busy junction by the volume of traffic. In contrast to human car-drivers, it is assumed that a self-driving car has no objectives other than those concerned with safely driving the car to its user-assigned destination, and as a result (and because of how it is designed) it does not experience unresolvable conflicts because it always has pre-established means for deciding what to do. Given these assumptions, consider now how criterial causation may figure in these two ways of realising a car-driving directive system.

5.4.5   According to independence indeterminism, but not determinism, specific instantiations of safe-to-cross patterns must be taken to be originated because they consist of joint-change composed of partly independently moving vehicles and other road users. This means that any response to such an originated pattern will itself be originated. But if the response is type-determined – as will always be the case with a fully automated car-driving system – then, according to the view of free will that has been adopted (1.4.14), no free-will processing will be involved in its production. However, with a human person there is room for free-will processing, as may be shown by continuing to develop and discuss the example of conflict just mentioned.

5.4.6   Suppose the driver who is rushing to get their seriously sick child to a hospital finds that their delay at the busy junction becomes quite extended, and that this leads them to contemplate taking a riskier approach to crossing the junction than they normally would. And let us suppose that in considering what to do they experience conflict – for instance, with thoughts about the consequences of causing an accident conflicting with thoughts about the need to get to the hospital as soon as possible. Assume that the driver has no pre-established means for resolving this conflict and that in consequence they engage in free-will processing in an effort to create a resolution. What sort of things may happen during this free-will process? Nothing can be said for sure because it is assumed to be a *creatively* originative process, but perhaps the driver's rising frustration leads them to think of a course of action such as switching on the hazard lights, sounding the horn, and edging-out into the traffic. However, in evaluating this plan the driver may become conscious of new dangers and perhaps experience new conflicts about whether or not to proceed with it.

5.4.7   It seems that criterial causation plays an important part in the process just outlined. For instance, rather than having a criterial detector for safe-to-cross patterns of traffic activity the driver will need ones that can recognise *degrees* of riskiness in crossing. And in trying to think of alternatives to a risky crossing, the driver will need criterial decoders that reject extreme options. For example, the option of getting out of the car and walking away to have a cup of coffee is very unlikely to receive any serious consideration, which suggests that criterial decoders will reject, suppress, or simply not respond to such alternatives, or operate in such a manner as to suppress their production altogether. Furthermore, it seems likely that in an unfamiliar situation of the sort considered that some criterial decoders will need to be originated on the fly to suit the particular circumstances. For instance, in contemplating taking a particular sort of serious risk in crossing the junction, criterial decoders will need to be originated that trigger thoughts about what may go wrong and what undesired consequences may follow from such an action.

5.4.8 One way of making sense of what might be going on in such a situation is to think of the person's mind-brain as, among other things, consisting of a large network of more or less well-established but flexibly responsive criterial decoders that are linked to a person's motivational, emotional, and executive selves and which seek to detect the presence of certain patterns of mind-brain activity – activity, for instance, emanating from processes of perception, memory recall, imagination, reasoning, and from the contents of consciousness – that are important to these parts of the self. For instance, thought of making a risky crossing of the junction may stimulate – through relevant criterial decoders – such motivations as wanting to avoid physical injury and pain to oneself, to one's child, and to other road-users; wanting to avoid damage to the car; wanting to avoid prosecution for dangerous driving and loss of one's licence; and wanting to avoid any further delay in getting the child to hospital. And accompanying the activation of these motivations may be stimulation of various associated emotions.

5.4.9 As time goes by without being able to cross safely, or decide on an alternative to just continuing to wait, the driver is likely to become increasingly stressed and this may lead to them to think of ways to deal with this. For example, the driver may decide to try to de-stress themselves – perhaps by using techniques they are familiar with, such as taking deep breaths and trying mindfulness or calming exercises. However, according to the view of free will that is being adopted in this book, no matter what course of action is ultimately carried out, for it to be produced by the driver carrying out free-will processing requires that it should not have arisen wholly through automatic or pre-established means but that some creative origination must have been involved.

5.4.10 Independence indeterminism explains the creativeness of the sort of free-will processing just discussed as being based on chance and directed independence interactions among various parts and processes of the person's mind-brain. For instance: independence interactions among the person's activated motivations and emotions, the condition of their executive self, and the products and processes of their perceptual systems, imagination, memory, reasoning, and consciousness. However, this explanation – one based on independence indeterminism – is not available to those who do not know

114

of this new metaphysics (or do not accept it) and so, as long as they accept that free will involves self-directed *creative* origination, they must look elsewhere for creativeness in the free-will process. As already discussed, Bob Doyle offers one scientifically credible account of how this may be achieved, and Peter Tse provides another partially similar account that makes use of his concept of criterial decoders.

5.4.11   Tse writes on this matter as follows.

Criterial decoders potentially interact with the uncertainty, noise, indeterminism, and randomness introduced by particle-level causality in at least two interesting ways. First, they clean up this noise by reducing a great variety of potentially noisy inputs into a single output, such as the firing of a neuron. Second they permit the "harnessing" of noise or randomness for the generation of novel information. By setting up criterial decoders in advance that convert many types of input into one type of output, systems that instantiate criterial causal chains effectively take control of randomness and use it to generate outcomes that are caused by the system, rather than outcomes that are determined by randomness per se. Yet these non-arbitrary outcomes are not predictable and could have turned out otherwise. Because solutions are not predetermined and can vary, yet still satisfy a given finite set of criteria, and because outcomes that satisfy lower level criteria can be compared, modified, and rejected in an open-ended fashion at the level of executive consideration of what has been generated by lower level systems, genuine novelty can result. This novelty is not itself random, because it meets the criteria that were preset. But a particular solution was not predetermined either. Criterial causality therefore offers a middle path between determinism and randomness. (Tse 2013, p. 131)

5.4.12   Although Tse recognises that this account is similar to a two-stage one in that indeterministic randomness is used to generate novelty at the alternatives or options level, he maintains that it is fundamentally different because it does not involve a division between a first stage in which multiple and possibly novel ideas are generated, and a second stage in which selection among these is made deterministically. Rather, he proposes a three-stage model involving cycles of activity taking place at various levels and over various time-spans within the mind-brain. The first stage in a cycle involves the setting or re-setting of criteria – in a neuron, or a neural circuit, or in an even larger neural system – on the basis of what preceding criteria have been met, and other factors such as the current purposes of the agent. The second stage involves the emergence of inherently variable (and to some extent indeterministically generated) inputs to the criterial decoders. The third stage consists in the inputs either meeting the criteria – so resulting in effects that influence future criteria-setting and action – or not meeting them (which may also influence what happens next).

5.4.13   Tse sees randomness playing a role in the first two stages but not substantially in the third. He sees quantum indeterminacy as the de novo source of this randomness, although, like Doyle, he accepts that this often expresses itself as noise of one sort or another. Drawing upon substantial research evidence, Tse argues that a particular molecular-level neuronal mechanism plays a key role. He writes:

> NMDA (N-methyl-D-aspartate) receptors [at synapses – the sites that informationally link one neuron to another] likely play a role in the magnification of microscopic randomness operative at the level of the behavior of a single magnesium ion to the level of spike timing. It is remarkable that this molecular device can play a role in physically realizing so many of the fundamental properties of information processing in neuronal circuits: rapid synaptic plasticity, amplification of microscopic randomness to randomness at the level of timing in neural circuits, bursting, LTP and LTD [long-term potentiation of synaptic weights, and long-term depression of synaptic weights, respectively], as well as information processing via bursting and synchronous bursting. (p. 96)

5.4.14   Tse points out that an agent cannot control what happens once criteria have been set and when no time remains for re-setting them. But what an agent can control, by appropriately setting criteria, is what *patterns* of events, among the multifarious happenings that may emerge in the future, will make a difference to it. That is, agents that operate as self-setting pattern-responsive systems have the inherent freedom of determining some aspects of their future.

5.4.15 The greatest strength of Tse's account is that it is solidly grounded in detailed scientific research, and that it is focused on criterial causation. Tse describes, sometimes in considerable detail, how particular systems and functions relevant to realising self-originative free will may be physically realised within the mind-brain. The serious weakness in Tse's account is that, at bottom, the only source of de novo origination is quantum indeterminacy, which is something over which an agent has no influence or control. But what Tse does show – through his idea of criterial causation and the way an agent has control over setting and re-setting criteria – is that such uncontrolled randomness need not deprive an agent of control over their choices and actions, and may provide them with a means of creatively originating novel ways of dealing with various aspects of their life.

5.5 Ultimate Responsibility – Kane's Account of Free Will

5.5.1 Robert Kane is perhaps the leading naturalistic libertarian of the day. Kane is a strong supporter of what he describes as the traditional view of free will: 'The power of agents to be the ultimate creators (or originators) and sustainers of their own ends and purposes.' (Kane 1996, p. 4) Kane recognises that free will requires that an agent who exercises it must have been able to have done otherwise. But he argues – following a line of reasoning initiated by Aristotle – that to be *ultimately* responsible for its actions an agent must be ultimately responsible for those aspects of its self that led it to do what it did. Kane acknowledges that ultimate responsibility (UR) is a difficult concept to pin-down, nevertheless he proposes the following formal definition.

> An agent is *ultimately responsible* for some (event or state) E's occurring, only if (R) the agent is personally responsible for E's occurring in a sense which entails that something the agent voluntarily (or willingly) did or omitted, and for which the agent could have voluntarily done otherwise, either was, or causally contributed to, E's occurrence and made a difference to whether or not E occurred; and (U) for every X and Y (where X and Y represent occurrences of events and/or states), if the agent is personally responsible for X, and if Y is

117

an *arche* (or sufficient ground or cause or explanation) for X, then the agent must also be personally responsible for Y. (p. 35)

5.5.2 The responsibility condition (R) has been widely discussed and is sometimes taken to be the central issue in the free-will debate. Showing how it may be naturalistically realised does not seem to be impossible – Doyle and Tse, for example, have indicated how it may be achieved. However it has been quite widely argued that the ultimacy condition (U) cannot be naturalistically satisfied. The problem, as Kane states it, is this: 'If our characters and our motives (together with background conditions) provide an explanation for our actions [...] then we must, according to the U condition, be responsible for forming our character and motives by earlier actions, and so on indefinitely.' (p. 37) In other words, fulfilment of the ultimacy condition implies that a natural agent must be able to realise an infinite regress, which is not possible. This impossibility has been recognised by several philosophers, and some of them have railed against the injustice of attributing *ultimate* responsibility to humans. For example, Friedrich Nietzsche strongly objected to the view promulgated by some religions (Catholicism, for example) that God has endowed humans with a special faculty of will which makes them ultimately responsible for their morally significant choices and actions. He condemned such teaching as 'the most infamous of the arts of the theologian for making mankind "accountable"' and declared that 'Christianity is a Hangman's metaphysics.' (Nietzsche 1889 (1968, p. 53)) Elsewhere Nietzsche writes:

> The *causa sui* [cause of itself] is the best self-contradiction that has been conceived so far; it is a sort of rape and perversion of logic. But the extravagant pride of man has managed to entangle itself profoundly and frightfully with just this nonsense. The desire for "freedom of the will" in the superlative metaphysical sense, which still holds sway, unfortunately, in the minds of the half-educated; the desire to bear the entire and ultimate responsibility for one's actions oneself, and to absolve God, the world, ancestors, chance, and society involves nothing less than to be precisely the *causa sui* and, with more than Baron Munchausen's audacity, to pull oneself up

118

into existence by the hair, out of the swamps of nothingness. (Nietzsche 1886).

5.5.3 In recent times the case for the impossibility of ultimate moral responsibility has been strongly stated by Galen Strawson who summarises what he calls the "The Basic Argument" as follows. '(1) Nothing can be *causa sui* – nothing can be the cause of itself. (2) In order to be truly morally responsible for one's actions one would have to be *causa sui*, at least in certain crucial mental respects. (3) Therefore nothing can be truly morally responsible.' (G. Strawson 1994, (2003, p 212)). Given the importance of the infinite regress problem to what Kane is arguing for it is worth spelling it out in a way that connects it with his approach.

5.5.4 To be ultimately responsible for its current doings – call them CD – an agent must be ultimately responsible for those aspects – call them s0 – of its current self that were decisive in the production of CD. (If those aspects of an agent's current self that were decisive in producing CD had their origin outside the agent – for example, in the agent's inherited biological makeup or socialisation – then the agent would not be ultimately responsible for CD.) According to the ultimacy condition, if the agent is indeed ultimately responsible for s0, then it must have been ultimately responsible for the actions (including mind-brain activity) it performed that were necessary for the production of s0. Call these actions SFA:s0 (short for self-forming actions producing s0). Now, in order to be ultimately responsible for SFA:s0 the agent must have been ultimately responsible for those aspects of its self – call them s-1 – that were decisive in the production of SFA:s0. However, in order to maintain ultimate responsibility for CD it is also necessary for the agent to have been ultimately responsible for those self-forming actions which played a decisive role in the production of s-1 – self-forming actions which may be labelled SFA:s-1. And in order to continue to maintain ultimate responsibility for CD it is further necessary for the agent to have been ultimately responsible for those parts of its self (call them s-2) which played a decisive role in the production of SFA:s-1. And logically this cycle has no end and so must continue in an infinite regress.

5.5.5 Kane addresses this problem by arguing that by carrying out what he calls self-forming willings (SFWs) an agent is able to create changes to its self for which it is ultimately responsible. Kane suggests that the process of carrying out self-forming willings may involve quantum indeterministic events occurring within the mind-brain of an agent which get amplified by chaotic dynamics that arise when the agent is in a condition of conflict over what to do, and is making an effort to resolve this conflict. He suggests that on such occasions, and in times of soul-searching, the outcomes that arise are strongly influenced by various conflicting and competing parts of the agent's self, but that they are not completely determined by these influences because quantum indeterminacies occurring within the mind-brain constantly affect what is going on. Peter Tse's detailed examination of possible mind-brain mechanisms may help in identifying some of what is involved in such an originative process. However, Tse's book was published after the work discussed here so Kane could not call upon it, but he does point to other scientific evidence that is consistent with the process he describes.

5.5.6   Kane acknowledges that his idea will raise objections and he discusses at length, and attempts to rebut, what he sees as the main ones. However, what he is unable to do is suggest anything other than quantum indeterminacy as the de novo source of origination in the process, and so he lays himself open to the criticism that a fully deterministic source of randomness in place of the quantum indeterminacy would make no difference to the process he is describing but would undermine the creatively originative nature of self-forming willings upon which his ultimacy argument rests. Furthermore, quantum indeterministic events cannot be controlled or influenced by the agent or anything else, so it may be argued that an agent cannot be held responsible if such events play a major part in creating its actions. Kane counters this latter line of criticism by explaining – in a similar way to Doyle and Tse – that the quantum indeterminacies are so intimately fused with macroscopic brain processes that the originations involved properly belong to the agent as such and not to the quantum processes alone. He writes:

> As long as effort is being made and the will is in tension, the micro indeterminacies are being fed upward to the neural net as a whole, which is continually reorganizing in response to micro indeterminacies and is in turn influencing individual neurons. There is an ongoing mutual feedback from the net to its parts and back, and this continuing process *taken as a*

120

whole is the experienced effort. One does not merely have in-determinism or chance (at the micro level) *followed* by a determinate effort, or a determinate effort *followed* by indeterminism or chance. Rather, the indeterminism and the effort are "fused": the indeterminacy is a property of the effort and the effort *is* indeterminate. (p. 151)

5.5.7   "Fusion-indeterminacy", as this process shall be called (Kane talks of it as "The Fusion Principle"), seems to be a naturalistically feasible creatively originative process, and one that so intimately involves the self that it may said to be a self-based creatively originative process. However, the fact that uncontrollable and randomly occurring quantum events are the only source of de novo origination occurring during the process rather weakens the role of the self in the specifically originative aspects of the process. However, quantum indeterminacy does provide a form of origination that is (according to mainstream ideas) entirely uninfluenced by anything and so would provide the ultimacy that Kane seeks. But Kane cannot have his cake and eat it: if an agent's self-forming willings arise in a way uninfluenced by anything then the agent can hardly be held responsible for what follows from them. Kane of course accepts this and this is why he introduces fusion-indeterminacy as a way of involving an agent's self in the creation of its self-forming willings. But in doing this it seems he must give up any claim to providing an account of *ultimate* moral responsibility because all natural psychological agents start with a mind-brain possessing features that are given (by biological inheritance or socialisation, say) and not created solely by the agent themselves. Were Kane's approach to incorporate independence indeterminism then it would yield a richer account of the free-will process than that which fusion indeterminacy based on quantum indeterminacy alone is able to provide – an account that would be able to give the self, and independence interactions (both undirected and directed) among its various relatively independently operating parts, an explicit role in the creatively originative processes involved. But independence indeterminism would not provide a basis for *ultimate* moral responsibility because it accepts that many factors not of a person's own creation play a part (directly or indirectly) in the production of their morally significant choices and actions.

121

5.5.8   Although *ultimate* responsibility for an action is a solid the-oretical basis for attributing moral responsibility, everyday moral practices do not seem to require it, as discussed next.

5.6   Moral Responsibility and Reactive Attitudes

5.6.1   Peter Strawson in his highly influential paper 'Freedom and Resentment' pursues a project of reconciliation between what he calls the optimists (compatibilists) who believe determinism is com-patible with moral responsibility, and the pessimists (incompatibilists) who believe it is not.

5.6.2   At the centre of Strawson's argument is his belief that hu-man moral life is based on "reactive attitudes" – attitudes and reac-tions such as resentment, hurt pride, gratitude, forgiveness, and love. These attitudes and reactions are highly dependent on how a person interprets what is going on. For instance, if a person feels that someone's failure to acknowledge them on a particular occasion was an understandable oversight, then they are likely to feel quite differ-ently about this than if they interpret what happened as a snub. Strawson distinguishes reactive attitudes from what he calls "objective attitudes". For Strawson objective attitudes arise when there are grounds for viewing an individual as 'psychologically abnormal – or as morally undeveloped'. Strawson suggests the objective attitude is indicated with the use of expressions such as '"He is only a child", "He's a hopeless schizophrenic", "His mind has been systematically perverted", "That's purely compulsive behaviour on his part".' Strawson says that 'To adopt the objective attitude to another human being is to see him, perhaps, as an object of social policy; as a subject for what, in a wide range of sense, might be called treatment; as something certainly to be taken account, perhaps precautionary ac-count, of; to be managed, or handled or cured or trained; perhaps simply to be avoided [...]' Strawson argues that to adopt a wholly ob-jective attitude towards a person precludes adopting any reactive atti-tudes towards them (Strawson P. 1962, (2003 pp. 78-79))

5.6.3   Having established the distinction he wants to make between reactive and objective attitudes, Strawson poses the question: 'What effect would, or should, the acceptance of the truth of a gen-eral thesis of determinism have upon these reactive attitudes? More specifically, would, or should, the acceptance of the truth of the thesis lead to the decay or the repudiation of all such attitudes? Would, or should, it mean the end of gratitude, resentment, and forgiveness; of all reciprocated adult loves; of all the essentially *personal* antagonisms?' (p. 80. 2003). It is quite reasonable to pose this question since were people generally to believe, completely whole-heartedly, that absolute determinism ruled every aspect of person's life it might seem logical that they would then adopt an objective-like attitude towards one another on the basis that no one can help doing what they do. Widespread adoption of such an objective-like attitude would not mean that people would view one another as abnormal, but it almost certainly would mean profound changes to human inter-personal interaction, and to various practices such as retributive punishment, that currently are typically part of human moral life.

5.6.4 Strawson accepts the theoretical possibility of the widespread adoption of such an objective-like attitude but he firmly rejects the practical likelihood of this coming about. He argues: 'The human commitment to participation in ordinary inter-personal relationships is, I think, too thoroughgoing and deeply rooted for us to take seriously the thought that a general theoretical conviction might so change our world that, in it, there were no longer any such things as inter-personal relationships as we normally understand them; and being involved in inter-personal relationships as we normally understand them precisely is being exposed to the range of reactive attitudes and feelings that is in question.' (p. 81. 2003).

5.6.5 Strawson believes that it is our reactive attitudes that are the basis of our moral life and that it is because, in their different ways, compatibilists and incompatibilists don't sufficiently acknowledge this that they are unable to reconcile their positions. He sees compatibilists as typically justifying practices of moral condemnation and punishment on the basis that they are important in regulating behaviour in socially desirable ways. And he sees incompatiblists as typically rejecting this view and wanting a deeper and fundamentally fairer basis for such practices – a basis if not rooted in persons being ultimately responsible for their actions, at least rooted in them being the self-directed originative source of their doings. Strawson argues that both sides would benefit from a more rounded appreciation of the fact that we possess reactive attitudes. Strawson is, however, crit-

123

ical of what, in the final sentence of his paper, he refers to as 'the obscure and panicky metaphysics of libertarianism.' (p. 93. 2003)

5.6.6 Strawson's paper has attracted a great deal of attention
and a strong following, but as far as human moral life goes people do
not live it solely on the basis of ingrained human reactive attitudes.
For example, many judicial systems base sentencing upon dispassion-
ate appraisals rather than reactive attitudes. In general, society has
moved away from justice based on lynch mobs, on vigilante groups,
and on overly retributive punishment. Reactive attitudes certainly play
a part in human moral life, but only a part.

5.6.7 Although Strawson is arguing for a reconciliation between
compatiblists and incompatibilists, he was writing at a time when
most English-speaking philosophers favoured a deterministic view of
human life rather than an originative one. Given this, and given the
central importance, from a traditional point of view, of seeing free
will as a necessary basis for moral responsibility, it is not surprising
that much work was done aimed at showing that determinism allows
a kind of freedom of the will that is worth having and which can
prove adequate as a basis for human moral life. One important contribution of this sort – which is discussed next – was published nine
years after Strawson's paper and argued that people have a special
sort of control over their wills that does not seem to be possessed by
animals and is such that it may give humans what is required for
moral responsibility.

5.7 Free Will and Higher-Order Desires

5.7.1 Harry Frankfurt, in his paper 'Freedom of the Will and
the Concept of a Person', argues that our possession of "higher-order desires" is essential to humans having free will, being persons,
and being full moral agents. A first-order desire, on its own or in a
coalition of supporting desires, is potentially able to move a person
to have a particular will – that is, a first-order desire is able to move a
person to act in some specific way. A second-order desire is potentially able to move a person to have, or not have, some one or more
first-order desires. Hence, second-order (and higher-order) desires influence and direct a person's possession and activation of first-order
(or higher-order) desires.

5.7.2 To take an example, consider a person with a strong first-order desire for food that leads them to eat to excess. Suppose that, because of their overeating, they have become unhappy with their weight and in consequence have formed the wish – a second-order desire – to no longer desire excessive amounts of food. This is a higher-order desire because it is a desire to *desire* differently, and it is of the *second* order because it is directed at changing a *first*-order desire that the person possesses – namely, their desire for eating. However, it is not only by forming higher-order desires that people are able to control their behaviour: very often they control their behaviour by forming new first-order desires aimed at defeating other, unwelcome, first-order desires. For instance, an excessive eater may adopt the resolution that in future they will not eat to excess. Their hope in adopting this resolution is that when they are in a situation that stirs their desire to overeat this new resolution will kick in with such strength that it wins out over their desire to eat. In this case they are trying to change their behaviour not by a desire to no longer desire to eat to excess, but by defeating this first-order desire with a stronger first-order desire.

5.7.3 The mere possession of a second-order desire does not mean it will be effective – it may fail to change the first-order desire, or desires, at which it is directed. For example, suppose the excessive eater being considered has in fact adopted the above second-order desire and is now at a dinner party where they have just enjoyed a generous first helping of a delicious dessert. Suppose they are now offered a second helping and that they come to the decision to refuse this offer, and they act accordingly. If their decision to decline the offer had resulted from them no longer desiring to eat more food, then their second order desire would have been effective because the first-order desire at which it was directed would have changed in an appropriate way. But suppose that in fact they had come to their decision not because this second-order desire was effective but because they had a stronger first-order desire: namely a desire not to look greedy among their fellow diners. In this case, although the end result was what would have been produced had the second-order desire actually been effective, the person may well feel a sense of failure in not having succeeded in satisfying their second-order desire to not actually feel any first-order desire for another helping.

5.7.4   To illustrate the notion of higher-order desires more fully, suppose the person finds that their second-order desire to desire only moderate amounts of food has got out of hand and they are now hardly desiring food at all and are dangerously under-eating. In such a situation they might now develop the third-order desire to control this second order desire so that they come to have a moderate and reasonable desire for food.

5.7.5   What this extended example has aimed to show is the complex nature of human desires and the ways they may interact to produce volition and action. Frankfurt argues that the possession of higher-order desires means that humans *care* about what desires they possess and the volitions they form. He classifies all volitional beings that don't care about what desires they have as "wantons". Frankfurt takes animals, and very young children to be wantons; and he accepts that some adults may be wantons. He says: 'Nothing in the concept of a wanton implies he cannot deliberate concerning how to do what he wants to do. What distinguishes the rational wanton from other rational agents is that he is not concerned with the desirability of his desires themselves. He ignores the question of what his will is to be. Not only does he pursue whatever course of action he is most strongly inclined to pursue, but does not care which of his inclinations is the strongest.' (Frankfurt 1971, (2003, pp. 327-328))

5.7.6   Having established these concepts Frankfurt then goes on to argue for the soundness of his main thesis, which is: '[T]hat it is only because a person has volitions of the second [or higher] order that he is capable both of enjoying and lacking freedom of the will.' Frankfurt sees human persons as 'a type of entity to whom freedom of the will may be a problem.' He asks: 'Just what kind of freedom is freedom of the will?' And he answers by saying that enjoying freedom of the will means (1) being free to do what one wants to do, and (2) being free to will as one wants to will. With regard to (2) Frankfurt continues: 'It is in securing the conformity of the will to his second-order volitions, then, that a person exercises freedom of the will. And it is in the discrepancy between his will and his second-order volitions, or in his awareness that their coincidence is not his own doing but a happy chance, that a person who does not have this freedom feels the lack (2003, pp. 331-332). The first of these two aspects of the freedom of the will is uncontentious. But the second is not, because it implies an infinite regress, for it may be asked: What determines what one wants to will? and answer: Another want. But what determines that want? presumably, yet another want. And so on endlessly.

5.7.7 Frankfurt argues that what is needed to end this infinite regress are higher-order desires with which a person may ultimately *identify* themselves and in so doing halt the regress. If such desires can be found then, since higher-order desires are formed by the rational and evaluative efforts of a person and are not inherited desires, it may be argued that they belong to the human person (in contrast to the human being – see 1.6.1) more strongly than do their genetically given biological desires. Frankfurt recognises that people may theoretically keep developing ever higher-order motivations with which to identify themselves. He argues that 'nothing except common sense and, perhaps, a saving fatigue prevents an individual from obsessively refusing to identify himself with any of his desires until he forms a desire of the next higher order.' He goes on to conclude: 'The tendency to generate such a series of acts of forming desires, which would be the case of humanization run wild, also leads towards the destruction of a person'. Perhaps realizing this argument for dealing with the infinite regress is somewhat weak, he continues: 'It is possible, however, to terminate such a series of acts without cutting it off arbitrarily. When a person identifies himself *decisively* with one of his first-order desires, this commitment "resounds" throughout the potentially endless array of higher orders.' (2003, p. 332) But this raises the question: What leads a person to identify themselves *decisively* with one of their first-order desires? Is this an act of an Indifferent Will? Is it determined by such things as the person's genes or their upbringing? Or, is it a matter of chance? Without making clear his answer to this key question Frankfurt is far from having resolved the problem of free will. Nevertheless, Frankfurt makes several important points, and his work deserves to be valued and taken into account by all those interested in understanding the nature of human free will.

5.7.8 Frankfurt, and many who have followed his lead, are compatibilists and therefore do not accept that the formation of higher-order desires can be a self-directively originative process. However, if it could be established that having the ability to form and act on higher-order desires was in itself a sufficient condition for a person to possess moral responsibility then compatibilism would have over-come one of its major weaknesses. However, there is a key moral principle that has nothing to do with whether or not people are able to form or act on higher-order desires – a principle that is discussed next.

5.8 Compatibilism and a Fundamental Moral Principle: PAP

5.8.1 Although self-originative free will seems to offer the best basis for human persons having what is required to make them full moral agents, it should not be forgotten that this form of free will remains, relative to compatibilism, the weaker contender in the free-will debate. Indifferently originative free will, or the Liberty of Indifference (see 1.4.7/13), was for many centuries the leading contender. However, with the rise of science, this kind of free will increasingly came to be seen as existing outside the natural order. In recent decades, models of the sort discussed above based on quantum indeterminacy have made self-originative free will seem to be a scientific possibility, but they are all open to the criticism that the de-novo origination is based on quantum indeterministic events and that these are beyond the control or influence of the agent. Although the three accounts that have been discussed – Doyle's two-stage model, Tse's criterial causation view, and Kane's fusion-indeterminacy account – go far in countering this criticism they don't altogether defeat it. And this is perhaps one of the key reasons why at present compatibilism remains the dominant position in the debate.

5.8.2 However, compatibilism, being based on an acceptance of macroscopic determinism if not absolute determinism, suffers from a major problem when attempting to provide an adequate basis for human moral life: namely, that to be consistent it cannot accept that true alternative possibilities exist. And this means it cannot reconcile itself with a fundamental moral principle, the principle that:

People should only hold a person morally responsible for what they do if they could have done otherwise.

5.8.3 This principle, which is often referred to as the Principle of Alternate (or Alternative) Possibilities (or PAP), is accepted by most compatibilists. For example, the logical positivist and compatibilist philosopher A.J. Ayer writes: 'When I am said to have done something of my own free will it is implied that I could have acted otherwise; and it is only when it is believed that I could have acted otherwise that I am held to be morally responsible for what I have done. For a man is not thought to be morally responsible for an action that was not in his power to avoid'. (Ayer 1954) And in a similar vein the compatibilist (or "reconcilist") philosopher Bruce Aune writes: 'According to both libertarians and reconcilers, people can reasonably be held responsible only for things they freely do or for things that are foreseeable consequences of what they freely do. An action for which we are morally responsible is one for which we are appropriately blamed, and if it is seriously wrong, even punished; but it is clearly immoral (as well as decidedly stupid) to punish people for things they cannot help doing'. (Aune 1986, pp. 196-197)

5.8.4   Under absolute determinism, once everything is taken into account, a person never has it in their power to avoid what they do; and what they do they cannot help doing. This means that absolute determinism is not compatible with PAP. However, there are related moral principles that *are* compatible, and one obvious example is the moral principle that says: *It is acceptable to punish people if to do so is likely to deter them from doing wrong in the future.* But, as Ayer and Aune make clear, the principle of alternate possibilities is a highly important prin-ciple and one that would make a good deal of difference to human life were it to be entirely abandoned. This means that compatibilists must, in some way or another, come to terms with it. Many ap-proaches have been attempted, and some of the more important ones are discussed next.

5.9   Attempts to Deal with Alternate Possibilities

5.9.1   One major approach that compatibilists have pursued in attempting to come to terms with PAP is to reinterpret what is un-derstood when it is said that a person "could have done otherwise." This so-called conditional analysis approach was given particular at-tention by one of the founders of analytical philosophy, G.E. Moore, in his book *Ethics*. He proposed a specific interpretation of "could have done otherwise" that, he argued, was not only the interpretation that most people normally assumed when they used or encountered the phrase but was one that was compatible with determinism. He wrote: '[W]e proposed [in Chapter 1], purely for the sake of brevity, to say that an agent *could* have done a given action, which he didn't do, wherever it is true that he could have done it, *if* he had chosen; and similarly by what he *can* do, or what is *possible*, we have always meant merely what is possible, *if* he chooses.' (Moore 1912, Ch. 6 third paragraph) Moore is well aware of the hard determinist view that in one very strong sense of what "could" means we can never do otherwise than what we actually do. But he insists that in everyday usage there is a weaker meaning which is that a person could have done otherwise had they chosen to do so and providing that they had the ability and resources to do so.

5.9.2 Another way to achieve a definitive understanding of the meaning of "could have done otherwise" may lie in analysing the meaning of the words and phrases involved. J. L. Austin, a leader of linguistic philosophy, adopted just this approach in the 1950s. In his well-known paper 'Ifs and Cans' (Austin 1956) Austin provides a thorough analysis of Moore's argument that "S could have done otherwise" is equivalent to "S should (would) have done otherwise if he had chosen (to do otherwise)." Austin convincingly demonstrates that "if" and "can" are words with a large and subtly different range of meanings, and he succeeds in casting doubt on Moore's interpretation, but he does not succeed in providing a definitive meaning of "could have done otherwise." Analysis of this key phrase has continued with detailed points being made on both sides, but no widely agreed meaning has become established.

5.9.3 A quite different approach appeared in a paper by Harry Frankfurt published two years before his one on higher-order desires discussed above, in which he sought to establish that alternative possibilities are not actually required for moral responsibility. Frankfurt, opens his paper 'Alternate Possibilities and Moral Responsibility' by noting the important role that the Principle of Alternate Possibilities (PAP) has played in the free-will debate, and the fact that almost no one has challenged this principle – a principle that he himself believes to be false. He starts the defence of his view by arguing that coercion does not necessarily mean that the agent to whom it is applied is not morally responsible for doing what was demanded since they may themselves have already decided to act in just the same way and did so not because of coercion but on the basis of their own freely made decision. The point Frankfurt is making is that although coercion may mean that the agent to whom it is applied could not have done otherwise, there are situations – such as the one just described – in which an agent could still be morally responsible. However Frankfurt recognises that this argument is inadequate as it stands since coercion does not necessitate in the way that determinism does – indeed, it is potentially open to an agent to resist coercion and do other than what is demanded of them. Frankfurt therefore introduces a scenario which he feels does properly establish his view that alternate possibilities are not necessary for moral responsibility.

5.9.4   The scenario is as follows.

Suppose someone – Black, let us say – wants Jones to perform a certain action. Black is prepared to go to considerable lengths to get his way, but he prefers to avoid showing his hand unnecessarily. So he waits until Jones is about to make up his mind what to do, and he does nothing unless it is clear to him (Black is an excellent judge of such things) that Jones is going to decide to do something *other* than what he wants him to do. If it does become clear that Jones is going to decide to do something else, Black takes effective steps to ensure that Jones, decides to do, and that he does do, what he wants him to do. Whatever Jones's initial preferences and inclinations, then, Black will have his way. (Frankfurt 1969, (2003 pp. 172-173))

5.9.5   After discussing various ways – through coercion, giving him a potion, hypnotising him, for instance – in which Black may get Jones to do as he wants, Frankfurt suggests a more reliable means by which to ensure that Jones could not have done otherwise. He writes: '[L]et Black manipulate the minute processes of Jones's brain and nervous system in some more direct way, so that causal forces running in and out of his synapses and along the poor man's nerves determine that he chooses to act and that he does act in the one way and not the other.' (2003, p. 173) Frankfurt maintains that with such a setup – made stronger if required by allowing Black to be replaced by a machine, and, although he does not explicitly say this, by giving the machine the power to monitor all of Jones's relevant brain processes – it seems it is theoretically possible to ensure that under no circumstances can Jones do otherwise than Black wishes. Frankfurt continues:

> Now suppose that Black never has to show his hand because Jones, for reasons of his own, decides to perform and does perform the very action Black wants him to perform. In that case, it seems clear, Jones will bear precisely the same moral responsibility for what he does as he would have borne if Black had not been ready to take steps to ensure that he do it. It would be quite unreasonable to excuse Jones, for his action, or to withhold the praise to which it would normally entitle him, on the basis of the fact the he could not have done otherwise. (p. 173. 2003).

5.9.6   Frankfurt's argument has attracted a lot of criticism (as well as a lot of followers). From a libertarian perspective, it is clear that Frankfurt makes at least two unacceptable assumptions, and that therefore his argument fails. The first of these is Frankfurt's assumption that Jones must be morally responsible for his decisions and actions because 'Jones, for reasons of his own, decides to perform and does perform the very action Black wants him to perform.' But, for libertarians, simply deciding for "reasons of his own" does not make a person morally responsible for what he does because, if absolute determinism is true, the "reasons of his own" will have been fully predetermined to arise on the occasion in question before the person was born, and so he cannot be truly morally responsible for possessing them and acting on the basis of them. From a libertarian perspective, if Jones is to be morally responsible then he must be the self-directed *creative originator* of "the reasons of his own" that lead him to do what he does, and this means he might have produced different reasons since creatively originative processes do not have a predetermined or type-determined outcome. Hence, for libertarians, Frankfurt has not shown that alternative possibilities are not required.

5.9.7   The second major assumption that Frankfurt makes and which cannot hold if Jones is exercising originative free will is that Black can always predict what Jones is going to choose *before* he does so. It is necessary for Black be able to do this so that he may, if required, be able to intervene to get Jones to do what he wants if he can see Jones is going to choose to do something different. In a fully deterministic world it may be possible (at least in principle) for Black

132

to always be able to make such a prediction, but with a creatively originative process this is not possible. Hence what Frankfurt proposes is not realisable once it is accepted that free will entails a creatively originative process. And if it is argued that Black may wait until Jones has, in a libertarian way, decided what he is to do before he intervenes, then the voluntariness condition for being morally responsible will not be met because Jones will not be doing what he had already freely chosen to do.

5.10 More Views on Moral Responsibility and Compatibilism

5.10.1   In fairly recent times, ancient views of what is required for moral responsibility have been resurrected. Socrates (470-399 BCE) wrote nothing and the main record of his thought comes from the extensive writings of Plato (c.428-347 BCE), his student. One of Socrates's best-known views is that no one does wrong, or fails to "hit the mark", voluntarily but does so through lack of knowledge and wisdom. This view has been summed up in the dictum attributed to him that "Knowledge is virtue". The point Socrates is making is that were a person to reason clearly and correctly about doing wrong they would never voluntarily choose to do so. Of course, Socrates accepts that many people have insufficient knowledge, wisdom, and reasoning skill, or are unable to control their passions, and so often fail to avoid doing wrong. Plato was not happy to see moral codes and principles as merely of human devising and so sought an absolute source for them. Plato introduced the concept of a non-material realm of Forms and Ideas – Forms find imperfect expression in the entities of the natural world, and Ideas in the imperfect concepts that humans develop. In this higher realm, the Good is supreme. According to Plato, humans are special in that they are born with a Rational soul that has had some sort of acquaintance with the Realm of Forms and Ideas. It is their power of Reason and their (imperfect) access to Ideas – such as those that constitute what the Greeks saw as cardinal virtues: Wisdom, Courage, Temperance, and Justice – that qualify humans as moral agents.

5.10.2   In recent decades, several philosophers have returned to the classical and medieval position of regarding right action to be a matter of true appreciation of the Good. For instance, Garry Watson and Susan Wolf, working independently, have adopted this approach and provided contemporary accounts of what it is that makes a person morally responsible.

5.10.3 Watson writes: 'The problem of free action arises because what one desires [in the sense of what Appetite or Passion demand] may not be what one values [in the sense of what Reason determines as Good such as steadfastness, integrity, and even-handedness], and what one most values may not be what one is finally moved to get.' Just as Frankfurt argues that guidance of human volitions and actions by higher-order desires gives people a degree of responsibility for their doings that they would not have if they only had first-order desires, so, Watson argues, possession of and guidance by *values* gives human persons a degree of responsibility that they would not have were they driven only by appetites and passions. Watson suggests that the existence and persistence of appetites and passions is independent of a person's judgement of the Good, and that it is because of this independence that a conflict between valuing and desiring is possible. (Watson 1975, (2003 pp. 343-344)) For Watson, a key requirement is that 'The free agent has the capacity to translate his values into action; his actions flow from his evaluational system.' He goes on to say: 'One's evaluational system may be said to constitute one's standpoint, the point of view from which one judges the world. The important feature of one's evaluational system is that one cannot coherently dissociate oneself from it *in its entirety*. [...] one cannot dissociate oneself from all normative judgements without forfeiting all standpoints and therewith one's identity as an agent.' (2003, p. 347) This has resonances with Frankfurt's belief in a person decisively identifying with certain first-order desires and by so doing stabilising their identity as an agent. But the open question that remains unanswered by Watson is: To what extent is a person's evaluational system produced or changed by the person's own self-directed creative processes? If a person's evaluational system, and all that it does, is a deterministic consequence of the condition of the world before they were born then this greatly diminishes the person's responsibility for their possession of it.

5.10.4 Susan Wolf has looked to classical thinking for a slightly different approach to seeing human persons as sufficiently special

134

that they may be counted as full moral agents. She proposes what she calls the "Reason View". In her book *Freedom Within Reason* she writes: 'According to the Reason View, a person's status as a responsible agent rests not only on her ability to make her behavior conform to her deepest values but also on her ability to form, assess, and revise these values on the basis of a recognition and appreciation of what I have called the True and the Good.' (Wolf 1990, p. 117) Wolf uses the term "the True" for a person's capacity to see and appreciate the world correctly in factual terms, and she uses the term "the Good" for their ability to use their faculty of reason to determine what is valuable and what is worthless in the world and in their own lives. She rejects, in favour of a naturalistic account, Plato's view that the Good finds proper expression only in the realm of Ideas and that human persons, through their faculty of Reason, have some sort of special access to that realm. However, she does believe that values have an objective existence and that a natural faculty of reason can access them. Yet she also recognizes there are cultural differences in values and so, to some extent, she accepts relativism. Her position on the relationship between the Reason View and determinism is fairly represented by the following extract from her book.

> [W]hile the Reason View acknowledges what any plausible account of freedom and responsibility must acknowledge – that part of freedom and responsibility consists in an individual's ability to govern her behaviour in accordance with her deepest values – its originality lies in the claim that the other part of freedom and responsibility lies in the agent's ability to form or revise her deepest values in light of the truth. Thus, it analyzes what fear of determinism remains, after the recognition that determinism is compatible with the ability to govern one's own actions by one's values, as the fear that determinism implies a form of blindness to all or part of the truth. In other words, it analyzes what fear of determinism is left as the fear (as it happens, unjustified) that determinism implies that all values are a product of indoctrination, or, perhaps, that the distinction between indoctrination and reasoned conviction cannot be intelligibly applied. (pp. 140-141)

5.10.5   It is not the fear of "a form of blindness to all or part of the truth" that libertarians find most unacceptable about determinism, but rather that it means *how* a person forms their "deepest values" and *whether* they are able to "form or revise [their] deepest values in light of the truth" is ultimately not up to them at all but has been predetermined since before they were born. Determinism means that no one – indeed, no natural thing at all – ever has any power of self-directed origination; in other words, under determinism nothing in a person's life is truly up to them. At bottom it is this that libertarians cannot accept about determinism, and not that determinism may be compatible with the publicly observable valuational, reasoning, and executive behaviours of a person. Yet compatibilists have continued to press the point that our extraordinary powers of self-evaluation and executive control give us all that is required for a free will worth wanting. Daniel Dennett is a major proponent of this line of thinking.

5.10.6 Dennett argues that the nature of human mentality gives people a form of compatibilist free will worth wanting. The following statement, taken from his book *Elbow Room: The Varieties of Free Will Worth Wanting*, expresses his position.

> Among the questions facing a sophisticated self-controlling agent are: could I revise my basic projects and goals in such a way as to improve my chances of satisfaction? Are there grand strategies or policies that are better than my current ones? Is there a style of operation that would suit my goals better than my current style? Will my current policies lead me into tight quarters with little room to manoeuvre and great risk of disaster? What should my general policy regarding risk be? What kind of an agent do I want to be or become? [...] There are in general no "book" answers to these questions and so, as in the mid-game in chess, one must abandon the book openings and strike boldly out into the territory of risky, heuristic reasoning. (Dennett 1984, p. 86)

5.10.7 Dennett is at pains to point out that people should not think of what happens to them as merely a matter of luck. Rather, he argues, a person's executive and directive abilities give them both the power to avoid things happening to them that they don't want to happen, and the power to make things happen that they do want to happen. Indeed, in his later book, *Freedom Evolves* (Dennet 2003, p. 56), he goes further than this and challenges the idea that determinism

136

means that what happens to us is inevitable. His approach is to resurrect the obsolete word evitable – which means avoidable, according to the Oxford English Dictionary. He then uses this word, and its close relative "inevitable" (meaning not avoidable), in the following logical argument:

In some deterministic worlds there are avoiders avoiding harms.

Therefore in some deterministic worlds some things are avoided.

Whatever is avoided is avoidable or evitable.

Therefore in some deterministic worlds not everything is inevitable.

Therefore determinism does not imply inevitability.

5.10.8   The trouble with this argument is that within an absolutely deterministic world it does not work. When talking about directive behaviour it is often meaningful to talk about the behaviour being directed at avoiding certain events, conditions, or states of affairs, where "avoiding" is used in its dictionary sense of something, usually an agent of some sort, "keeping away from, or at a distance from", or "shunning" certain things. For example, prey-animals tend to avoid their predators, and have various means for achieving this. Clearly Dennett is latching on to just this fact. However, once the totality of happening that is going on in the universe is taken into account then, in an absolutely deterministic world, this totality of happening can't be said to be "avoiding", or "keeping away from, or at a distance from", or "shunning" anything at all. The reason for this is that, in such a world, the totality of happening is consistent with only a single future, and this means that the universe cannot be said to be operating in such a manner that it is avoiding anything – and in particular it can't be said to be avoiding certain sorts of possible future without endowing the universe with a some sort of purposefulness. However, in a universe in which origination is commonplace the "totality of happening" does not wholly fix the future, and if such a universe contains appropriate kinds of directive systems (prey-animals, for example), then it may legitimately be said that those systems are indeed working to avoid certain sorts of future coming into existence. Hence, it is independence indeterminism that properly supports Dennett's argument, not determinism.

5.10.9   Libertarians are unconvinced by the many accounts of moral responsibility that compatibilists have produced. They are unconvinced because, in their view, none of these accounts establish that a person could, in an absolute rather than in a conditional sense, have done otherwise than they actually did. Nevertheless, most naturalistic libertarians would accept that what compatiblists have achieved are many insightful understandings and helpful descriptions of the hugely complex social and mind-brain processes that are involved in the production of morally significant human doings. However, in attempting to establish a basis for full moral responsibility, libertarians have their own difficulties because in their efforts to give a naturalistic account of being able to "do otherwise" they have had to rely on quantum indeterminacy as the source of de novo origination, and quantum indeterministic origination is not open to influence or control by anything, let alone a person. What is minimally required is a place in the universe for directed origination, and creative self-directed origination – a place that independence indeterminism is able to provide. Given, then, its central importance in helping to resolve the problem of free will, and also of moral responsibility, over the next three chapters this new naturalistic metaphysics is further discussed and developed in order to better establish it as a credible and worthy replacement for determinism.

6 The Assumption of Independence of Change

6.1 Why so Long Coming up with Independence Indeterminism?

6.1.1   The assumption that true independence of change is extremely common in the universe is the single primary assumption upon which independence indeterminism is based. It is not a complex assumption and it appears to be tacitly accepted by almost everyone. However, it does deserve further discussion simply because of its central role in this new metaphysics. In what follows, an effort has been made to avoid repeating points that have already been raised and discussed, but some repetition is unavoidable.

6.1.2   There seems to be nothing about the assumption of independence of change that could not have been thought of as soon as people started to develop naturalistic metaphysical theses – that is, at least from the time of the early ancient Greek philosophers. So, before embarking on further discussion of this concept, it is worth briefly considering why it has taken so long for this idea to become the basis of a metaphysical thesis.

6.1.3   All humans – scientists included – hold implicit metaphysical assumptions about the nature of existence. For example, almost all scientists are realists. That is, they hold the metaphysical assumption that there is a real world that corresponds, in more or less systematic ways, to the perceptions, and conscious thoughts and understandings that humans collectively and individually have about what exists. On the other hand metaphysical idealists (of which there are many, but few of whom are scientists) reject this realist view and hold the assumption that human consciousness is but part of a universal consciousness, or Mind or Spirit, and that it is this that is the only true reality.

6.1.4   One implicit metaphysical assumption that is shared by most realists and idealists is that existence is a unity – that is, a wholly integrated entity with everything related to everything else. Perhaps one reason why this view is so widely held is that human consciousness appears to consists of a more or less unified and coherent 'world' and not (generally) of a hotch-potch of unrelated sensations, perceptions, recollections, feelings, and thoughts. For example, when a person walks down a street they 'see' (or rather, are conscious of) a world of physical objects and activities related to one another in space and time. However, considering this apparent wholeness from the perspective of the multitude of inanimate non-conscious things in it, all these things 'see' are those things they interact with: they don't 'see' all the things whose change is making no difference to them. It is as if consciousness "connects up the dots" to make a whole – a whole that does not actually exist in the absence of the consciousness. It is, perhaps, because of the 'world' or 'unity' that human consciousness produces that people feel that existence must in actuality be unified as well. And this would perhaps explain why many people intuitively feel that the real world cannot be disjointed, non-unified and full of independence of happening and with many gaps within and between the causal networks of existence. Determinism, unlike independence indeterminism, is compatible with the real world being unified so it is perhaps not surprising that this metaphysics seems to many people to be true, particularly when it is coupled with a belief in the law of cause and effect – a belief which makes it seem reasonable that all interactions, even between apparently independently changing things, are fully caused. Hence, it may be that since a metaphysics based on independence and non-unity has little appeal, it has not previously been taken seriously.

6.1.5 There is one further point worth making again (see section 3.6 for earlier discussion) because it supports the belief that determinism applies to the coming into being of what are apparently independence interactions. Human have a well-developed ability to anticipate some *near-future* independence interactions, and this encourages them to believe that, if they had all the relevant information, far-future interactions would also be predictable. But the evidence is that humans have no reliable ability to make *far-future* predictions of independence interactions. However, rather than taking this as evidence to support independence indeterminism, most people seem to see this failure as a consequence of people not having sufficient knowledge and data. Independence indeterminism does not deny that far-future independence interactions are a product of very complex sequences of dependence and independence interactions. What it

140

denies is that these sequences are all fully predetermined because it concludes – based on its single primary assumption that true independence of change exists in our universe – that independence interactions arise indeterministically, which is something absolute determinism denies. The key difference between the two views is that absolute determinists believe that apparently independently changing things are – if only the "big picture" was available – actually changing in lockstep whereas independence indeterminists do not believe this. Rather, they believe there is nothing in existence that fully links, governs, or describes how independently changing things jointly change.

6.1.6   What has just been said may be summarised in the following way. Just prior to the occurrence of an independence interaction, determinism often seems to be true, and independence indeterminism often seems to be false. However, when an independence interaction is in the far-future it is, in practice, impossible to identify exactly what exists in the present that necessitates its later occurrence and so determinism seems to be false, and independence indeterminism seems to be true.

6.1.7   That independence indeterminism should have taken so long to emerge remains something of a puzzle. However, the main business of this chapter is to further discuss the assumption of independence of change, and to that end the assumption shall be slighted modified to state that **stretches of change that to some extent run truly independently of one another are extremely common in our universe.**

6.2   Clarification of Terms and Concepts

6.2.1   Nothing out of the ordinary is implied or meant by the phrase "stretches of change". However it is important to appreciate that in using this phrase particular *instances* of stretches of change are being referred to, not *types* of stretches of change. So, for example, a period of flight of a particular bird on a particular occasion would constitute a particular instance of a stretch of change. However, this would also be a particular instance – or token – of the general type of change, "bird-flight". The type/token distinction used here is well-established within semiotics and philosophy.

141

6.2.2 "Stretches of change that to some extent run truly independently of one another" are such that how each stretch of change runs is not *completely* fixed by how the other stretches of change run. What is important is that there is *some* independence of running, not *complete* independence. For example, when I take our dog Nellie for a walk using a long (7 metre) spring-loaded extendible leash she has a good deal of independence of movement and action relative to me, but not complete independence, and because of this partial independence between what she does and what I do, our respective behaviours may be assumed to be two "stretches of change that to some extent run truly independently of one another." If complete independence of change were required then this would be something that would be difficult to justify since all forms of mass/energy exert some (however slight) gravitational influence over one another. On the other hand, *partial* independence of change seems to be very common. And because most things appear to have very little influence on most other things, it seems obvious – to both scientists and lay people – that independence of change is extremely common. Furthermore, partial independence of change is common even when things are in some sort of interaction. For example, although the translational motion of the Earth is highly constrained by its gravitational relationship with the sun, the moon, and the other planets, most of its geological activity – e.g. earthquakes, volcanoes, tectonic plate movements – runs in ways that are largely independent of this dependency relationship. Similarly, the continuous activity within the nucleus of an atom runs largely independently of the activity of the electrons bound in shells around its nucleus. And in a human organisation, although some of the activity of its participants contributes to realising and sustaining the operation and continuing existence of the organisation not all of their activity does. These examples illustrate an important general point: namely, that the constituents of a system and the participants in a RENOIR generally maintain a good deal of independence from one another while at the same time giving up some independence to make their contribution to the realisation of the higher-level entity. Indeed, it is for this reason that as well as being able to say that a system is *more* than the sum of its parts because it has properties its parts don't have, it is also correct to say that a system is *less* than the sum of its parts because not all the properties and activity of its parts participate in realising the system.

6.2.3   The assumption of independence of change refers to how stretches of change "run". This term is used to emphasise that it is not stretches of change considered as static blocks that is being re-ferred to but stretches of change that are "ongoing", "in process", "proceeding", or "evolving." Were stretches of change taken to be static blocks then the process view of nature that is adopted by inde-pendence indeterminism would be denied. And were stretches of change to be described as "unfolding" (rather than "evolving") then again the process way of thinking would be denied since "unfolding" implies that what is to come already pre-exists in some sense. Accept-ing the assumption of true independence of change becomes more difficult if these familiar ways of thinking are used and that is why they are generally avoided in the present work.

6.2.4   Concurrently running stretches of change are usually what are of interest, but the assumption of independence of change ap-plies equally to non-concurrently running stretches. For example, not only may the independence of what persons A and B are doing over the same period of time be considered, but also, say, the independ-ence of what person A is doing today relative to what person B was doing yesterday. It should be clear from what has been said about ab-solute determinism that under this metaphysics not only are all con-current changes in a fixed relationship to one another but so are all changes – including those separated in time by a considerable period. This follows because under absolute determinism the history of the universe is seen as a predetermined totality brought into existence at the point the universe is created, or as having been eternally fixed if the universe had no point of creation.

6.2.5   As well as causal *independence* existing, it is important not to forget that there also exist many particular dated and located stretches of change which seem to be in relationships of causal *de-pendence*. For instance, the sun and planets of the solar system are in tight relationships of gravitational interdependence, and this means that their motions are fairly well synchronised – well enough syn-chronised to allow accurate predictions to be made about such things as eclipses. However, this particular network of influence relations only determines the gross translational motion of the planets and the

143

sun, and it does not determine everything that is happening in or on these bodies. This exemplifies an important point: there may be (very near) synchronicity between *some* of the types of change that two or more things are undergoing, while there is no synchronicity between *other* types of change. For example, although at the level of overall motion the cogs and the hands of a mechanical clock manifest stretches of change that run in a synchronised manner, no such synchrony exists between the vibrational motion of the atoms and molecules that constitute the parts of the clock. Examples to support this general point are common: for instance, the behaviours of the players in the same section of an orchestra – e.g. the violin players – may show a fair degree of synchronisation at an overall level but not at a detailed level, and not in terms of their thoughts and other internal processes. Similarly, while the flight-path of birds moving in formation is fairly well synchronised at the gross level, it is not at the detailed level.

6.2.6   It worth emphasising that the assumption of independence of change refers to stretches of change that are running in a *truly* causally independent manner, and are *truly* non-synchronised. Stretches of change that only *appear* to be meeting these criteria but do not actually do so are excluded. For example, some of the activities of the actors in a play or a movie may appear to be taking place more or less independently of one another but in fact they are not because, at the overall level, all these activities have been scripted to happen just as they do. And it is of course possible for people to be mistaken about the physical world. For example, it requires careful observation and accurate records, and appropriate analysis of these records, to establish that the planets (the "wanderers") do not move independently of one another. However, given that people can only work on the basis of what they believe to be the case, it must be accepted that they might be mistaken about some of the stretches of change that they currently think are running truly independently.

6.2.7   Although not much discussion has been given to this, it should not be forgotten that stretches of change may lack independence not because they are influencing one another directly but because they are subject to some third-party influence. Such third-party causal influence is common: for instance, the behaviour of individual plants and animals is affected by the third-party influence of the

144

changing seasons, and this often results in a good deal of correlation and some synchronisation among the changes and behaviours plants and animals undergo during the year.

6.3 Type and Token Independence of Change

6.3.1 Most of the time people act in the world as if the assumption of independence of change were true: that is, they act as if what they do is truly independent of the doings and activity of most other things. For instance, I am currently acting under the tacit assumption that my typing activity is going on truly independently of the vast majority of other stretches of change that happen to be taking place at the same time. For example, truly independently of what is going on in the seas around Britain; truly independently of what my wife Jill is doing; truly independently of what the people in my local town of Chesham three miles away are doing; and truly independently of the motion of the leaves on the trees in the wood next to our house.

6.3.2 Although most people in their thoughts and daily activities implicitly accept the truth of the assumption of independence of change it is not possible to obtain logical or empirical proof that this assumption is correct, and it is for this reason that it must be taken to be a metaphysical belief. The reason it cannot be proved by logical reasoning is because its truth is a contingent matter: it depends on whether or not humans happen to live in a world in which it is true; or, alternatively, happen to live in a world in which it is false – with both such worlds being logically possible. And the reason why no empirical evidence for its truth can be obtained is because it refers to *particular* instances of change – to *uniquely dated and located stretches of change* and not to *types* of change – and these cannot be re-run to see if they may run differently with respect to one another because it is not possible to re-run the history of the universe.

6.3.3 The phrase "dated and located" has been used without discussion because its meaning seems to be clear. However, according to mainstream physics, its meaning is not clear – indeed, it seems to have no empirically definable meaning. The theory of special relativity asserts that the time of occurrence of an event is relative to the frame of reference of the observer, and that there is no evidence for a universal frame of reference. That is, the theory tells us that no empirical methods exist for establishing a single moment of "now" for the universe as a whole. This means that it is technically incorrect to talk of uniquely dated and located stretches of change and that we should be referring to events with a unique placing in four-dimensional space-time. However, bearing this clarification in mind, this convenient phrase shall continue to be used.

6.3.4 Given that every stretch of change is a uniquely dated and located happening, it might seem that since the universe will have only one history (whatever that may turn out to be), it is necessarily true that every *particular* stretch of change belonging to the history must exist in a completely fixed relationship to every other *particular* stretch of change, including future ones. In an absolutely deterministic universe this is true, but in a universe in which the future is yet to be originated it is not. To give an example to clarify this, consider the quantum indeterministic generation of a random sequence of numbers. Up to any given point, a definite sequence of numbers will have been generated, and each of these numbers will be in a fixed relationship in the sequence to every other one. But no such fixed relationship exists between the numbers so far generated and those yet to be generated because, according to mainstream thinking, what these future numbers are remains indeterminate until they actually arise as a result of the occurrence of quantum indeterministic events such as the disintegration of atomic nuclei.

6.3.5 It is easy to think that true independence of change does actually exist because it seems to be so widely apparent. However, in thinking like this care is not being taken to distinguish between *token independence of change* and *type independence of change*. Using this distinction, it would be more accurate to say that true *token* independence of change is assumed to be extremely common in our universe – i.e. that specific dated and located stretches of change that to some extent run truly independently of one another are assumed to be extremely common. However, the simpler statement of the assumption of independence of change (that true independence of change is extremely common) will generally be used, with it being understood that it is the more accurate version that is being referred to.

6.3.6 Although it is not possible to provide empirical evidence to support the assumption of *token* independence of change (because the history of the universe cannot be re-run), it is possible to do so for *type* independence of change – indeed, how this might be done in the case of my typing activity and the simultaneous activity of our cat Purdy was discussed earlier (see 2.1.4). However, two things are implied by type independence of change. Firstly, that a given type of change may take place concurrently with many different types of stretches of change. And secondly, given two (or more) types of concurrently running stretches of change there will be little or no correlation between the *details* of how each type runs on particular occasions. It was this second aspect to which attention was drawn earlier, but the example did not establish the first sort of evidence for type independence of change, so to remedy this consider a similar imagined investigation of a kind that would show both sorts of evidence and allow some other points to be made.

6.3.7   This second imagined investigation concerns two types of stretches of change: type-A consisting of the motion of the pendulum of a very accurate clock, and type-B consisting of stretches of human voice sounds of different subtypes such as "singing", "speaking", "whispering", "shouting". In the experiment, measurements would be made (perhaps based on high-speed video recordings) of 100 stretches of change of the motion of the pendulum – with each particular dated and located stretch consisting of, say, 10 swings, with the bob starting from the same position each time. Concurrently with making these measurements, high fidelity recordings of the voice sounds of a cooperating person would also be made – voice sounds that for a single dated and located stretch are all of the same subtype but with the subtype and content of each such stretch being randomly selected by the investigator. If this investigation were actually conducted it would be expected to show that the details of the video recordings of the 100 stretches of pendulum motion would be very similar to one another – perhaps, as *recordings*, even identical. But the details of the recordings of the particular dated and located stretches of voice sounds would not be expected to show the same degree of similarity, although the degree of similarity between stretches of the same subtype would probably be greater than between stretches belonging to different subtypes.

6.3.8   The presumed results of the investigation could be used to illustrate and confirm the existence of evidence for both forms of type independence of change noted above. Firstly, it would be clear that one type of stretch of change – "pendulum swings" – may co-exist with a variety of different types of stretches of change, namely the various subtypes of voice sounds ("singing", "speaking", "whispering", "shouting"). And secondly, it would be clear from comparing the pairs of simultaneous recordings that there was little or no correlation between the details of the recordings of the pendulum swings and the details of the recordings of the voice sounds for any particular subtype. So, for example, the details of cases of stretches of change of type "pendulum swings" occurring concurrently with details of stretches of change of type "speaking" would show little or no correlation. For instance, there would be little or no correlation between the bob reaching the extremities of its swing and what spectrum of sound frequencies existed at the same time. Such an investigation would demonstrate evidence for the existence of *type* independence of change (in both its forms), but it would not demonstrate *token* independence of change. However, some people might be inclined to think otherwise since they might suppose that because the details of the 100 stretches of change involving the pendulum were so similar, they must in fact be *identical* tokens of the type of change "pendulum swings". If this was indeed the case, then evidence for token independence of change would have been demonstrated since the same token of one type of change would have been found to arise with different tokens of another type of change. But the 100 stretches of change "pendulum swings" are not actually identical, even though the video recordings may be, because each is a differently dated (and located, once the rotation of the Earth, etc. is taken into account) stretch of change. And were *all* the change going on in each swing – including the particular thermal motions of the atoms and molecules of the pendulum – taken in to account then it would be quite clear that the swings were not identical.

6.3.9   Evidence for type independence of change is extremely common. And it is all too easy to point to such evidence to persuade people that the assumption of (token) independence of change is true. Indeed, this has been done in giving the examples of independence of change mentioned a little earlier when it was suggested that my typing activity was going on truly independently of what was going on in the sea around Britain; truly independently of what my wife Jill was doing; truly independently of what the people in my local

148

town of Chesham three miles away were doing; and truly independently of the motion of the leaves on the trees in the wood next to our house. What was being tacitly appealed to was the solid evidence that exists that the details of such *types* of change are not correlated. However this does not provide evidence that *particular* dated and located stretches of change run truly independently of one another – to provide evidence for this would require performing experiments on the history of the universe, which can't be done.

6.4 Type Independence of Change and Absolute Determinism

6.4.1   In a universe in which absolute determinism rules there can be no true independencies of any sort – token, type, or whatever. However, in such a universe empirical evidence may be gathered that would seem to suggest that true *type* independence of change does exist. The purpose of this section is to illustrate and discuss this point. To begin with, the notion of "laws of nature" needs to be clarified.

6.4.2   The first part of van Inwagen's argument (see 3.4.4) implies that the present instantaneous total state of the universe and the laws of nature fully determine the next total instantaneous state, and so on for all subsequent states. What form may such laws of nature take? One possibility is that there is only one law of nature: a single law that specifies how every instantaneous total state of the universe changes into its immediately succeeding total state. For example, consider an extremely simple universe with only four instantaneous total states: a, b, c, d. The law of nature for such a universe might be: . . . a > b > c > d > a . . . That is, a law that states that if "a" is the present instantaneous total state then its immediate successor instantaneous total state is "b", and that if "b" is the present instantaneous total state then its immediate successor instantaneous total-state is "c", and so on, endlessly. Different sequences of these four total states are possible (e.g. c > b > d > a > c) and each of these would represent a differently running universe.

6.4.3   Is there a sense in which such a universe – a universe with a single law that defines how total states change – may contain evidence for independently changing *types* of stretches of change? The general answer must be "No" because such a law has no necessary place for separate sub-states within total states, and therefore no place for separate types of change involving such substates. However, if the laws of nature are such that they do refer to sub-states of existence, as the laws of nature so far established for the real universe do, then different *types* of stretches of change may occur, hence it is this kind of universe that shall be discussed.

6.4.4 The imaginary universe to be considered may be thought of as like a very large (idealised) billiard table with a number of balls in motion upon it. The table has no pockets, its cloth offers no resistance to the balls, the cushions are perfectly elastic, and the balls collide with one another and the cushions without any loss of energy. What changes from instant to instant in this universe are the positions of the billiard balls. At what shall be taken as time-zero, imagine that about 1000 balls are in various kinds of motion. The sub-state laws (which are modelled on Newton's laws of motion) are as follows, and each is a fully time-determinate law. (1) A ball at rest or in uniform motion remains at rest or in uniform motion unless it is in collision with one or more other balls or with a cushion. (2) When balls collide their momentum (i.e. the product of their mass and their velocity) will be changed in a fully determinate way that depends upon their positions and momentums at the moment of contact. (3) The total magnitude of the momentum of the balls involved in a collision remains constant throughout the process. (4) When a ball collides with a cushion it is reflected with no loss of speed but with the angle of reflection being equal to the angle of incidence (and with the directional component of its momentum normal to the cushion being exactly reversed). These are sub-state laws in that the refer to individual balls, to subsets of balls (e.g. those involved in a collision), and to parts of the cushion. They do not refer to the total state of this billiard-ball universe. The laws are also type-based in that they specify conditions that are true of certain *types* of changes and attributes rather than being true only of *particular* instances of these. For example: law (1) refers to the type of change, "uniform motion", a type of motion which individual balls may possess in different quantities at different times; and law (2) refers to types of attribute – "momentum" and "position" – which individual balls may possess with different values at different times.

150

6.4.5   Given these laws, and the initial positions and momentums of the balls at time-zero, the position and momentum of all the balls at every subsequent instant of time is fixed. That is, this is a universe in which change is entirely governed by time-determinate sub-state laws and in which, therefore, absolute determinism is true. Hence, all instances of stretches of change that occur in this universe are in a completely fixed relationship to one another – they run in perfect lockstep, even though this may not be apparent to an observer. This means that no true independence exists between any *particular* instances of stretches of change that arise in this universe. And it also means there can be no true independence of change between the occurrence of stretches of different *types* of change. Nevertheless, there remains *evidence*, of the sort discussed above, for there being type independence of change, as shall now be indicated.

6.4.6   Many different types of stretches of change may be defined in this universe, such as: "balls in collision", "ball in cushion reflection", "ball in uniform motion", "stationary ball", "ball moving roughly parallel with a long side", "two balls heading towards one another", and so on. Now there is going to be a lot of evidence that one *type* of change may occur concurrently with different *types* of stretches of change. For example, observation of the occurrence of a stretch of change of the type "ball in uniform motion" is not sufficient for an observer to fix what other types of stretches of change may also be observed as occurring at the same time (even though this must be fixed in such a universe). So, for instance, on one occasion "ball in uniform motion" may be observed accompanied by the type of change "balls in collision" and on another occasion by the type of change "ball in cushion reflection". But with about 1000 balls moving on the table there are going to be many co-occurring types of change accompanying any observation of, say, the type of change "ball in uniform motion", thus satisfying the first requirement of evidence for type independence of change. And as far as satisfying the second requirement, there is going to be little of no correlation between the details of different instances of particular types of change that are observed to be running concurrently. For example, there is going to be little of no correlation in the details of various instances of "ball in uniform motion" and the details of various instances of "ball in cushion reflection".

6.4.7   If nothing is known about this universe being wholly ruled by absolute determinism, and if its nature is known only through what has been observed, then it may seem that not only is there type independence of change but that there is token independence of change as well. However, once it is known that a universe is operating according to absolute determinism then it is also known that there can be no independencies at all – whether token independence of change or type independence of change. So, returning to the imaginary billiard-ball world, where it is known that absolute determinism reigns, it follows – for instance – that the occurrence of a specific ball undergoing uniform motion at a particular time is not doing so truly independently of the simultaneous occurrence of another specific ball undergoing a particular cushion reflection because these two particular dated and located concurrent stretches of change were predetermined to occur exactly as and when they did ever since time-zero. And although the evidence suggests that type-independence of change is true for this universe, this is not actually the case because every occurrence of a given type of change bears a fixed relationship to every occurrence of all other types of change. Which means that although there may be ample evidence, as in the real world, for there being true type independence of change, this does not actually prove that there is such independence. What this emphasises is that metaphysical matters are being dealt with that cannot be resolved empirically or logically.

6.4.8   Support for absolute determinism reigning in the real world requires, at the very least, evidence that all human-identified laws of nature are time-determinate laws. Many of the laws of classical physics, and also some quantum-based ones, are time-determinate, but not all of them are. In particular, quantum-indeterministic change (so-called "collapse of the wave function") is not time-determinate since when such change will occur is indeterminate. Compared to physics the biological and human sciences have very few time-determinate laws, and it seems these cannot be reduced to time-determinate ones. Indeed, according to independence indeterminism this reduction is not possible because what happens in such domains depends greatly upon independence interactions – interactions which, by being indeterminately arising occurrences, do not happen according to a time-determinate schedule. Hence, there is little evidence that the real world is ruled by absolute determinism.

6.5 Identifying Likely Cases of Independence of Change

6.5.1 It has been argued that however intuitively reasonable it may be to say that there are truly independently running stretches of change in the universe, it can never be proved by logical or empirical means that this is so. It is this that makes independence indetermin-ism as much a metaphysical thesis as absolute determinism. However, if the primary assumption of independence indeterminism is accep-ted without further discussion then it is accepted that there are a very great many instances of independence of change in the universe. And this being the case, it would be helpful to have some criteria for distinguishing between likely and unlikely instances of such change. This matter has already been discussed in Chapter 2 (see 2.1.5) and there it was noted that in practice people tend to assume that inde-pendence of change exists when they (usually tacitly) believe that three conditions are jointly met:

(i) that the stretches of change of the types concerned are not completely causally linked;

(ii) that no third party is fully determining how such types of stretches of change jointly run; and

(iii) that such types of change do not run in a perfectly syn-chronised way.

6.5.2 Very little can be empirically established about particular *instances,* or tokens of types, of stretches of change other than through recognising they have features of certain *types.* Specifically, it cannot be established whether or not a cause and effect relationship exists between particular *instances* of stretches of change: all that can be established is evidence that the *types* of change involved do or do not have causal connections. Similarly for there being third party in-fluence at work: all that can be established is evidence for whether or not such *types* of change are or are not subject to having their joint-change determined by certain *types* of third-party influence. And the same holds for synchronicity: it is only evidence for the presence or absence of synchronicity between *types* of change that can be established. This is why the three conditions are stated in type-based terms and make no reference to particulars other than them being of certain types. So, for instance, in discussing the raindrop and the leaf example (see 2.1.6), type-based evidence was used to support assumption (i) that causal independence of change exists between falling raindrops and leaves moving down a stream. And the absence of type-based evidence of third party influences determining the joint-change of raindrops and the leaves was used to support assumption (ii). And type-based evidence was also used to support assumption (iii) that there is little synchronicity between such types of change. Absolute determinists, although for practical purposes they accept these type-based conclusions, believe that were the "complete picture" available then all apparently independently running stretches of change would be seen to be taking place in completely predetermined lockstep, and there would be no true independence of change of any sort – something William James was well aware of when he wrote that determinists believe that '[t]he whole is in each and every part, and welds it with the rest into an absolute unity, an iron block, in which there can be no equivocation or shadow of turning.' (see 3.2.5)

6.5.3   The non-synchronicity condition deserves further discussion. Experience of the world leads most people to believe that the vast majority of stretches of change do not run in synchrony unless they are appropriately causally linked, or a third party is ensuring that they do so. Just by observing two (or more) specific dated and located stretches of change, and without drawing on any evidence about the types of change involved, it is not possible to determine whether they are, or are not, running in synchrony. However, very often there is relevant evidence of the ways in which such types of change run, and this knowledge will often lead people to believe that specific instances of such types of change do not run in perfect unison. However, there do exist types of change that seem as if they are running in synchrony even when there is no apparent causal connection between them or third party ensuring this. For example, the swings of two causally disconnected pendulums of identical design and near identical construction set to swing in the same locality will, for shortish periods at least, run in very near synchrony. How may such stretches of change be shown *not* to be running in perfect synchrony? Over a short period, and without accurate observation of all the detail of what is going on, this may be difficult. But over a long period, obvious differences may begin to appear: for instance, two swinging pendulums may get progressively out of step and this would indicate that they are not running in perfect synchrony. But if the changes (e.g. the swings of the pendulums) are in widely separated locations so that they cannot be observed together then how may it be discovered that they are *not* running in synchrony? One way of doing this is by using clocks.

6.5.4   Perfect clocks are devices, or purely natural phenomena, that although running in causally independent ways and with no third-party intervention, keep in perfect step with one another – that is, they change in perfect unison or synchronicity. No perfect clocks exist, but if they did then they could be used to determine the synchronicity or non-synchronicity of stretches of change which are not jointly observable. For example, the synchronicity or non-synchronicity of two pendulums in widely separated parts of the world could be found by timing the swings of each using a perfect clock local to each pendulum: if the timings for the pendulums agreed then this would provide evidence for them running in perfect synchrony. But if the clocks were not perfect, then this method would not give reliable results. Given the importance of clocks to the matters being considered, and particularly because they provide cases of natural changes that run in an almost time-determinate manner, they deserve to be discussed in their own right.

6.6   Some Notes on Clocks

6.6.1   According to currently available empirical evidence there are some – but, relatively speaking, few – long-lasting stretches of change that run in very near synchronisation but which, as far as can be determined, are causally independent of one another and involve no third-party coordination. One reason for the lack of such cases is that there seem to be (relatively speaking) very few long-lasting stretches of change that run in an extremely regular manner. Celestial phenomena provide most of the cases. For example, the motion of the Earth relative to stars is very regular but, in the modern world, not regular enough to provide an adequate world standard of time – indeed, leap-seconds occasionally have to be added to keep our most precise time standards in line with less regularly changing celestial time. But quite apart from this weakness, celestial time provides a highly inconvenient clock – one, in particular, that cannot at all easily be used to measure short intervals of time. There are however some celestial phenomena that could, at least in principle, be so used. The best known of these are pulsars. These were discovered in the 1960s and are rapidly rotating neutron stars. They emit a narrow beam of radio-frequency electromagnetic radiation which sweeps across space rather like a lighthouse beam, and when such beams happen to be in line with the Earth, their sweep results in a brief illumination which can be detected by radio telescopes. These pulses arise with a period of recurrence of a few milliseconds to a few seconds, and with a regularity of the order of 1 part in a billion. Since there are many pulsars in the universe, they provide a large collection of (apparently) causally independent long-lasting stretches of cyclic change which show a high degree of synchronisation. Nevertheless, the synchronisation is not perfect, and furthermore very elaborate (and expensive) equipment is required to detect them.

6.6.2 The creation of readily available and highly regularly-running stretches of change that people may use as practical time-measuring devices has long been an objective within the realm of civilization. The daily motion of the Sun has often been used as the basis of such devices – sundials are a familiar example – but they only work when the sun is out and they cannot "tell the time" very precisely. Water clocks were developed by the Ancient Egyptians, and were widely used by the Ancient Greeks – but they, like candle clocks, are not very regular. Escapement clocks first appear in ancient times and typically used water to drive the escapement mechanism. Later, the Arabs constructed water clocks incorporating gears and weights. The crown wheel (or verge) escapement was invented in the 14th century and led to all-mechanical clocks, including spring-driven pocket watches. Recognition, by Galileo, that the swing of a pendulum (through a small arc) was very regular, led (in the 18th century) to the first highly accurate clocks.

6.6.3 A step change in the time-keeping precision of clocks arose in the 1920s with the development of electronic quartz clocks – which obtain their precision from the highly regular piezo-electric oscillation of quartz crystals. The next large advance came in the 1950s when atomic clocks were introduced. These devices use the highly stable frequencies of the electromagnetic radiation emitted from atoms that undergo certain very specific energy transitions. Atomic clocks currently form the basis of international time standards, of which there are several.

6.6.4   Clocks accurate to a fraction of a billionth of a second are vital components of many modern technologies such as telecommunications, the internet, global satellite-based navigation, modern astronomy, and interplanetary space exploration. At these accuracies procedures must be adopted to correct for deviations due to relativistic effects. For example, the atomic clocks aboard the satellites of global positioning systems run about 1 part in 10^{10} slower because of their speed relative to ground-based atomic clocks, and about 5 parts in 10^{10} faster because of the lower gravity at the heights at which they operate compared to the surface of the Earth. Without correcting for these relativistic time-distorting effects satellite navigation systems would be useless because errors in position of many metres would be inevitable.

6.6.5   Relativistic slowing and speeding applies to every kinds of physical change. The effect is extremely small – except in the presence of very high gravitational fields, and/or where relative speeds approaching those of light in vacuum (about 3×10^8 meters a second) are involved. Some indication of how even very slight relativistic influences can affect the rate at which change takes place is given by the fact that the most accurate atomic clocks are so regular that raising such a clock by just one meter in the Earth's gravitational field is sufficient to produce a measurable speeding up of the rate at which it runs – a speeding up that is a consequence of the very slightly weaker field within which it then operates.

6.6.6   Enough about the assumption of independence of change has now been said to provide a basis for moving on and further considering two very important consequences of adopting independence indeterminism: namely, that it has a place for *directed* origination, which is discussed in the next chapter, and for *creative* origination, which is considered in more detail in Chapter 8.

7   More on Directed Origination

7.1   Introduction

7.1.1   The idea of directed origination was introduced in Chapter 2 (see sections 2.3 and 2.4). In this chapter the aim is to develop and add to the ideas mentioned there. Throughout the discussion, the assumption of independence of change is taken to be true. The chapter begins with several sections relevant to the conceptual basis of directed origination. It then continues by considering some common methods for implementing directed origination. The chapter ends by introducing the notion of executive controlling agents, and it is suggested that most of the time human persons operate as self-evaluating executive controlling agents – or SEECing agents.

7.2   Some Key Concepts and an Unfamiliar Terminology

7.2.1   Unfortunately, although the topic being discussed, has received a good deal of attention during the past 100 years or so, and although it is still an active field of research and thinking, it does not have an agreed set of clearly defined concepts, nor does it have a settled vocabulary. Given this, a set of concepts, and a vocabulary to go with them, will be introduced that is somewhat non-standard. Nevertheless, the ideas and intuitions that shall be drawn upon are common within the field. A good account of many of these ideas and intuitions, and a review of much of the early development of the field, may be found in Andrew Woodfield's book, *Teleology* (Woodfield 1976). And Michael Weir's book *Goal Directed Behaviour* (Weir 1984) presents a novel approach to explaining goal-directedness based on the concept of path rather than state.

7.2.2   In what follows it will be helpful to have available a concrete example, and the one that shall be used – that of a particular lion chasing and catching a particular antelope at a particular time and place – is similar to the dog-chasing-rabbit example that was discussed briefly in section 2.3. Prior to such a chase there is likely to be a good deal of true independence between the activities of the lion and the antelope and this means that the event of them coming into initial interaction (e.g. seeing one another) is likely to be mainly a chance independence interaction. Once the chase begins chance play less of a role but it does not disappear. Throughout the chase both animals retain a good deal of independence of action because each is an autonomous agent, but they will influence one another. Each animal will also be influenced by factors common to them both – such as the nature of the terrain, the vegetation, and the presence of other animals – but each will tend to react to these influences somewhat differently. Given these independencies, during the chase each animal will enter into many independence interactions – e.g. with one another, with other animals, and with the environment. This means that the eventual capture of the antelope by the lion will be a de novo originated event.

7.2.3   The first new term to be introduced is "directed happening". This term shall be used to indicate that some happening appears to embody "directedness", and that the situation being considered seems to manifest such happenings. Directedness is a quality that people readily attribute to many happenings, indeed, perhaps they attribute directedness rather too readily – for example, some people may read into certain purely chance events the workings of Fate; or they may see divine intervention behind all that goes on in the universe. This suggests that care must be taken in attributing directedness to a happening.

7.2.4   Unfortunately it does not seem possible to give a simple and universally acceptable definition of what it is about a happening that gives it the quality of directedness. So instead a cluster of concepts which jointly seem to allow this quality to be captured shall be introduced. A directed happening will be taken to be a stretch of change which appears to manifest one or more directed outcomes. By a directed outcome is meant (1) a non-chance outcome whose existence requires there to be a system, known as a directive system, operating in an appropriate environment, that (2) is so matching its actions to independently arising and/or changing circumstances that the outcome tends to be produced, and (3) the outcome tends to be produced even though the circumstances alone do not tend to give rise to it, and they may often be such that they interfere with, disturb, or oppose its occurrence. The term directive activity is used to refer to that activity of a directive system that is relevant to the system's production of directed outcomes. Some directive entities are better understood as RENOIRs, but for simplicity throughout the present discussions the term system will generally be used.

7.2.5 While the presence of directive activity and directed outcomes may often be inferred by an intelligent agent such as a person, their presence cannot be objectively identified by observing or meas- uring features of a single particular stretch of change taken in isola- tion. The reason for this is that identification of the above three con- ditions for the presence of directive activity and directed outcomes has to make use of complex type-based knowledge which may only be obtained by observing and analysing several cases of more or less similar behaviour. For instance, an event can only be identified as non-chance by taking it to be a member of a class of events that col- lectively seem to possess the characteristic of being non-chance (i.e. not randomly arising) events. Similarly, it is only possible to infer whether actions are indeed being matched to independently arising and/or changing circumstances by relating particular instances of ac- tions to a set of similar actions for which, as a set, this seems to be true. And whether the circumstance alone do not tend to give rise to the outcome (and whether something may be interfering with or dis- turbing its occurrence), may only be determined for a set of similar stretches of change and not for a single stretch of change considered in isolation. For cases of a familiar type it may be relatively easy to ar- rive at an uncontentious conclusion regarding fulfilment of the above conditions and therefore of the existence of directive activity and dir- ected outcomes. However when dealing with a novel one-off case, achieving a conclusion may be a good deal more difficult. Neverthe- less, because humans have a very wide familiarity with directive activ- ity, it is often possible for a group of observers to reach agreement that directedness is present.

7.2.6 Assuming the lion/antelope example being considered is typical then conditions (1) to (3) for the presence of directed happen- ing may be assumed to hold, as the following reasoning shows. Clearly, a specific dated and located stretch of change is being con- sidered, but because it is typical it may be taken to belong to a large class of similar stretches of change and so general type-based know- ledge relevant to this class may be used. The most obvious candidate for being a directed outcome is the capture of the antelope by the

160

lion, and type-based knowledge suggests this event is not a matter of chance and that it requires that there be a directive system – a lion – operating in an appropriate environment (one in which the lion can conduct a chase and which contains animals capable of being chased and caught). Hence, it seems condition (1) is met. It might be that the actions the lion takes during the chase are not matched to independently arising and/or changing circumstances (such as the movement of the antelope, or of changing terrain), but that they arise as a matter of chance, or a consequence of blindly executing a pre-set sequence of movements. However, type-based knowledge gained from observing several such chase episodes suggests that in the present typical case the lion's actions are (mainly) matched, by the lion, to the current independently arising circumstances of the chase in such a way that capture of the antelope results. Hence, it seems condition (2) is met. Finally, again from understanding obtained from observing several such chase episodes, there is no reason to believe that the circumstances under which the lion is operating are such that by themselves they delivered the antelope into the lion's grasp without any effort on the lion's part. Rather, it is clear that the lion must take appropriate action in order for this event to occur. Hence, it seems condition (3) is met. It is not essential that the latter part of condition (3) be met for directed happening to exist but many cases of directive activity do involve opponents or competitors. The present case is one since the antelope behaves in such a way that what it does tends to "interfere with, disturb, or oppose" the occurrence of the directed outcome of the lion catching the antelope. Since all three conditions have been found to be met in the lion/antelope episode being considered, it may be taken to involve directed happening.

7.2.7   At this stage a couple of points of clarification are needed. Firstly, by the circumstances associated with a directed happening is meant things (including events, etc.) that influence, directly or indirectly, the coming into existence of the type of directed outcome in question. The things that exert influence may be divided into those in the agent's environment, and those concerning the agent itself. With respect to the lion/antelope example, the environmental circumstances in which the directive activity of the lion takes place include the partly independently occurring activities of the antelope, the activity of other animals, the terrain, and the visibility conditions.

Those things concerning the agent itself that are taken to be part of its circumstances include its current physical and mind-body state, its current activity, and its placement within its environment.

7.2.8 Secondly, directive activity does not guarantee the production of the directed outcome(s) it tends to produce. However, it is often possible to identify the existence of directive activity even when a directed outcome is not achieved. For example, although the success rate of a single lion catching its prey is quite low – somewhat less than 20% – it is generally easy to identify that prey-chasing directive activity is taking place even when the lion fails to catch its prey.

7.2.9 The terms directed happening and directed outcome do not commonly appear in the literature. The terms goal-directed behaviour, goal-oriented behaviour, and goal, objective, and aim are much more commonly used. The term directive activity has been used in the past – for example, see *The Directiveness of Organic Activities* by E. S. Russell (1945) – but it is not in common use today. The term directive system is also little used, with other terms such as goal-directed system, goal-seeking system, end-directed system, and control system being in more common use. Unfortunately, in common usage the word goal – 'A point towards which effort or movement is directed; the objective point or terminus that one is striving to reach; the end aimed at: the *goal* of one's ambition.' (*Webster's Dictionary* 1998) – is too strongly associated with purposive activity for it to be used as a general term when referring to directedness since non-purposive directive systems (such as a thermostatically controlled home heating system) show directedness.

7.3 Directive Systems Originate their Directed Outcomes

7.3.1 Most determinists would accept that directedness is a feature of much of the happening that takes place in the living and human worlds, but they would not regard it as entailing the *origination* of the associated directed outcomes. However, independence indeterminists most certainly would. In order to establish this conclusion, it is necessary to consider what is entailed in the production of different kinds of directed outcome.

7.3.2 Directed outcomes in which the directive system producing them is an autonomous agent – as is the case with a lion producing the directed outcome of capturing an antelope – are quite straightforwardly de novo originated outcomes. The following reasoning shows this to be so. To produce a directed outcome a directive system must match its actions to independently arising and/or changing environmental circumstances in such a way that the directed outcome tends to result. By definition, an *autonomous* agent (such as a lion or an antelope) is taken to be able to commence, cease, and direct (some of) its actions independently of (but not necessarily without regard to) its environmental circumstances. This means that the directed outcome produced by an autonomous agent is a product of interactions between two partially independently running stretches of change – a stretch of change involving the agent and how it generates its autonomously produced actions, and a stretch of change involving the environmental circumstances under which the agent is operating. And because independence interactions are involved this means the directed outcome the agent produces must be a de novo originated event.

7.3.3 However, there are (at the functional level) deterministically operating directive systems that have no autonomy because all their actions depend upon their fixed operating rules, their present internal condition, and the current environmental circumstances under which they are operating. If it is to be established that all directive systems carry out de novo origination of their directed outcomes then it must be shown that this is true for non-autonomous as well as autonomous directive systems.

7.3.4 To simplify the discussion consider the operation of a specific deterministically operating directive system – namely, a simple thermostatically controlled home central heating system. Such a system, when operating correctly and in a suitable environmental situation, will tend to produce the directed outcome of a roughly constant temperature in the home. A central heating system is usually designed to be able to produce a range of different fairly constant temperatures and it will generally have some means for the home-dweller to easily set an internal condition of the system (via, say, a dial on the thermostatic switch of the system, or by entering a digital value into an appropriate part of the system's controller) that corresponds to the temperature in the home that the system will then work to produce. In engineering control theory such an internal correlate of the directed outcome that a directive system is working to produce is known as its set-point. In less technical discussion it is often referred to as the goal of the system but, for reasons just discussed (7.2.9), this usage shall be avoided and be reserved for when speaking specifically about purposive systems (see 2.3.8).

7.3.5   A simple thermostatically controlled home central heating system does not directly match its actions to changing environmental conditions but acts solely on the difference between the temperature corresponding to its set-point and the current temperature in the home. In fact, the system does not take action on the difference between these two temperatures as such but rather on some condition within itself that is correlated with this difference. If the difference is negative (i.e. the temperature in the home is less than the set-point temperature) then this difference results in the switching on of the heating, providing it is not already on. And if it is positive (i.e. the temperature in the home is greater than or equal to the set-point temperature) then this difference results in the heating being switched off, providing it is not already off. (In practice there is usually a small spread between the switching-on temperature and the switching-off temperature to avoid over-frequent cycling of the system, but this shall be ignored to simplify the discussion.) Under what conditions may the roughly constant temperature be taken to be *originated* by the entirely automatically produced directive activity of the system? Before considering this matter, it is first necessary to establish that the roughly constant temperature in the home is a directed outcome according to the conditions specified earlier.

7.3.6   To be a directed outcome the existence of the roughly constant temperature must be such that the heating system (the directive system concerned) produces actions (turning the heating on and off) that are so matched to independently arising and/or changing conditions (e.g. the outside air temperature, the prevailing wind and sunshine conditions, whether supplementary heating is on or off, whether windows and external doors are open or shut) that this fairly constant temperature tends to result. Observation soon leads to the conclusion that this is indeed the case. It is required that the constant temperature be maintained in spite of the environmental circumstance not themselves giving rise to this condition. In general, this is true – except on those occasions when the outside temperature pretty well matches the set-point temperature. And it is required that should some of the circumstances change in ways that affect the mainten-ance of the constant temperature (as will usually occur, for example, when there is a change in the external temperature, or windows and external doors are opened or closed, or supplementary heating is turned on or off), then the system's actions will be such as to tend to maintain the fairly constant temperature. Again, within limits, obser-vation shows this is true for a correctly operating thermostatically controlled central heating system. Hence, since all the required condi-tions are met it may be concluded that the roughly constant temperat-ure is indeed a directed outcome and that the actions of the heating system play an essential role in producing this.

7.3.7   Given then that the roughly constant temperature is a dir-ected outcome, can it be taken to be a directively *originated* outcome? Considering the central heating system from a detailed material per-spective, it would be possible to argue that the slight degree of inde-pendence that exists between the operation of the parts of the sys-tem – e.g. between the operation of its motors, pumps, switches, valves – means that it does not respond in a perfectly deterministic way to its inputs and so the roughly constant temperature must be taken to be originated. But this is not what is meant by asserting that under independence indeterminism the directed outcomes that are produced by the directive activity of directive systems are de novo originated outcomes. Rather, what is being asserted is that this is true even when the system, from a *functional* rather than a *material* perspect-ive, is operating deterministically. There is no problem if all that must be established is that the roughly constant temperature in the house is a *stale* origination because the central heating system – in being an artefact – is an originated entity, so whatever it does will be originated according to the definition of origination that is being used (see 1.2.4). Rather, the question is: How can the roughly constant temper-ature be a *fresh*, or de novo, origination given that (functionally) the central heating system does not run independently of its environ-mental circumstances but is organised to respond to them in a fully (functionally) deterministic way? This question is easily answered: without the activity of the central heating system the roughly con-

165

stant temperature would not be reliably maintained, so even though it is responding entirely deterministically to changing environmental conditions its operation plays an essential role in producing the directed outcome. But if this is so then for the directed outcome to be de novo *originated* the environmental conditions must change indeterministically. This is almost always the case in which home central heating systems run because independently varying factors – of the sort mentioned above, such as the external temperature, wind and sunshine conditions, windows being open or closed – make up the environmental conditions. But this is not necessarily true in artificially contrived situations, as shall now be discussed.

7.3.8   Imagine a scenario in which a laboratory for testing central heating systems has been constructed that allows researchers to investigate the performance of such systems under a variety of pre-set programmes of environmental changes. In such a case the environmental changes would, from a functional perspective, be predetermined, and therefore it would not be correct to say that the activity of the central heating system was (de novo) originating the roughly constant temperatures that it was able to achieve. But that this is so would only be apparent if it was known that the environmental conditions were changing deterministically – i.e. according to a pre-determined programme – and although this might be fairly obvious given a laboratory setup, it is certainly not obvious that it is so in the real-world environments within which ordinary central heating systems normally operate. Indeed, under independence indeterminism (but not absolute determinism) environmental circumstances cannot change deterministically if they are composed of independently varying factors, as is almost always the case in real-world situations such as one involving a thermostatically controlled home heating system.

7.3.9   Subject to accepting the assumption of independence of change, and because there is nothing special about the examples used, it may be concluded that in general directive systems do indeed originate the directed outcomes their activity tends to produce.

7.4   Natural Directiveness and Directed Origination

7.4.1   Having established the existence of directed origination under independence indeterminism, it is important to identify how it differs from what shall be referred to as "natural directiveness". There are several types of natural directiveness and to indicate its nature three specific cases shall be discussed. The first case is that of the directiveness suggested by Fermat's principle which states that the path taken by a ray of light (or any wave-motion) in passing between two points will always establish itself so that it minimizes the time taken for the propagation to occur. This means that should circumstance change that affect the course of a ray (e.g. the introduction or removal of lenses from an optical path), then the ray will change its course in such a manner that the directed outcome of minimum propagation time will be maintained. This is an infallible consequence of situations in which Fermat's principle applies – there is no sense in which the 'actions' involved can fail to produce a minimum propagation time. Nor is it possible to identify any subsystem – that is, a directive system – whose presence and correct functioning within the situation brings the directiveness with it. Rather, the directiveness and the infallible production of the associated directed outcome belongs to the whole situation and cannot be attributed to the presence of a specific subsystem within it. The second case is of the directiveness suggested by Hamilton's principle, which states that dynamical physical systems undergo changes only in ways that either maximize or minimize an abstract physical quantity known as "action" – a quantity with the physical dimensions of energy and time. (Interestingly, Hamilton's principle, while being a central concept of classical mechanics, has also found a role in quantum mechanics.) In situations in which this principle applies, achievement of the maximization/minimization cannot fail to occur. And neither can any subsystem be identified within the overall system that is responsible for producing this directed outcome; nor is there any sense in which a malfunction may occur that destroys the directiveness. The final case is that of Le Chatelier's principle which asserts that if a chemical system experiences a change in concentration, temperature, volume, or partial pressure, then the equilibrium shifts to counteract the imposed change and restore a new condition of equilibrium. This happens infallibly, and no directive system responsible for the directiveness can be identified as a subsystem within situations where the principle applies; and malfunctions that destroy the directiveness are not possible.

7.4.2   Natural directiveness differs from the directiveness associated with directive systems in the ways mentioned in the three examples just given. Firstly, natural directiveness operates infallibly in bringing about the relevant directed outcome. Secondly, it belongs to the whole situation and not to the presence of a subsystem within it. And thirdly, there is no sense in which a malfunction may arise that destroys the directiveness. In sharp contrast, the directiveness of directive systems does not possess any of these features. That is, the directiveness cannot guarantee to bring about its associated directed outcome; the directiveness is always associated with a subsystem (the directive system) that is in principle separable from the overall system or situation to which it belongs; and malfunctions may arise that destroy the directiveness.

7.4.3   With the foregoing discussion of mainly conceptual issues related to directed origination in mind, it is appropriate to consider some of the ways in which this important kind of activity is implemented in the biological world and in the realm of civilization. Although implementation methods will generally be discussed individually, it should be remembered that very often methods are combined in the execution of a particular kind of directive activity – as they are, for example, in the case of a lion chasing an antelope.

7.5   Some Methods of Directed Origination

7.5.1   Perhaps the most basic method is error-reduction control (also commonly known as feedback control). This method, in its simplest form, has already been mentioned when the operation of a thermostatically controlled home central heating system was outlined. It is used widely in the biological, human, and technological realms, and it is often a part of more complex methods of directed origination.

7.5.2   In carrying out the error-reduction method a directive system takes actions that tend to reduce the error, or difference, between a target value of some variables (e.g. those defining a set-point, or an objective) and the current value of these variables. A directive system using this method takes action based on the error or difference between conditions internal to the directive system that are correlated with the target and actual values rather than on the difference between these values as such. The condition representing the actual value is generally based on the directive system sensing relevant variables in some way – as, for example, when a heating system uses the state of a bimetallic strip or some electronic sensor as a proxy for the actual temperature in the home. The condition representing the target value is usually built-in or is set by some external system, sometimes another directive system – as for example occurs when a home-dweller adjusts the thermostat of their heating system. This internal target condition is correlated with the directed outcome that the operation of the system works to achieve.

7.5.3 "Bang-bang" error-reduction control is the term used to describe the method found in central heating systems of the kind discussed earlier. It is called bang-bang because the corrective action is either all on or all off: that is, the corrective action cannot be varied in strength. Continuously variable error-reduction gives smoother control and is frequently used. For instance, it is often required that certain engines or motors maintain a constant output speed even when the load they are driving varies. For example, a steam engine used to drive machinery in an old-fashioned textile mill needs to be regulated so that the speed of the drive-shaft feeding the various machines maintains a constant speed in spite of a varying load. Error reduction control – often involving quite sophisticated implementation – is also used in servomechanisms: directive systems for ensuring that heavy machinery (e.g. an anti-aircraft gun) can accurately track a moving target, or rapidly achieve a given target condition without overshoot. Error-reduction control is used within the living realm to ensure the constancy of many biological conditions – a constancy that is required for the effective running of certain biochemical processes. As mentioned earlier (2.3.10), homeostasis is the term generally used to refer to this sort of biological directive activity. For example, as well as maintaining core body temperature constant, human homeostasis includes the regulation of levels of blood sugar, calcium, iron, osmotic pressure of body fluids, and the pH (i.e. acidity/alkalinity balance) of blood plasma.

7.5.4 It is appropriate at this point to introduce and briefly discuss the meaning of several terms that are in common use. "Closed-loop control" includes error-reduction control and exists whenever the action a directive system takes depends directly or indirectly on what previous action it has taken and what effect this has had. In general, a directive system must be appropriately responsive not only to relevant disturbances and disruptions, but also to the effects its actions are producing. There is therefore a need for the system to "close the loop", that is for there to be a more or less continual process of performing an action, identifying the effect produced, assessing what to do next, performing a further action, and so on with this loop only ceasing when success is attained or a decision is made to abandon the endeavour. In many cases of error-reduction control this loop is implemented in a fixed and mechanical way with the "identifying the effect" step being realised by the system simply using the current error between target and actual values, and the "assess what to do next" step being built into how it operates. But in more sophisticated forms of directed origination this is often far from being the case, particularly when the directive system is dealing with unfamiliar circumstances, or trying to work out an appropriate set of actions to achieve some goal. And sometimes an agent has to be more or less creative in trying to identify (or understand) just what the effect of their actions has been, and in trying to decide what to do next to achieve their goal when they are uncertain about how to proceed. And almost always one of the options available to such an agent is to abandon pursuit of a goal. However, in abandoning a particular endeavour, they may still have some higher-level motivation that remains unsatisfied and this may lead them to seek out and pursue another goal aimed at satisfying the motivation. Or, they might give up their attempts to satisfy the motivation in question and try to learn to live with their dissatisfaction. These latter points are made to emphasise that the directive activity of human agents in particular can be extremely complex and convoluted even though, at a rather abstract level, what they are engaged in is a fairly basic pattern of directive activity.

7.5.5   One of the weaknesses of the error reduction method is that the directive system's action always depends solely upon an error existing between the target value and the actual value: the system has no means to anticipate and so is not able to prepare for, or avoid, oncoming disturbances, or changes in the target value. "Feed-forward control" incorporates a simple form of anticipation in that the directive system assesses the current situation and on the basis of what it finds it selects an appropriate objective and means of achieving it. This may be illustrated with the simple example of a person using a domestic washing machine. A modern washing machine generally offers the user several wash programmes, each suitable for producing a good result given a load consisting of items all with the same general characteristics. Typically, a user organises their washing into batches of items suitable for being satisfactorily washed together and then selects, and sets going, an appropriate wash programme for the load. This initial phase is the situation-assessment and action-selection step. During execution of the selected wash programme the machine carries out a predetermined sequence of actions considered suitable for achieving a satisfactory wash for the types of items in the load. However, an ordinary washing machine does not check the effectiveness of its washing actions, meaning it operates blindly in an "open-loop" manner: closure of the overall control loop is carried out by the user after they have removed the washed items from the machine and examined them to see if they have been cleaned satisfactorily. At this point, if items have not been satisfactorily washed the user may re-wash them using the same programme or carry out other actions such as applying a stain removal agent before re-washing – or perhaps they may decide to simply discard an item as no longer of use for its original purpose. However, it might be that at this assessment stage the user comes to believe the wash has failed to work satisfactorily for some other reason, such as a failure to add detergent, or because of a malfunction of the machine. The varied nature of the human contribution illustrates how what may start out as a very ordinary activity can end up involving quite complex forms of directive activity that sometimes leads to non-trivial decision-making and free-will processing. For instance, with a malfunctioning washing machine, a person may be faced with conflict over what to do: either call someone out to look at the machine – but who may charge for the visit while also concluding that it is not economical to repair it – or go straight for buying a new machine.

7.5.6 Although it might seem that feed-forward control would always work best if the selected actions were carried out in a closed-loop way involving monitoring of their success as they are executed, this is not always the case. For example, in a game of golf, a player typically first assesses the situation they are currently in, and on the

171

basis of this they decide on a particular aim or target for their shot and on the club to use to achieve this. They then execute the chosen shot in an open-loop manner. Experienced golfers know that trying to actually execute a golf-swing using error-reduction control during the swing is not recommended as it rarely produces good results – indeed, the inclination to do this is something that a novice golfer may have to learn to control. What has just been drawn attention to is a general feature of many complex types of directive activity. That is, the directive activity involves a manager or supervisor directive system that selects targets and organises directive systems to achieve them, but which does not get involved in the directive activity of these systems unless it identifies problems that need its attention.

7.5.7   The next common method of directed origination that shall be considered is the control of sequences of separate directive activities. However, although sequence control usually makes use of both feed-forward and error-reduction control, and includes open-loop and closed-loop activities, it is considered to be a type of directive activity in its own right for two main reasons. Firstly, because the directed outcomes it produces are generally achievable only by satisfactorily managing and sequencing several subsidiary activities. And secondly, with more complex forms, because often the sequence will need to be appropriately adjusted – perhaps with new procedures needing to be created – to take account of the particular circumstances that obtain. An example from the biological realm will serve to illustrate a relatively straightforward case of sequence control.

7.5.8   A bird in building a nest carries out sequence control since to build a satisfactory nest requires successful fulfilment of several subsidiary stages, each of which involves executing a sequence of directive activities. First, an appropriate site for the nest must be found. This is far from being a blind automatic activity even though the criteria that a bird seeks to satisfy seem to be largely laid down genetically rather than being mainly acquired through learning or being up to the bird to decide more or less creatively for themselves. Finding a suitable nest site entails search activity. (Search is in itself another common form of directive activity, and one that may involve a good deal of complex subsidiary activity. However, to avoid an overlong presentation, it shall not be discussed further even though much work has been done investigating and devising various search methods and strategies). Once a site has been located, the next phase of directive activity entails building the nest. This usually consists of a sequence of directive activities aimed at achieving a succession of directed outcomes that together result in a finished nest. For example, the first step may consist of obtaining sticks and twigs to construct the support and basic structure of the nest; the second step may involve obtaining smaller twigs to build a bowl-shape within the basic structure; and the final step may entail lining the bowl with suitable materials – possibly of several layers composed of such things as moss, fibres, and mud. All of these stages require that the bird (or birds, if the nest is made by a mating pair) carry out quite complex directive activity to achieve the directed outcome in question. Should the nest suffer damage – from a storm, say – then the bird must decide whether to implement a sequence of directive activities to repair the nest, or to abandon it and build a new one.

7.5.9 Used by individuals and when working cooperatively, the above methods – in combination with the use of knowledge, intelligence, and in the human case with language and symbolic representations – make possible highly complex forms of directive activity. Directed *creative* origination plays an important role in human life, but a less important one in animal life. There are many methods that claim to stimulate or enhance human directed creative origination but, for lack of space, these shall not be discussed. A little more about human creative origination is included in the next chapter in paragraphs 8.4.14/15.

7.6   Executive Controlling Agents

7.6.1 Executive control is the final form of directive activity that shall be discussed in this brief survey, and although relatively simple forms of it have been implemented in the technological realm – a computer operating system is an example – the concern here is with executive control as it is found in psychological agents, and humans in particular.

7.6.2 The executive self is that part of a psychological agent that carries out the function of intelligent executive control. Executive control is simply one mode of operation among several found in animals and humans and it may be displaced or overridden by more primitive modes such as those based on instinct, unthinking habit, and emotion-driven action. The superordinate objective (or prime directive) of an executive controller is to successfully organise (e.g. create, initiate, guide, coordinate, and terminate) directive activity to satisfactorily attend to a set of potentially conflicting tasks while doing so with limited resources and powers, with various constraints on its actions, and in the face of conflicting priorities and demands. The executive branch of a human organisation provides a familiar example of an intelligent executive controller. Its job is to organise directive activities to successfully carry out the tasks or goals given to it by the policy-making part of the organisation (e.g. its board of directors or governors) under constraints imposed by this part, by the capacities and resources of the organisation, and by the environment within which the organisation operates. Higher animals, when operating in their executive mode rather than when operating in another mode (such as responding purely instinctively), may be understood as having the superordinate objective of successfully serving and satisfying their physiological and other motivations according to (mainly) genetically given priorities and evaluation criteria while taking into account environmental and other constraints, including those imposed by their emotional self.

7.6.3   A bird building a nest provides an example of animal executive control. Building a nest is one of the motivations that a bird's executive controller (or executive self) must attend to, but a bird also has other motivations such as obtaining food and water, finding a mate, rearing its young, defending its territory, and avoiding predators. Although birds learn about their environment and acquire some new skills, they are mostly reliant upon genetically given means for serving and satisfying their motivations. However, with animals operating in executive controller mode, what is not given genetically is how they organise their activities to satisfactorily attend to these different motivations given the particular circumstances they find themselves in. Rather, this is something they must do by using their intelligence. Generally, the task priorities that a bird (or other kind of higher animal) operates under when in executive controller mode are given genetically. So, for example, preserving their life tends to take priority over other motivations, although this may not always be the case as when, say, an animal risks their life to protect their young, or to obtain food when starving. Similarly, what an animal's executive self takes to be success in serving the animal's motivations tends to be given genetically and, for most animals, consists mainly in them being able to actually satisfy their motivations according to their genetically given priorities. However, sometimes conflict will arise and the animal, while operating in executive controller mode, will try to resolve this and may then perhaps engage in some (usually relatively weak) form of free-will processing. For example, in searching for suitable material for its nest a bird may spot horse-hair on a brush in a stable yard and be motivated to get some for lining its nest. But it may experience conflict – e.g. fear of a predator: a cat sleeping nearby, say – and not have prefigured means for resolving this conflict. In such a case it may engage in some mind-brain struggle in deciding what to do: a struggle that, in the case of animals (and often humans, too), may involve its taking tentative actions towards first serving one competing motivation, and then another. For example, the bird might carefully advance toward the brush, and then get frightened and retreat. But later it might try approaching the brush again. And it may be that exactly how the bird ends up resolving this conflict is not prefigured. However, what is not clear is whether the non-prefigurement is wholly down to the indeterminacy of future events (e.g. the cat awakening and getting up) or also involves some indeterminacy within the mind-brain of the bird over what to do. The assumption made in the present work is that in some higher animals (possibly including birds), and in some situations, resolution of internal mind-brain conflict about how to act is not solely a matter of how circumstance change but partly a result of non-prefigured internal mind-brain interactions, adjustments, and mutual accommodations. That is, it is assumed that some free-will processing may take place.

7.6.4   Intelligent executive control has proved to be a highly successful evolutionary development. And with the emergence of human persons it seems evolution has scored another success by producing beings capable of operating as self-evaluating executive controlling agents – or SEECing agents. The assumption that is being adopted in the present work is that humans express self-evaluating executive controlling capabilities in three main ways. Firstly, through being able to create their own methods and priorities for satisfying their ge-

175

netically given motivations (and in so doing, partly overriding these given methods and priorities). Secondly, through being able to adopt (e.g. from their social group), or create – based on their own experiences (including past successes and failures), on their past learning, and as a result of thinking things over for themselves – their own criteria for what they believe does or would make them themselves successful executive controllers. And thirdly, by being able to carry out their own evaluations, according to their own criteria, of their success and failure as an executive controller. None of this means human persons necessarily wholly disregard their genetically given criteria of success and failure (e.g. as indicated by pleasure and pain signals), nor that they shall necessarily wholly disregard the influence of their peers and other social and cultural factors. But it does mean that humans have a degree of freedom in how they operate as an executive controller that does not seem to be available to animals or to any other natural agents. The key to the sort of self-evaluation being identified here is the creative capabilities of human persons – their capacity to establish for themselves modes of activity that are not wholly prefigured by their given nature and nurture.

7.6.5   One important consequence of humans having evolved powers of self-evaluation is that it allows society (or nurture), rather than genes (or nature) alone, to influence what priorities and criteria of success and failure in conducting their life an individual person may adopt or create. And this makes societies based on and regulated by human-devised rules of acceptable and unacceptable conduct possible because members of such a society may be influenced (through socialisation, teaching, peer pressure, and other societal influences) to incorporate the values, norms, standards, etc. of the society into the criteria they adopt or create for what shall count for them as a satis-factory way to live their lives. The point is that these criteria need not be linked directly to pleasure and pain signals or other genetically given values but may have a more abstract basis – for example, the sort of abstract basis that religions make use of in laying down their rules for living.

7.6.6   Free-will processing plays a prominent role in the activity of a self-evaluating executive controlling agent (a SEECing agent) because such an agent does not necessarily rely solely on genetically given or socially conditioned priorities and evaluation methods to help them resolve conflicts and indecision. Rather, they are able to use more elaborate and personally adopted and created priorities and evaluation criteria. Furthermore, it seems that human persons have an intrinsic capacity to question and possibly change these priorities and criteria – a process which in itself is another source of conflict within a person. Further comments on humans as SEECing agents are made in section 10.7, but the present work is not the place to fully develop this idea. (Note, viewing humans as self-evaluating executive controlling agents was introduced by the author in his paper 'A Cybernetic Analog For Human Behavior' Elstob, 1976.)

8 Creative Origination

8.1 Introduction

8.1.1 A good deal has been said about creative origination already. In this chapter the discussion of this important concept is broadened. However, since much of the chapter does not directly concern free will but rather tries to establish creative origination more widely, it is worth re-expressing, but largely holding to one side, the view adopted in this book about the role creative origination is seen to plays in the exercise of free will.

8.1.2 The basic view that has been adopted (see 1.4.14/15) is that an agent who has free will is able to self-directively originate satisfaction of their needs and wants. But often this may be done by the agent using well-established methods (e.g. by using instinctive, habitual, or fully-learned procedures) and free will is generally understood to require more than this – namely, the capacity to do otherwise: i.e. for an agent to be able to satisfy their needs and wants in non-necessitated but self-determined ways. It has been argued that this requires that an agent carry out a self-directed creative process, what has been called the free-will process: a process that it is assumed arises when an agent is experiencing conflict or indecision about what to do and has no prefigured means for resolving matters. In humans it has been suggested that the creative origination involved in the free-will process mainly finds expression in what has been referred to as the ARCS of free-will processing: that is, in the creative origination and modification of alternatives and reasons; in the creatively originative playing out of internal conflicts; and in the transformation of aspects of a person's self (see 1.5.4). Some of the methods of creative origination that are used in the ARCS of free will processing are mentioned in this chapters, but a great deal is left unsaid not only because of space limitations but because of a lack of sufficient knowledge and understanding.

8.2 Some Preliminary Points

8.2.1 Although intuitively fairly clear, the notion of creative origination is difficult to pin down precisely. The strongest intuition behind the idea is that whereas most originations are of types of things that are quite strongly prefigured by the nature of the domain in which they arise, some others are not and that it is these others that are thought of as having been creatively produced. Specifically, what is being said is that creative origination is involved when what is produced cannot be explained by the natural laws, constraints, systems, RENOIRs, and structures that constitute the established nature and dynamics of the domain in question. Of course, according to independence indeterminism, no origination (considered as a dated and located particular) is *fully* prefigured, so it might seem reasonable to say that creative origination is involved in the production of all originations. However, if this were done the notion of *creative* origination would become redundant since all origination would count as creative. Since the vast majority of originations are type-determined it might seem that it would be sufficient to say that creatively originative processes are those processes that produce novel originations – that is, originations of a new, non-prefigured, type relative to the domain concerned. This would cover many cases but it would exclude creative origination being involved in the resolution of conflicts where the types of possible outcome that may occur are prefigured but the process by which any particular outcome is originated is not prefigured – as, for instance, occurs with predator/prey interactions, competitive team games, market competition, and warfare. To accommodate such cases it would be sufficient to say that a creatively originative process is one that follows a course that is of a non-prefigured type (relative to the domain concerned) and which often, but not necessarily, produces a novel type of outcome. However, this looser definition may lead to some originative processes being counted as creatively originative when they are at best only marginally so.

8.2.2   Chance plays a part in the creative origination of most novel entities, but chance alone only very rarely results in the creation of a complex entity with significant properties distinctly different from those of its parts. Jumbles and relatively haphazard collections of objects may be novel entities but unlike a system or a RENOIR they rarely have any significantly novel properties as the totalities they are. Chance alone may creatively originate relatively simple systems – possibly even something as organised as some of the more complex building blocks of life. But without the domain containing directive systems able to exploit chance events to create novel entities then the complexity and significance of the created entities will be limited. For example, without a framework of biological reproduction and natural or artificial selection in place, chance genetic mutations will not result in novel advantageous changes within a species; and without a suitably engaged and prepared human person or group, chance events will not advantageously influence their creative activities.

8.2.3 The first issue to be addressed in this chapter is what sorts of things qualify as having been creatively originated. A start is made by discussing where type-boundaries are to be drawn. If the types that are used for describing entities that are originated are too high-level then little creative origination will be apparent. For example, if a new work of fiction is taken to be merely another instance of a book belonging to a familiar genre then it shall not count as being a creative origination. But on the other hand, if an overly fine-grained approach were adopted then almost all products of human endeavour would be seen as having been creatively originated even when they are run of the mill. To further clarify this issue, and return to an earlier example, consider the origination of a bird's nest.

8.2.4 Birds build nests of a type that is largely fixed by their genetic inheritance. Nests with coarse-grained differences may be readily distinguished. For example, a chaffinch's nest is quite different from a crow's nest, as the following descriptions from a popular website shows. 'Chaffinches build a neat cup nest from moss, grass, and feathers bound with spiders' webs, lined with feathers and wool, and decorated with lichen and flakes of bark. The nest is usually in a fork of a tree or shrub.' And the same website says: 'A Carrion Crow's nest is built in the fork of a tree, cliff edge or even electricity pylon and is a large construction of twigs lined with hair and bark.' (From www.garden-birds.co.uk). However, nests of both of these general types vary in their specific details, so should such minor variations mean the nests are of different types? It is not clear how to answer. If they are to be treated as different types then at what point should the boundary be drawn since treating every nest as a unique type seems to undermine the reason for introducing the idea of types? And taking too general a view may lead to no distinction being made between nests with consistent differences made by the same species of bird but in different types of environment. What is being con-

180

fronted here is a general problem and it is not clear how to resolve it. In later discussion some suggestions are offered, but these do not provide a definitive resolution of this issue.

8.2.5 Closely related to the type-boundary problem is another one: namely, that creative origination varies in degree or strength. At the low-end are what shall be referred to as weak forms of creative origination – weak in the sense that they produce outcomes of a pre-figured general type but which produce novel subtypes. Such originations are prefigured to the extent that they are produced by established type of structures, systems and RENOIRs, and through types of interactions that are more or less common within the domain concerned. But they are novel to the extent that the originations produced have significant differences and belong to such a large set of possible originations that it cannot reasonably be said that the emergence of a particular member of this set is prefigured. Later, a couple of examples of this kind of weak creative origination are considered: the formation of snowflakes, and the origination of gametes (e.g. sperm or egg cells). Another common kind of low-end creative origination arises when outcomes of a familiar and often quite restricted type are originated by situations involving competitive and conflictual interaction.

8.2.6 Mid-range creative origination arises when, relative to the domain concerned, novel *types* of systems, RENOIRs, structures, procedures, and interactions are originated rather than only novel *subtypes*. But here again there is the problem of drawing a line between a novel *type* of entity and a novel *subtype*. However, rather than trying to provide rules for doing this, it shall be accepted that mid-range creative origination covers a broad spectrum, and that at one end it merges into the low-end and the other into the high-end. Learning and inventiveness are the mainstays of mid-range creative origination in that they are the usual ways by which novel, non-prefigured types of entity are produced by agents. Simple and limited forms of learning do arise as part of some kinds of low-end creative origination – learning that consists of tuning the parameters of some system to optimise its performance or to allow it to adapt to a changing environment are examples.

8.2.7 High-end creative origination is understood to be a process that is not carried out by individuals alone. Rather it is taken to

181

be a group phenomenon, and one of the defining features of large and complex creative realms, of which the most significant are the realm of life and the realm of civilization. Creative origination in the latter realm is much more widespread and operates on a much shorter time-scales than in the former. For instance, creative origination is constantly at work in the adaptive evolution of domains within the realm of civilization such as those of politics and government, media and entertainment, defence and security, education and training, science, technology, transport, agriculture, commerce and industry, law and justice, medicine, and in the various fields of artistic and cultural endeavour. These domains are characterised by their own distinctive types of created entities and the distinctive ways these typically interact and influence one another. All of these domains are strongly reflexively creative in the sense that they creatively renew and extend themselves and are strongly involved in their own evolution. And because these domains all belong to the realm of civilization they are more or less influenced by one another, and often in creative ways.

8.2.8   In the following sections more shall be said about the three broad categories of creative origination that have just been mentioned, but much will be left unsaid, not only because of a lack of space but also because at present relatively little is understood about how creative origination works.

8.3   Low-End Creative Origination

8.3.1   Before continuing it is worth indicating what kinds of origination shall not count as being even weakly creative. It has been said those originations whose type is prefigured in present existence don't count, unless the course by which they are produced is being creatively originated. Science is good at identifying processes of noncreative origination because its forte is the description of happenings that have a repeatable and lawful way of occurring and running. At present, science does not recognise the very widespread existence of macroscopic origination that independence indeterminism says exists. But even if it did – and perhaps it will in the future – it would still be most successful in dealing with types of happening and phenomena that are regular, repeatable, and more or less predictable at the type level. What science is good at is understanding and explaining *dependence* interactions, not *independence* interactions. This means science is often good at explaining what happens once an independence interaction has actually taken place and more or less deterministic interactions and changes ensue. Humans, and animals too, are good at coming to know what types of prefigured events might happen within domains with which they are familiar, but they are not good at predicting specific instances of independence interaction until their occurrence becomes relatively certain – as they often do when the things involved in the interaction are set on relatively time-determinate courses of change and seem to be heading towards an interaction. Unexpected disruptions may occur – such as an earthquake taking place, a bomb going off nearby, a malfunction occurring – but since these generally rarely arise it is found that in practice many happenings run in more or less expected ways even when they entail origination.

8.3.2 What qualifies something as being a product of creative origination is sometimes not obvious, and much of the difficulty comes from deciding where to draw type boundaries. If candidate entities are classified too coarsely then little creative origination will be apparent, but if they are drawn too finely then too much shall be seen. For example, if all snowflakes are taken to be of a single type then no creative origination will be seen, whereas if each individual snowflake is taken to be a distinct subtype then a great deal will be seen. But if humans and their personal judgements are determining the type boundaries then the matter becomes rather subjective. One way of partially overcoming or avoiding this weakness is to tie differences in type (and subtype) to there being significant differences in the objective (rather than subjective) effects that the different types produce. For example, molecules originated within a chemical reaction are considered to be of the same chemical type if the are individually indistinguishable with respect to their chemical properties and behaviours.

8.3.3 Many originative processes have only a single type of outcome, and generally such processes are not taken to be creative. For example: a thermostatically controlled home central heating system tends to originate the single type of outcome of a roughly constant temperature in the home; organisms tend to grow towards a single type of mature form characteristic of their species; and chemical reactions tend to produce specific types of product. However, simply because an originative process produces a single type of outcome does not necessarily mean it cannot operate creatively to achieve this. For instance people, and some animals, are sometimes able to creatively originate a pre-specified type of outcome when they lack the skills and knowledge to do so by non-creative means. For example, a person may need to operate creatively to solve a brain teaser or puzzle which has a well-defined target condition (trying to solve the Rubic Cube is an example), or a chimpanzee may have to be creative in order to break open a nut — a task with a single well-defined target condition.

8.3.4   Processes that produce a single outcome that is drawn from a prefigured and relatively small set of possible outcomes are generally not considered to be creative processes. For example, according to independence indeterminism, where the ball will land for a particular spin of a roulette wheel is an originated event, but rather than there being only one type of outcome there is a fixed set, and the design of the wheel and method used for playing roulette generally means these outcomes arise with fixed probabilities. For these reasons roulette is not considered to be a creatively originative process. Neither do many similar processes count as being creatively originative, such as the throw of dice, the rotation of a lottery tumbler, or the random generation of numbers by quantum indeterministic means. Nevertheless, there are some originative processes that might reasonably be classified as being at least weakly creatively originative because they are capable of originating a very large number of distinct subtypes, meaning that what particular thing or outcome they produce on any specific occasion may be regarded as unexpected and not prefigured. However, to qualify as even a weak form of creative origination the subtypes produced must, at least within some contexts, have significantly different features. In order to develop these points two examples shall be considered: the production of snowflakes, and the generation of gametes.

8.3.5   If we take snowflakes to be all of a single type then snowflake production will not be seen as a creatively originative process. However, if we take a much finer-grained view of snowflakes — indeed, literally a microscopic view — then we shall see that individual snowflakes are almost all different. They are not only different because each ice crystal from which they are composed has a unique 6-fold symmetric structure but also because, under natural conditions of snowflake formation, these crystals often become stuck together in a variety of different ways. What is involved in snowflake production is outlined in an article in *New Scientist* which states that '[Snowflakes] usually form when [through an independence interaction] a super-cooled water droplet freezes around a speck of dust to form a basic six-sided crystal. This crystal grows and becomes more complicated as it steals water vapour from the air and starts to fall [a process involving innumerable independence interactions between the crystal and water vapour molecules in the air]. At -2°C, simple hexagon and star shapes form. Between -5 and -10°C, it's columns. Then below -15°C, the six-siders appear again. What's more, each tiny snow crystal experiences a gamut of temperatures and humidities as it falls [experiences that all involve independence interactions], and often collides with other crystals [more independence interactions]. A snowflake can consist of a single crystal, or it can be many thousands of these crystals joined together. "Every snowflake that falls to earth has its own unique history," says ice physicist John Hallett of the Desert Research Institute in Reno, Nevada.' (Pilcher 2013). Two things are worth noting. Firstly, as has been indicated with the additions to the above passage, under independence indeterminism, each snowflake may be seen to be the product of many independence interactions and so is taken to be an originated entity. And secondly, it seems that many of these independence interactions influence the precise form that the resulting snowflake will have. Under independence indeterminism roulette, throwing dice, lottery-tumbling, and many similar processes are also seen to involve independence interactions in the origination of their outcomes. However, they produce only a relatively limited number of distinct types things or conditions, whereas with snowflake production the number of distinct subtypes produced is extremely large, and it is this that suggests snowflake production may be taken to be a creatively originative process. However, it should be regarded as only a weakly creatively originative process because, firstly, the process does not entail the origination of any new type of system, process, or procedure, and secondly, because the enormous variety of distinct snowflake subtypes that are produced do not lead to anything like an equivalent variety of distinct consequences in the natural world. However, from the human perspective, a huge variety of distinct forms of snowflake ice crystals may be distinguished.

8.3.6   The second example, one which has a stronger claim to be a creatively originative process than snowflake production, concerns the production of gametes – a highly regulated process known as meiosis. Individual gametes, unlike individual snowflakes, do not rely simply upon human powers of discrimination to give them a distinct identity. Rather, each gamete, should it participate in the origination of a particular individual living organism, expresses its specific identity in the uniqueness of that organism. Throughout the following discussion of meiosis, independence indeterminism is presumed to hold and the fairly detailed account that is given aims to make clear how biological evolution has found a way of combining several stages of chance (i.e. non-directed) origination to make huge genetic diversity available to the reproductive process – something that greatly enhances the robustness of the biological evolutionary process and the continuance of complex life.

8.3.7   Independence interactions occur during all the key processes involved in sexual reproduction: for instance, in mating (or pollination), in fertilisation (whereby a particular male gamete unites with a particular female gamete to form a particular zygote), and in meiosis – the process by which male and female gametes (e.g. sperm and eggs) are produced. The intracellular independence interactions involved in meiosis are capable of randomly originating an enormous number of genetically similar but distinct gametes and this contributes to ensuring that genetic diversity is maintained within the gene pool of a species, so helping to ensure that natural selection has many options available to it. The following discussion relates to human beings but the basic process is common to many species.

8.3.8   Every somatic (body) cell, and every germ cell in the gonads (i.e. in the testes in males, and in the ovaries in females), contains 22 (unjoined) pairs of genetically similar but not precisely identical chromosomes. One of each pair contains genetic material derived (via the father's sperm) from the individual's paternal ancestry, while the other contains genetic material derived (via the mother's egg) from their maternal ancestry. In females, the 23rd pair – the sex chromosomes – consists of a further two genetically similar chromosomes, but in males this 23rd pair consists of partly dissimilar chromosomes to the extent that the paternally derived chromosome is much shorter and contains genes that control the development of male characteristics. The immense genetic diversity that meiosis generates is achieved in three stages. First, in the crossing over (exchange) of genetic material between paternally and maternally derived chromosomes. Second, in the process of forming two daughter cells from a single germ cell. And third, in the splitting of each of these daughter cells to produce individual gametes – sperm in males, eggs in females. These stages involve a large number of intracellular independence interactions – interactions between, for instance, chromosomes, DNA, proteins, and the various intracellular structures and systems (such as microtubles, centromeres, kinetochors, and spindle apparatus) that carry out the processes concerned.

8.3.9   Meiosis starts with replication of the 23 pairs of chromosomes in a germ cell. This is a complex process common to all cell division within humans (and many other organisms) and after it is complete each original chromosome and its replicate are joined at a single point – a centromere – to form a pair of what are known as sister chromatids. (There are at this point 92 chromatids – i.e. distinct strands of DNA – consisting of 23 chromosomal sets each containing four genetically similar chromatids: two paternally derived, two maternally derived.) Next, the two pairs of sister chromatids belonging to each of the 23 chromosomal sets are moved to the equatorial plane of the germ cell and a process called crossing over takes place. Crossing over involves the maternally and paternally derived sister chromatids of a set interweaving and sometimes swapping stretches of DNA with one another. Exactly which stretches of DNA get exchanged is a result of chance independence interactions between the chromatids concerned and the various proteins and structures that carry out the interweaving, cutting, and swapping operations.

8.3.10   After crossing over has taken place the paternally and maternally based sister chromatids in a set are separated from their interweaved state and are moved, randomly, to one side or the other of the cell. This is another complex process that involves such things as the spindle apparatus (with microtubles playing an important role in its operation), kinetochors, and various proteins. Which side (and therefore which future daughter cell) gets a paternally derived pair of sister chromatids and which gets a maternally derived pair depends upon chance independence interactions occurring in the initial stage of the moving process. Once this migration is complete the germ cell divides to form two daughter cells. Each of these contains 23 pairs of sister chromatids – some being paternally based and the rest maternally based with the exact mix being a matter of how the chance independence interactions just mentioned played out for each of the 23 sets of chromatids. Those sister chromatid pairs in which some crossing over occurred will consist of dissimilar sisters, whereas those pairs involving no crossing over will consist of identical sisters.

8.3.11   The final stage of meiosis involves the division of each daughter cell into two gamete cells each of which will contain 23 in-dividual chromosomes. Some of these chromosomes will be wholly paternally derived, and some wholly maternally derived but some (because of crossing over) will consist of a mix of paternally and mater-nally derived DNA. This final cell division starts with the 23 pairs of sister chromatids in a daughter cell being moved to the equatorial plane of the cell. The sister chromatids are then separated and moved to opposite sides of the cell through a process involving chance inde-pendence interactions similar to that described earlier. This final stage ends with the division of each of the two daughter cells into two sep-arate gamete cells.

8.3.12   A calculation of approximately how many genetically dis-tinct gametes may result from meiosis may be made as follows. The interweaving process may not always produce a crossing over of DNA between chromatids but suppose (as an unfounded and purely illustrative assumption) that on average this happens with 10 of the 23 chromosomal sets of sister chromatids. Furthermore, to keep things as simple a possible, assume that in each of these 10 sets only one of the two paternally derived chromatids exchanges DNA with only one of the two maternally derived chromatids, leaving the other paternally and maternally derived chromatids unchanged. This means that within the germ cell as a whole 20 (out of 92) chromatids have their DNA altered through crossing over. It is unclear in how many different ways an exchange of DNA between paternally and mater-nally derived chromatids may occur but it is likely to be a great many. For this approximate and illustrative calculation, suppose it to be one thousand (this is probably a large underestimate). This means that crossing over among any given set of 10 pairs of sister chromatids may result in any one of 1000^{10} (10^{30}) genetically different variants. But over a million different sets of 10 sister chromatids may be drawn from the 23 sets available. Taking this into account, and under the assumptions made, this indicates that after crossing over has taken place any one of about 10^{36} genetically different sets of 92 chromatids may result.

8.3.13   After crossing over has occurred, division of the germ cell takes place. As already noted, this involves the chance and random assignment of the paternally and maternally derived sister chromatids to opposite sides of the cell prior to its division into two daughter cells. This random assignment can lead to any one of 2^{23} (i.e. about 8 x 10^6) pairs of genetically different daughter cells being produced. However, as has been explained and with the assumptions being made, crossing over changes the genetic makeup of a germ cell into any one of about 10^{36} genetically different variants, and since any one of these variants may lead to about 8 x 10^6 distinct pairs of daughter cells the first two stages of meiosis taken together may produce any one of about 10^{42} different pairs of such cells.

8.3.14   However, there is more to come because there is still the final stage of meiosis to take into account. The division of each daughter cell involves the movement of the sister chromatids to the equatorial plane, their separation into independent chromatids, and then the random assignment of these to opposite sides of the cell to form the genetic makeup of each of the gametes that result when this final stage of cell division is complete. If no crossing over had occurred then this division would result in two identical gametes since each sister chromatid pair would consist of identical sisters and it would not make any difference to which side of the cell (and there-fore which gamete) a sister chromatid moved. But, with the simplifying assumptions that have been made, on average 10 pairs of sister chromatids are involved in crossing over and that therefore 10 pairs of sister chromatids (out of the 23 pairs in total) will have genetically different sisters. Now each of these different sisters may be assigned randomly to one or other of the gametes, giving 2^{10} (about 1000) ways in which gametes may be constituted in this final step of the process of meiosis. Taking this additional variation into account, and

189

given the assumptions made, the process of meiosis will produce four gametes from a germ cell with each of these gametes being randomly drawn from a set of about 10^{45} possible genetic variants. This is a truly immense number, and although the main genetic differences among these is likely to come from the particular mix of paternal and maternal contributions, the genetic diversity that comes from crossing over is not necessarily insignificant.

8.3.15   It is worth emphasising that while the function of meiosis is to produce genetic diversity among the gametes it produces, the process itself is one that depends for its successful execution on a great deal of complex and exquisitely coordinated directive activity. This directive activity ensures that certain specific *types* of chance independence interactions occur at specific stages in the process – it does not, of course, at all determine what *tokens* of these types the process will produce.

8.3.16   Is meiosis a creatively originative process? According to independence indeterminism, it is a process in which any particular genetically distinct gamete it produces cannot be said to be prefigured, or expected, simply because the number of possibilities is so vast. However, this would be a valid conclusion only if taking individual gametes to be distinct subtypes was justified. So, can this be justified? As already noted, the distinctiveness of a type of entity may be identified with the set of distinctive effects or consequences that an instance of such a type of thing produces within a particular kind of context. That is, if the effects produced by the different instances are the same then the instances are taken to be of the same type (or subtype), and if different then of different types. To see how this works in practice consider some of the cases considered earlier. On each spin, roulette results in the ball landing in one of 37 numbered slots on the wheel (38 slots in American roulette with its double zero) and from a strictly physical point of view there is little to distinguish one outcome from another: namely, a ball at rest within a slot. But from the point of view of players of roulette there is a good deal of difference – a difference that shows itself in the various betting payoffs associated with the human-allocated categories or types to which each slot has been assigned – e.g. its unique number type, its colour type (red, black, or green), its parity type (odd, even, neither), and its set type (its membership of various subsets of numbers). This suggests that in a human game-playing context but not in a purely physical context, the slots come in several (but not a huge number of) different types rather than just one. With snowflakes, again they may be considered in either a strictly physical context or a human one. In a strictly physical context snowflakes reveal themselves in how they pack together to form, say, wet slushy snow or dry fluffy snow. In a purely physical context the vast variety of microscopic differences that exist between snowflakes do not reveal themselves, but to human observers using microscopes their differences become apparent, and a huge number of microscopically different snowflakes seem to be possible. Gametes considered within a straightforward chemical context – i.e. simply as complex molecular structures – do not reveal their distinct differences. But within the context of biological reproduction their differences are important because a gamete partly specifies the particular characteristics of an individual organism – characteristics that are not purely a matter of human categorisation. Furthermore, as discussed above, meiosis is capable of producing an immense variety of distinct gametes.

8.3.17   Is creative origination involved in the spin of a roulette wheel? No, because only a relatively small set of types of outcome are possible. What about snowflake production? Here the decision is more difficult, but because snowflake production only reveals the detailed differences in the snowflakes it produces to human observers and not independently of them it seems reasonable to say that, at most, it is at the extreme lower end of creative origination. However, gamete production through meiosis does seem to just about qualify as being a creatively originative process because each gamete has a significant contribution to make to the objective identity of the living organism to which it may help to give rise. But meiosis should be taken to be a very weak form of creative origination because the systems and structures that control and realise the processes involved are a pre-existing part of the biological domain concerned, and the processes themselves follow, in overall terms, a prefigured type of course. Nevertheless, it does seem that gametes, as the particular distinct entity each is, are not prefigured and so should be regarded as being creatively produced.

8.3.18   There are many borderline cases of weak creative origination of the gamete sort in the human and animal worlds. For instance, when humans produce speech they are being weakly creatively originative when what they say is not strongly prefigured in the situation concerned. Speech utterances belong to an indefinitely large set and so, except in banal conversations, may be taken as newly originated subtypes in much the same way as individual gametes may be taken to be newly originated subtypes. Some birds produce quite varied songs but it is questionable whether these carry the huge variety of meanings that human speech carries, so the production of highly varied birdsong is probably, at most, a borderline case of weakly creative origination. Many commonplace directive activities such as tying shoe laces, putting on clothes, shaving, brushing one's teeth, eating, and washing the dishes hardly ever count as being even weakly creative activities, but if things don't go smoothly then some, usually weak, creatively originative intervention may be needed to achieve the desired directed outcome. The same is true of many commonplace animal activities. However, although a good deal of the everyday life of humans and higher animals requires little creativity, when an end is sought for which no well-established method for its pursuit already exists, humans and higher animals use various methods – including learning, problem-solving, and the exercise of intelligence and inventiveness – to try to obtain what they want. Such activity is definitely creatively originative – but much of it only relatively weakly so.

8.3.19   Although borderline cases may be difficult to deal with, it is relatively easy to exclude from being counted as creatively originative the very large number of randomly originative processes that produce mere jumbles or haphazard arrangement of things with little or no collective, or systemic, identity. For instance, my desktop as I write this consists of a relatively jumbled arrangement of papers, books, letters, notes, jottings, pens, pencils and a good many other items. This jumbled arrangement is not a highly complex unity, nor even a system because it has few significant properties as a whole. Rather, any properties the desktop does have tend to belong to the individual items on it, or some subsets of items (such as groups of related sheets of paper). Certainly, specific states and jumbles of things may play an important secondary role in creative origination, but they don't play a primary role. For example, in searching through a pile of papers on my desktop I may on some (rare) occasion notice two separate and unrelated pieces of text that jointly trigger a new thought.

However, the processes and interactions that led to the (more or less random) placing of these sheets, and my rummaging activity, should not themselves be regarded as being even weakly creatively originative. Rather, the primary source of creative origination lay within my mind-brain – although the creative process involved was essentially dependent upon the particular arrangement of my desktop at the time, and my more or less chance interaction with it.

8.3.20 Conflictual and/or competitive interaction between purposive agents has been taken to be a creatively originative process when there if nothing prefiguring how the interaction will run on any particular occasion. However, much of this sort of interaction should be taken as only weakly creatively originative when the outcome belongs to a small, well-defined set of types of possible outcome – as happens in competitive games, for example.

8.4   Mid-Range Creative Origination

8.4.1   In the space available, only brief consideration can be given to this vast topic. Some relevant points shall be made but a great deal will not be mentioned. Again, independence indeterminism is presumed to hold and it is assumed that creative origination is heavily dependent upon independence interactions – both chance and directed ones – taking place within the mind-brains of the agents concerned and between the agents and their environments. Most forms of learning and relatively straightforward kinds of problem-solving constitute the bulk of mid-range creative origination and it is these topics that shall mainly be discussed, although some mention will be made of invention.

8.4.2   Trial-and-error learning is the simplest means by which new or modified skills and procedures may be acquired by an animal or a human. Edward Thorndike studied this common form of learning in the final years of the 19th century. To take a well-known example, in one series of experiments a hungry cat is placed in a box from which it can see food outside. The door of the box can only be opened if the cat correctly manipulates a lever. In the first trial, the cat carries out a great deal of clawing, biting, and moving about in a futile attempt to get out of the box before, more or less fortuitously, it happens to move the lever and the door opens. On subsequent trials, although there is no sudden grasping of the relationship between moving the lever and the door opening, the time taken before the cat moves the lever tends to decrease until eventually the cat almost immediately moves it when placed in the box. It is possible to train animals to perform quite elaborate procedures using a form of trial-and-error learning known as operant conditioning (also known as instrumental learning, and in AI as reinforcement learning). The method consists in rewarding an animal (or human) when they happen, more or less by chance initially, to perform a certain action when placed in a certain situation, or when presented with a certain stimulus. In this way an animal's behaviour may be shaped in quite complex ways. For example, pigeons may be trained to get a food reward by pecking at a particular place when the string of letters PECK is displayed, and by turning when the string TURN is presented. There is no suggestion that the pigeons understand the meaning of "peck" and "turn" – they have simply learned to respond in a particular way to a particular visual pattern in order to obtain a food reward. Some hard-line behaviourists – such as B.F. Skinner, who did a great deal of experimental work on operant conditioning – argue that human behaviour is almost entirely a product of implicit and explicit operant conditioning that is linked to the often complex and subtle rewards contained within the social environment of humans. On this view there is no place for free will, although it may be argued, as Skinner does in his book *Beyond Freedom and Dignity* (Skinner 1971), that a society founded on a humanely and strictly organized system of operant conditioning would offer humans the most satisfactory kind of life that is possible.

8.4.3 Animals do not learn new skills and solve problems by trial-and-error learning alone, often the process involves some reasoning as well. For instance, rodents such as squirrels and rats show remarkable ingenuity in obtaining food. And some animals (and humans to a much greater extent) are able to use what is known as insight learning in which relationships and understanding arise seemingly all at once and not slowly through trial and error. For example, in experiments with birds (e.g. crows, ravens), it has been observed that some are able to bend a length of wire to form a hook in order to remove food from a tube. In recent decades, understanding of the range and complexity of the apparently insightful problem-solving that some animals can achieve has grown greatly, but studies into insight learning have their roots in work done over a century ago, and it is some of this research that shall be discussed as it illustrates several important points.

8.4.4 Between 1913 and 1917 Wolfgang Kohler carried out extensive studies of the learning and problem-solving behaviour of captive chimpanzees, and he gave an account of his work in his book *The Mentality of Apes* (Kohler 1928, 1957). The seven or so chimpanzees he studied lived in relatively free conditions in a compound on Tenerife. Kohler and his assistants observed the activity of the chimps in a range of test situations in which some desired object, usually fruit, was visible to the animals but placed out of their easy reach, or beyond their present skill to retrieve. Kohler found strong and striking evidence for the more or less sudden development by the chimps of procedures by which they could obtain the desired object. His conclusion was that the suddenness of the change in behaviour suggested that the procedures were produced by the use of insight as well as trial-and-error learning. In what is known as the single-box experiment, Kohler attached food (such as a banana) to the top of a chimpanzee's cage well out of the chimp's reach. However, the food could be reached if the chimp first moved a box under the food, climbed on it, and then jumped up to snatch the food. Only the most intelligent chimp, Sultan, was able to learn to do this unaided – other chimps learned how if they were helped by having the box placed under the food, or if they observed other chimps using this method. Kohler went on to investigate a more difficult problem in which a chimp must place, in a way that is stable and climbable, a second box on top of the first before they can reach the food. Some chimps – those familiar with the solution to the single-box problem – seemed to be able to acquire the key insight of "one-box-on-another", however none of them seemed to be able to acquire the additional insight of the need for stability and climbability – they only achieved this knowledge through trial-and-error learning.

8.4.5 Kohler did further experiments on insight learning with one involving chimps having to use sticks to rake in food placed outside their cage beyond their unaided reach. Again, once the skill had been learned, a chimp placed in a similar situation immediately looked for a stick, rather than using trial-and-error. However, Sultan was the only chimp who was able to go one step further in that he eventually learned how to join two bamboo sticks together to make a joined-stick long enough to rake in the food. It is worth giving a more detailed account of what happened because it seems to shows clear signs of a process of creative origination taking place within the mind-brain of Sultan – a process that seems to involve the non-pre-figured connecting up of notions, understandings, memories, etc. that were previously independent of one another. (The following account and the included quotations are from the English translation of Kohler 1957, pp. 111-114)

8.4.6   Near Sultan were placed two hollow-ended bamboo sticks – one of a lesser diameter than the other so that it was possible to in-sert an end of this stick firmly into the open end of the larger dia-meter one to make a rigid longer stick. Outside the bars of the en-closure several bananas were placed too far away to be reached by either stick alone. Sultan started by trying hard to reach the fruit by using a single stick, but he eventually gave this up. Kohler tells us that at this point Sultan made a "bad error" in that he pulled a box from the back of the room towards the bars, but he soon realised that this was a pointless move and he abandoned it. Sultan then immediately did something which Kohler identified as a "good error": he pushed one of the sticks with the other out towards the fruit. To make con-tact with the fruit in this way is a tricky thing to achieve, but Sultan persevered and eventually succeeded, which seemed to give him a good deal of satisfaction.

8.4.7   There are several things in this first stage of the experi-ment that are characteristic of most creative origination of this prob-lem-solving and insight-based kind. Firstly, it is generally highly mo-tivated directive activity in that the agent persists with it in spite of failures – which seems to be strong evidence that the agent has a clear and valued goal in mind. Secondly, it seems that higher animals (and humans) generally don't like to give up on a valued goal once pursuit of it has commenced – indeed, persistence in pursuit of a goal is a mark of all purposive activity. A third feature of much of this sort of behaviour is that the value the agent attaches to achieving the goal does not seem to lie solely in the intrinsic worth of the goal – e.g. in Sultan's case, having a tasty item of food to eat – but also in the satisfaction to be obtained in achieving a difficult end. It seems some higher animals, and humans to a very great extent, gain considerable satisfaction in proving their competence to themselves (and often, at least in the case of humans, to others as well).

8.4.8 A fourth important feature of much complex goal-directed activity that is illustrated by Sultan's efforts to get the fruit, is that the agent concerned is able to transfer the value they attach to attaining their ultimate goal to the achievement of preliminary and intermediate goals. This is what Sultan seemed to be doing when he worked so persistently in trying to push one stick with another in order to touch the fruit – he seemed to have come to believe that achieving the sub-goal "Make contact with the fruit" would help him achieve his ultimate goal of actually acquiring the fruit. What he had failed to appreciate is that merely being able to touch the fruit with the sticks doesn't on its own enable the fruit to be raked in – a rigid rod capable of doing this is needed, and this he had not appreciated. A fifth point worth making is that in trying to achieve a goal when an agent lacks the skill or knowledge to do so – i.e. when they have to resort to creative origination – sometimes results in an agent trying a method they are familiar with for obtaining the sort of goal in question even when the method is inappropriate in the given situation. This makes some sense since often a solution to a new problem can be created by modifying, or partly making use of, an existing method. Indeed, the creative origination of complex entities rarely starts from nothing – it almost always builds on systems and procedures that already exist. Sultan's "bad error", as Kohler called it, seems to be an example of this: Sultan seemed to think that climbing on boxes would help in some way. However, once he retrieved a box he realised that this approach wouldn't help. Humans are able – through using their powers of imagination-based reasoning – to dismiss as infeasible many potential approaches to finding a solution to a problem without having to try them out in practice. Nevertheless, human do often test ideas out in reality (or in representations of reality) in an effort to properly appreciate their strengths and weaknesses. And in doing this, humans often get ideas for new approaches. Higher animals, lacking the advanced cognitive capabilities of human persons, mainly have to try ideas out in practice before they can see their relevance or usefulness – or indeed, use*less*ness. Some further points worth making relate to what happened next.

8.4.9 To try to help Sultan see how a rigid stick might me constructed by pushing one stick into the other, Kohler tried moving his finger into and out of the end of one of the sticks. But Sultan didn't see the significance of this. This exemplifies another general point – the sixth mentioned so far – namely, that giving hints and clues towards a solution, or simply having them available in a problem-solver's environment, is generally not much help unless the agent is in an appropriately receptive condition, which usually means that they have almost seen the suggested way forward themselves. Again, this is something that seems to be a common feature of the sort of creative origination being discussed: creating the new is generally done incrementally rather than wholesale, but with occasionally a vital insight being created that joins up several previously relatively disconnected ideas. The occurrence of such an "ah-ah" moment is apparent in what Sultan did next. This happened after Sultan had lost interest in retrieving the out-of-reach fruit, even after the sticks were thrown through the bars again in order to encourage him to have another try with them. At this point the experiment had lasted over an hour, and Kohler had decided that Sultan on his own was never going to understand that he could join the sticks. Kohler therefore decided to leave the Keeper in charge so that he could attend to other matters, but it is shortly after this that something really interesting happened. The Keeper reports on what this was as follows.

> Sultan first of all squats indifferently on the box, which has been left standing a little back from the railings; then he gets up, picks up the two sticks, sits down on the box and plays carelessly with them. While doing this, it happens that he finds himself holding one rod in either hand in such a way that they lie in a straight line; he pushes the thinner one a little way into the opening of the thicker, jumps up and is already on the run towards the railings, to which he has up to now half turned his back, and begins to draw the banana towards him with the double stick. I call the master: meanwhile one of the animal's rods has fallen out of the other, as he has pushed one of them only a little way into the other; whereupon he connects them again.

The keepers report covers a period of barely five minutes. Kohler then took up observation and reports as follows.

Sultan is squatting at the bars, holding one stick, and, at its end, a second bigger one, which is on the point of falling off. It does fall, Sultan pulls it to him, and forthwith, with the greatest assurance, pushes the thinner one on again, so that it is firmly wedged, and fetches a fruit with the lengthened implement. But the bigger tube selected is a little too big, and so it slips from the end of the thinner one several times; each time Sultan re-joins the tubes immediately by holding the bigger one towards himself in the left hand and the thinner one in his right hand and a little backwards, and then sliding one over the other. The proceeding seems to please him immensely; he is very lively, pulls all the fruit, one after the other, towards the railings, without taking time to eat it, and when I disconnect the double-stick he puts it together again at once, and draws any distant object whatever to the bars.

8.4.10   It is worth noting – as a seventh general point – that Sultan's ah-ah moment did not seem to have come entirely out of the blue. He had been working with several sticks and knows that he can reach the fruit with two of them end-to-end. He had failed to get the fruit because he didn't have a rigid stick that was long enough. He had repeatedly and persistently tried to get the fruit using the sticks individually and had finally given up. He had been shown that a finger fits in the end of a bamboo stick, but had not seen that this suggests one stick may fit into another. In other words, Sultan was fairly deeply engaged with the problem and had explored ways of solving it prior to having his ah-ah moment. This is almost always true of ah-ah moments as they arise in problem-solving and invention. Sultan's mind-brain was prepared, and, although he voluntarily took a break, we may assume he was still partially pre-occupied with memories of his recent endeavours, failures, and successes relating to his fruit-getting efforts. This seems to be typical of creative origination of the sort being described: a prepared mind-brain and one sufficiently occupied with pursuing some current goal, even if sub-consciously so, for the possible emergence of new connections. Having "explored the territory" also seems to be a necessary prerequisite: a creative solution rarely comes to those who have had no engagement with the problem domain in question. However, there is another point (the eighth to be made so far), which seems to partially contradict it:

namely, that often a creative breakthrough comes when an agent has temporarily disengaged themselves from a problem – or at least disengaged themselves consciously. There are many examples of this in the human world. For instance, to take a case from the author's own experience, in the early 1970s I was involved in studying how computer engineers identified (and then repaired) faults in mainframe computer systems and I noticed how frequently a breakthrough came during a coffee or meal break when an engineer's mind was temporarily disengaged from what they had earlier been working on so intensively. Much of the sorting and linking that leads to the solving of a problem (or the resolution of a conflict within the self) seems to benefit from being detached from consciousness. Any person who does crosswords will have experienced how the solution to a clue may suddenly spring to mind when they are doing something else, or will be immediately available to their consciousness when they take up the puzzle after a break. This underlines the well-known fact that much of great importance goes on subconsciously or unconsciously. For instance, in his 2015 book *Freedom Regained: The Possibility of Free Will*, Julian Baggini discusses (pp. 88-92) the importance to an artist or writer of allowing their unconscious free rein.

8.4.11   Finally, it is worth re-emphasising that Sultan seemed to be motivated not merely by the need for food – he was not starving – but by something less tangible: namely, the need to achieve a goal he had set for himself, a goal that challenged his abilities, and the achievement of which seemed to satisfy a need within him to prove his own competence. The existence of this "need for achievement" motivation seems to underlie Sultan's keenness to rake in all the fruit rather than just what he required to satisfy his appetite: it seems he wanted to repeatedly demonstrate to himself just how clever and capable he is. This need for achievement and success is very strong within humans, but it seems it may exist to some extent in some animals as well.

8.4.12   In the foregoing discussion little has been said about human-based mid-range creative origination. The reason for this is that there is so much human mid-range creative origination that it is difficult to know what to mention without suggesting that what is discussed is the most widespread or important. With this proviso in mind, consider some of the learning-based creatively originated achievements of a typical person in the modern world as they live their life. These achievements include such things as acquiring proficiency in the language and rules of conduct of their family and community; gaining the basic skills of everyday life (e.g. how to wash and dress themselves, do simple chores, eat food, operate household equipment); and in learning how to read and write and do simple arithmetic. And a typical person learns all sorts of facts – not just school facts, but facts about their family, their friends, their home, their locality, their family's religion, and their nation's culture and history. Later in life they carry out much directed learning of such things as facts, knowledge, skills and understanding, and they do so at school, college and university, in their jobs, and in conjunction with their various hobbies, sports, and projects. And they learn a great many other things, such as how to drive; how to cook, clean, garden, sew, decorate; how to play a musical instrument; how to draw and paint; how to swim, dance, and sing; how to use computers, smartphones, etc.; and how to carry out the specialist skills that their job may require. And a further large and important area of learning concerns how people come to identify and create the values, goals and specific objectives that may help them achieve their higher-level ends and purposes, or help them satisfy unsatisfied motivations such as a desire for self-actualisation.

8.4.13   In addition to learning – and often as part of it – human persons (and some higher animals) also engage in inventiveness. In the discussion of Sultan's ah-ah moment some general points were made about what is typical about such processes of creative origination. Many attempts have been made to understand and explain what is involved in individual human creative origination of the inventiveness or ah-ah sort. Graham Wallas in his book *The Art of Thought* (Wallas 1926) identified five stages. (1) Preparation: exploration and clarification of the problem; initial attempts to find a solution; recognition that something new is required; frustration in not being able to readily solve the problem. (2) Incubation: temporary abandonment of conscious pursuit of the problem; unconscious processing continuing. (3) Intimation: a feeling that there is a new way forward; a conscious desire to revisit the problem. (4) Illumination: the ah-ah breakthrough occurs. (5) Verification: refining and firming up the new idea; checking it out, and implementing it; revising it as necessary. Wallace drew upon the work of others on human problem-solving and inventiveness (that of Herman von Helmholtz and Henri Poincare, in particular), and many other writers have since developed their own multi-stage models of the process but, it seems, generally with little of great significance being added.

8.4.14   Although the stages that a person typically goes through during mid-range creative origination are fairly clear, it is much less clear how novel (i.e. non-prefigured) things are actually originated. Biological evolution seems to be based on at least three principles that are also commonly used in human creative origination. These are: (1) create the new by successive modifications of the currently existing; (2) modify copies or fresh versions of the currently existing, not the currently existing itself; (3) evaluate the new against certain criteria and purge those that fail to come up to the mark. However, unlike biological evolution through natural selection, humans are cap - able of *directed* creative origination. Directed creation, apart from re - quiring intelligence also seems to use at least three further principles, as follows. (4) Create the new by forming and working with repres - entations of the existing, rather than with the existing real things themselves. (5) Use analysis, as well as chance, to produce new pos - sibilities. And (6), use representations (e.g. plans, blueprints, simula - tions) of new things to guide their actual production. With directed creative origination these principles may themselves be applied to the *application* of these principles. For instance, these principles may be used to help creatively originate some of the evaluation criteria that are used in a creative endeavour; or they may be used to creatively originate some of the representational techniques to be used; or to creatively originate some of the analytical methods. It is the ex - traordinary powers of directed creative origination that humans indi - vidually and collectively possess that have contributed greatly to the emergence and growth of the realm of civilization.

8.4.15   One further thing worth pointing out about human direc - ted creative origination is that people are able to identify and preserve items that they have either found or created that seem to them to have value but of a specific sort that they have not yet been able to fully recognise or exploit. For example, some novelists keep note - books containing such things as fragments of conversations, or sen - tences, phrases, ideas, or character outlines that come from their personal observations and experiences, or have been created by them and which seem to them to have value but of a sort they cannot yet incorporate into a larger creative production. And artists and other creative workers do much the same thing.

8.5 High-End Creative Origination

8.5.1	Some things have already been said about high-end creative origination and little shall be added in this final section of the chapter because attempting to address it more fully would not be appropriate in this book. The reason why this is so is that it has been assumed that high-end creative origination is something belonging to groups and not to individuals. For example, biological evolution by natural selection is a group process not an individual one, although without individual living organisms there would be no biological evolution. Similarly, in the human world high-end creative origination always takes place within groups, but again it would not exist without individual human persons who make up the groups concerned. Of course, in the human world high-end creative origination has often been greatly influenced by the significant creative contribution of particular individuals, but without these contributions being taken up by others they would not have the widespread impact that marks out high-end creative origination as being different from what goes on in the mid-range.

8.5.2	High-end creative origination is a process that itself creates many of the entities that play a key role in realising and sustaining the process in question. For instance, living organism play a key role in the process of biological evolution but are themselves a creative outcome of this very process. And, as another example, many of the ideas, skills, and artefacts that were created in the early stages of the industrial revolution played a key part in the further creative development of that revolution.

8.5.3	The emergence and continuing evolution of technological civilisation provides a stunning example of high-end creative origination. The industrial revolution – out of which full-blown technological civilisation has emerged – arose less than three hundred years ago, yet since then it has led to an utterly extraordinary extension to existence: an extension realised by the hugely powerful, highly reflexive, and multi-stranded process of purposively directed creative origination that is part of the realm of technology and human civilization as it exists today. This realm differs from the realm of biology, upon which it (at present) depends, because it makes use of purposively and intelligently directed creative origination rather than solely the kind of non-purposive creativity found in biological evolution by natural selection. Furthermore, the realm of technological civilization is characterised by the creation of artefacts – entities that are *constructed* using skill and intelligence rather than being *grown* as living things are. It seems that with the emergence of purposively and intelligently directed creative origination that a new realm of existence has come into being – what perhaps may be called the "realm of the artificial" – and this seems to be a remarkably important event in the evolution of the universe.

9 Independence Indeterminism: Its Wider Significance

9.1 Introduction

9.1.1   Independence indeterminism has significance beyond being able to help resolve the problem of free will. After making some further general comments below, in the second section a critique of absolute determinism is given which lends support for arguing, in the third section, that a better case may be made for accepting independence indeterminism rather than determinism as our default naturalistic metaphysics. The next five sections are concerned with how independence indeterminism may help resolve some philosophical disputes other than the problem of free will. The final section of the chapter argues that while independence indeterminism is compatible with naturalism it is not compatible with physicalism.

9.1.2   It seems clear that independence indeterminism offers a novel worldview. Some people will readily grasp that it reinforces the belief that humans have tremendous powers of directed origination and also of directed creative origination, and that this means that people can, in some respects, truly make their own future. Furthermore, this new naturalistic metaphysics supplies arguments for the existence of these powers that can stand up to traditional criticisms from scientists and philosophers that such powers cannot possibly exist. But there are aspects of independence indeterminism that many people who would welcome much of what it says would feel disturbed by. One of these aspects is that it sees the universe as lacking full definiteness – something that seems to be simply wrong to many people. Nevertheless, mainstream physics already accepts that indefiniteness exists because Heisenberg's uncertainty principle asserts that an irreducible indefiniteness exists between the values of what are known as conjugate variables. The best known example of this irreducible indefiniteness is that which exists between the values of the momentum of a particle and its position. This indefiniteness is not, as is often supposed, a result of a measurement of the value of one variable disturbing the value of the other variable – rather it is taken to be an intrinsic feature of the nature of the quantum world.

Mainstream physics also accepts that there cannot be a common moment of "now" for the universe, which adds to its indefiniteness. But since these kinds of indefiniteness do not belong to the world of everyday experience they tend not to challenge most people's belief in the definiteness of reality. However, the claim of independence indeterminism that independence of change is extremely common *does* apply to the everyday world, and this assumption implies that how independently changing things jointly change is indefinite – something which many people may find difficult to accept. And there is a further aspect of independence indeterminism that will disturb some people: namely, that it does not see the world as a unified whole with everything having a necessary place within it, but rather it takes the universe to be a non-unity which is loosely connected with many gaps within and between causal networks and in which most things get on with their business quite independently of what most other things are doing.

9.1.3 The really positive feature of independence indeterminism is that it has a naturalistic place for creative origination. That is, it allows connections (and disconnections) to be originated that are of types that are not prefigured to come into existence. Hence it has a place for the creation of genuine novelty. And with the biological evolution of intelligent purposive beings such as human persons it provides a place also for *directed* creative origination and the opening up of the realm of civilization and the realm of the artificial.

9.2   A Critique of Absolute Determinism

9.2.1   Various accounts of absolute determinism have been offered (see section 3.2) but for the purposes of this critique the approach adopted by Peter van Inwagen will be considered because it is particularly explicit and it has already been discussed (see section 3.4). His account consists of two (informal) assumptions, or theses, that shall be referred to as A and B.

Thesis A   For every instant of time, there is a proposition that expresses the state of the world at that instant.

Thesis B   I f p and q are any propositions that express the state of the world at some instants, then the conjunction of p and the laws of nature entails q.

9.2.2   Thesis A refers to "every instant of time" and "the state of the world" at an instant of time. "Instant", used as a noun, means: **1** a particular point in time; the moment which in passing may be called now. **2** a very brief portion of time; moment (*Webster's Dictionary* 1998). It is unclear in what sense van Inwagen is using the word instant, but in the literature on determinism an instant is generally taken to be a point in time in which nothing changes. However, this notion needs to be examined in more detail.

9.2.3   Treating an instant as a true point in time gives rise to problems. Perhaps the most notable is how to get change from non-change: a problem recognized by the ancient Greeks. Zeno of Elea (c. 470 BC) in his "Arrow Paradox" argued that at every instant of time a flying arrow must be at rest in a single definite place, for nothing can change within a true instant of time. But if the arrow is motionless at each instant then how can it change location from instant to instant and so be flying? Henri Bergson, writing in the early 20th century, put this point quite bluntly when he wrote: '[E]very attempt to reconstitute change out of states implies the absurd proposition, that movement is made of immobilities.' (Henri Bergson 1911, p. 325)

9.2.4   However, Bergson rather overstates his point since it is possible to represent *continuous* change using immobilities as Newton and Leibniz, working independently, showed in the 17th century. What they developed is known as the infinitesimal calculus. Some insight into the approach may be gained by considering one aspect of the motion of an arrow: namely, its speed at an instant in time. Average speed is not a problem: it is simply distance travelled divided by the time taken. What is a problem is instantaneous speed because an instant has zero duration and anything – such as distance travelled – divided by zero is infinity. But of course an arrow can't travel any distance at all in a true instant of time, so its average speed at an instant is equal to zero divided by zero – an undefined mathematical quantity. Yet, intuitively, it seems strange that something – such as the speed of an arrow – should have a meaningful value over an extremely

207

small duration of time, but no meaningful value when this small interval finally disappears altogether. The introduction of the infinitesimal calculus solved this problem and allowed variables that represent continuous change to be given a finite value at what is effectively an infinitesimally small mathematical point. This was done by taking the value to be that towards which the ratio representing the change tended as the quantities involved in defining it approached zero. However, many mathematicians and others remained unconvinced and it was not until the 19th century with the introduction of the formal mathematical concept of limits that the infinitesimal calculus was put on fairly sound conceptual and mathematical foundations. But even so, not all mathematicians have been satisfied and the matter remains an open topic.

9.2.5 Although many of the fundamental equations of physics, and other sciences, are expressed in terms of the calculus, discontinuous change cannot be described in these terms. Hence Bergson would be correct in saying that *discontinuous* change cannot be reconstituted from immobilities. Discontinuous change is common in the non-living world – for example, the breaking of a rock, phase transitions (e.g. the transformation of a substance from solid to liquid to vapour, and vice versa), and some sub-atomic processes such as the disintegration of a nucleus, or the emission of a photon from an atom. Discontinuous change is even more common in the biological realm – for example, cell division, hunting, mating, and nest-building are all processes containing many discontinuities of change. And in the human world discontinuous change is probably more common than continuous change.

9.2.6 Given the difficulty of defining an instant in a way that allows all forms of natural change to be accounted for, it seems that it is not obvious what is meant by the claim that 'For every instant of time, there is a proposition that expresses the state of the world at that instant'. It seems that what van Inwagen has in mind is some sort of Platonic notion of what the said proposition is – that it is something expressing an eternal truth that depends not at all upon whether means have been devised to actually express this truth.

9.2.7 Consider next the metaphysical status of van Inwagen's thesis B: that 'If p and q are any propositions that express the state of the world at some instants, then the conjunction of p and the laws of nature entails q.' This thesis ensures that, under absolute determinism, there is one history for the universe – one which is fixed at the beginning of time, or for eternity if time has no beginning. But it says more than this because it asserts that the fixed history of the universe consists of a succession of instantaneous states of the entire universe (total states) that are all linked according to the laws of nature.

9.2.8   The laws of nature as they are currently understood all involve sub-states or aspects of existence; none of them are laws referring to the total state of existence. These human-produced laws account for some of the pattern, structure, and order that is apparent in the world. But there is nothing in van Inwagen's Thesis B that says the laws of nature must be of this sort: they could, in accordance with the idea discussed earlier (see section 6.4), consist of a single list of items with each item fully describing each instantaneous total state of existence. If this were the case then there would be no need to incorporate instantaneously existing infinitesimals, or something similar, in order to fix how a sub-state – such as the position of an object – changes from instant to instant. If the true laws of nature – not the human-produced ones – are of this total-state form then the current sub-state laws approach of science is way off beam. But even if the sub-state laws approach is correct science is still very far from having identified anything like a final set of laws. Indeed, even without accepting the metaphysics of independence indeterminism, quantum indeterminacy means there can be no set of laws that completely determines future total states of the universe. At best, Thesis B is an assumption that is only partially supported by the findings of current science.

9.2.9   However, perhaps science is closer to a "Theory of Everything" than what has just been said. For many years, but with little widely agreed success so far, physicists have been trying to establish a unification of quantum theory and general relativity to produce a so-called theory of quantum gravity. But a unified account of fundamental physics is very far from being a theory of *everything*, as the distinguished physicist and cosmologist, Martin Rees makes clear.

> The sciences are in a hierarchy of complexity, from particle physics, through chemistry and cell biology, to psychology and ecology. But each of these sciences is autonomous, in that it depends on its own set of concepts that can't be ana-

lysed into anything simpler. To understand turbulent flow of water, a challenging and still unsolved problem, you must think in terms of wetness, whirls, eddies, and so forth: analysing the water into atoms doesn't help – indeed it erases all its distinctive features. And – to take a different example – what goes on in a computer could be described in electrical terms, but that misses the essence, the logic encoded in those signals. (Rees 1997, pp. 175-176)

9.2.10   It seems that without the emergence of life – and from this the emergence of the human world and the realms of civilization and the artificial – the universe would be lacking many distinctive kinds of things: things such as the specific living forms that have evolved, and the particular types of artefacts that have been produced by the purposively and intelligently directed creative activity of humans. Independence indeterminism sees creative origination playing a vital role in the emergence of many of the distinctive products of these two realms. But even if independence indeterminism is dismissed, as long as the current macro-deterministic and micro-indeterministic view of nature hold sway it is likely to be accepted that quantum indeterminacies (occurring in the interaction of nuclear radiation with genes, for example) have played a part in genetic mutation and therefore in influencing the particular course the evolution of life has taken. If this line of thinking is correct then the belief central to absolute determinism – that the past history of the universe, together with the laws of nature, completely fixes every detail of its future – is seriously undermined.

9.2.11   Are there other accounts of absolute determinism that would fare better in the support they are able to gain from scientific evidence? The most familiar and important thesis of determinism that might, at least at first sight, *not* seem to need to refer to the laws of nature and instantaneous states of the whole universe is that based on the so-called law of cause and effect. However, as has already been argued (see section 3.3), upon examination this thesis has serious weaknesses. Nevertheless, many writers on free will still rely on the law of cause and effect as grounds for asserting the truth of determinism. For example, Patricia Churchland (see 1.4.12) feels able to state, apparently as a matter of fact, that '[t]he problem [with the traditional view of free will] is that choices are made by brains, and

210

brains operate causally', and this leads her to dismiss the Indifferent Will and indifferently originative free will as nonsense. However, it is currently an open scientific question whether brains do operate wholly causally since there is some evidence (for example, recall the work of Peter Tse, section 5.4) that quantum indeterministic events – which, according to mainstream thinking, are events that do not arise in a causally deterministic way – play a role in some brain processes. But, as a few further examples will show, Patricia Churchland is not alone in simply assuming – as a matter of fact rather than as an acknowledged metaphysical presupposition – that cause and effect dominates how people function and think. Richard Oerton, in his book *The Nonsense of Free Will* feels able to assert as an obvious fact that 'determinism is causality'. (Oerton 2012, p. 7) And later he expands on this assertion by writing: 'Determinism is no more than a natural process of cause and effect which works its way towards our existence, then encompasses our existence and everything we think and feel and do, and then passes on, after our deaths to other things.' (p. 14) Tom Clark, who edits the naturalism.org website writes: 'Judged from a scientific and logical perspective, the belief that we stand outside the causal web in any respect is an absurdity, the height of human egoism and exceptionalism. [...] Everything is a function of, and participates in, the causal web; we are no exception.' And Sam Harris in his short but influential book *Free Will* writes: 'Free will *is* an illusion. Our wills are simply not of our own making. Thoughts and intentions emerge from background causes of which we are unaware and over which we have no control.' (Harris 2012, p. 5) Given these strongly-held assumptions it seems that belief in determinism is not likely to die out soon even though independence indeterminism is a more credible metaphysical doctrine, as shall now be argued.

9.3 The Case for Adopting Independence Indeterminism

9.3.1 A good deal has been said so far in this book about independence indeterminism and examples have been given, and arguments presented that support the view that this is indeed how the universe works. But it has been acknowledged all along that the thesis is metaphysical and that at bottom, no matter how reasonable and in accordance with common-sense it may be, independence indetermin-ism cannot be confirmed or denied by empirical or logical means. In this respect it is no different from the thesis of absolute determinism. But where independence indeterminism *is* different is in the much greater support it gets from science and common experience than does absolute determinism.

9.3.2   Recall that the primary assumption of independence inde-terminism asserts that **stretches of change that to some extent run truly independently of one another are extremely common in our universe.** This assumption is about non-repeatable, one-off particular dated and located stretches of change and not about types of stretches of change, and because this is so no experiments can be done to confirm or deny its validity. But what is remarkable about it in comparison with the thesis of absolute determinism, in the form discussed above, is that it calls upon no abstract concepts like "the state of the universe at an instant", and "the laws of nature". The phrase "stretches of change" may be unfamiliar, but once explained it is easy to find examples. Similarly, the idea of "true independence of change" is quite intelligible once it is explained what it means. Never-theless, in discussing whether or not "true independence of change" exists, care has been taken (see section 6.3) to say that it is only evid-ence for *type*-independence of change that is available, and not evid-ence for *token*-independence of change – which is what "independ-ence of change" refers to.

9.3.3   Quite apart from the truth or falsity of the assumption of independence of change, it is certain that in living their lives and go-ing about their business people believe that most specific dated and located stretches of change run in a way that is truly independent of how most other specific dated and located stretches of change run. That is, they believe that they can ignore almost all of what the rest of the universe is doing when they think about what it is that they might do. And this belief in the general independence of change is central to science. Science depends upon independent verification of findings: that is, upon the belief that it is possible – should any ap-propriately competent scientists choose to do so – to replicate the es-sential conditions and procedures leading to given findings and so confirm (or disconfirm) these for themselves. That is, scientists be-lieve that as long as they get the relevant conditions right – and they

212

see no reason why they are not free to do this as their inclination and resources allow – they can ignore what else is going on in the universe. Or put another way, they tacitly assume the truth of the assumption of independence of change. Furthermore, the sub-state laws of science – which are the only sort of laws science has at present – are based on the tacit assumption of independence of change because such laws assert that only the specific aspects of existence that figure in a law need to be taken into account in describing the phenomena concerned. Hence, whether scientists realise it or not, they are already deeply committed to the assumption of independence of change.

9.3.4   If a naturalistic metaphysics is based on assumptions that are simpler, easier to accept, and gain more support from science than those it competes with then these seem to be reasons enough for preferring it to its competitors. And since independence indeterminism does score over absolute determinism on these counts it seems it should be preferred to absolute determinism. But there is another important reason for preferring one naturalistic metaphysics over another, and this is because it gives rise to fewer irresolvable disputes, or problems. As has been already argued, independence indeterminism helps resolve the problem of free will – a problem that belief in absolute determinism is largely responsible for producing – but it also helps resolve a number of other long-standing disputes, as shall be discussed in the next five sections. However, before doing this it is important to recall some points made earlier.

9.3.5   It is generally accepted that when certain groups of things are related and interacting with one another in certain ways the group collectively has properties and behaviours that the things themselves don't have, and (usually) don't have when they are related and interacting in a different way. Such groups are usually understood as being systems, but thinking of them as RENOIRs (relatively enduring networks of influence relations) is often helpful when the particular participants involved in realising the system may vary and when they are in loose rather than tight relationships to one another as is frequently the case when the participants are humans. It is often difficult to explain exactly why a particular type of system or RENOIR has the holistic properties it does have but two general points are worth making. Firstly, a system or a RENOIR consists of a distinctive network

213

of dependencies or influences – a network that links together things which prior to their inclusion in the system or RENOIR changed more or less independently of one another, or were linked together in other ways. Secondly, these networks possess new causal powers – that is, they link events together into cause-effect, or input/output, relationships that in the absence of the network (or one functionally equivalent to it) would not exist. For example, a working mobile phone establishes (among many other things) a cause-effect link between speech sounds made by its user and correlated radio waves emitted by the phone – a cause-effect link that does not exist in the absence of the phone (or something functionally equivalent), and which is a cause-effect relationship that the parts of the phone separately are unable to realise. Few people deny the truth of these two points, but many people believe that the realisation of all such system-level causal links is fully reducible to a sequence – possibly a very complex sequence – of simpler cause-effect links, with this reduction bottoming-out with cause-effect links between simple fundamental entities.

9.3.6   One of the major contributions of independence indeterminism is that it challenges this widely held view. It does not deny that dependency relations or influence relations play a major role in determining what goes on in the world, but what it does deny is that such relations account for *everything* that happens. It denies this because it sees origination as playing a part as well. Most chance originations, and many directed ones, are type-determined and so have some sort of predictability. However, independence indeterminism accepts that some originated things (including events) are not prefigured to occur and are therefore not predictable. Such *creatively* originated things, and the processes responsible for producing them, will be seen to play a major role in helping to resolve the problems discussed next.

9.4   The Ontological Reductionism Problem

9.4.1   According to *The Oxford Companion to Philosophy* ontological reductionism is 'the belief that the whole of reality consists of a minimal number of entities or substances.' (Honderich 1995, entry on 'reductionism'). Mainstream physicists currently believe that the fundamental entities are space-time, energy, and matter with matter consisting of irreducible fundamental particles and accompanying fields. However, string theorists, who constitute a strong group of physicists, argue that rather than irreducible particles there are irreducible 'strings' of energy vibrating in perhaps ten or so dimensions. And, to add to how unclear scientists currently are about the fundamental nature of existence, mainstream cosmologists propose that in addition to ordinary matter, dark matter and dark energy should also exist – however, they cannot agree upon the detailed nature of these supposed additional fundamental aspects of reality.

9.4.2   A start may be made by addressing the question: What is meant by "the whole of reality"? If reality is taken to be all that exists at an instantaneous moment then it may be reasonable to see it as consisting of a minimal number of types of fundamental entity. But, even on this view not enough is being said because the quantity and configuration of the fundamental types of entity that exist at an instantaneous moment also need to be specified. And it is also necessary to know what sequence of instantaneous states constitutes the life-history of reality. On the basis of these two considerations, the thesis of ontological reductionism as stated in the form given above, must be dismissed as inadequate.

9.4.3   How may the thesis be more adequately stated? One approach is to continue with the instantaneous-state view but expand it according to van Inwagen's thesis of absolute determinism outlined in section 3.4. It may then be said that ontological reductionism is "the belief that the whole of reality consists of a pre-determined sequence of instantaneous total states each composed of a certain quantity and configuration of a minimal number of types of entities or substances, with the instantaneous states of the sequence deterministically related to one another by a fixed set of laws of nature." Put in these terms, all change is fully reducible. But if an alternative view is adopted, say one in accordance with mainstream science which has a place for quantum indeterminism and so for de novo originated events, then not all change will be fully reducible. And if independence indeterminism is adopted, then a very great deal of the change that is part of reality will not be fully reducible because it involves independence interactions which, according to this metaphysics, are de novo originated events whose occurrence is not reducible. So, from the perspective of independence indeterminism, it may firmly be asserted that ontological reductionism is not possible. Of course, this only helps to resolve the dispute if independence indeterminism is accepted.

9.5   The Problem of Emergent Properties

9.5.1   Turning again to *The Oxford Companion to Philosophy*: 'A property of a complex system is said to be "emergent" just in case, although it arises out of the properties and relationships characterising its simpler constituents, it is neither predictable from, nor reducible to these lower level characteristics.' (Honderich 1995, entry on 'emergent properties'.)

9.5.2   Properties that are an additive result of the properties of the components of a system don't present much of a reducibility problem. For example, the mass of an assembled mobile phone may readily be understood to be reducible to the sum of the masses of its components. But the phone's property of being able to send and receive voice messages is not one that any of its components possess and so the reducibility of this property is more of a problem. Nevertheless, it is widely believed that this property may be understood to be a consequence of how the phone's components interact and influence one another when related in the specific way they are in a working mobile phone. However, it should be recognised that an appropriate environment (one containing at least an active cellular phone network and users of it) is essential for the manifestation of this property.

9.5.3   This last point is important. Many properties of systems – including abilities, powers, and behaviours – are environmentally dependent and cannot actually exist without the existence of an appropriate system-environment coupling (and this includes systems understood as RENOIRs). Given this fairly obvious fact it seems somewhat surprising that such properties (and abilities, etc.) are taken to be properties of the *system*, rather than properties of the system together with an appropriate environment. Perhaps this way of thinking is one of the consequences of the dominant place that substance, rather than process, has played in thinking about what is the primary feature of existence. But whatever the reason for this view it is un-

216

deniable that many properties – particularly those properties seen as abilities or powers – only gain realisation through an appropriate kind of system-environment interaction. For example, the property of being able to walk requires that the walking system – a person, say – be able to interact in a certain way with an appropriate surface; and it is recognised that not all surfaces support the required form of interaction: for instance, liquid water and vertical surfaces do not support human walking. One consequence of this is that a system may have potentialities that never get actualised because the system never interacts with an environment that enables the relevant properties to manifest themselves. For example, a radio set in an environment without appropriate radio channels to tune into will never manifest its capacity to emit speech and music. And undoubtedly there are people with talents that they have never fully expressed, or even expressed at all, because the conditions that allow these to flourish have never arisen for them.

9.5.4   Once it is made explicit that interaction with an appropriate environment is essential for the actualisation of certain properties, the definition above will need to be modified. Here it is convenient to re-use the prefix introduced when talking about input/output dependent mind-processes (see 2.5.3). By an IOD-property is meant a property whose realisation depends upon the system that is said to possess it being engaged in certain types of input/output interactions with an appropriate environment. Using this term, it may then be said that "An IOD-property of a complex system is said to be 'emergent' just in case, although it arises out of the properties and relationships characterising its simpler components and how these interact with one another and with an appropriate environment, it is a property that is neither predictable from, nor reducible to these factors."

9.5.5   It has been argued that processes involving de novo originated events are neither wholly predictable nor wholly reducible because their course is not fully determined by prior conditions and the laws of nature. Hence, according to the revised definition just given, it follows that those IOD-properties of a system whose input/output interactions entail de novo originated events will be emergent properties simply because these events, being de novo originations (e.g. independence interactions, or quantum indeterministic occurrences), are not wholly reducible. What this means, for instance, is that the colour of an object should be taken to be an emergent IOD-property because its colour is realised by independence interactions between the various sorts of photons that constitute white light and the electrons, atoms and molecules of the object. However, because the originations (i.e. independence interactions) involved are strongly type-determined, most people would be reluctant to count such a property as emergent. It would seem sensible therefore to exclude those properties whose manifestation involves only type-determined originations from being classified as emergent properties.

9.5.6 Under independence indeterminism, all that is required for a *closed* system to manifest a property that is neither predictable nor reducible is for the process that expresses this property to involve independence interactions among the internal parts of the system. For example, a lottery tumbler regarded as a closed system with the property of ejecting numbered balls in a random sequence is manifesting a property that is neither predictable nor reducible because the ejections are a consequence of many independence interactions taking place within it. But again, it seems sensible to exclude those properties whose realisation depends solely upon type-determined originations among the component parts of the system concerned.

9.5.7 Given the decision to exclude many properties from being classed as emergent that seem to qualify according to the definitions presented above, how may it be further revised to accommodate this decision? One obvious way is by requiring that at least some of the de novo originations involved in realising the property (or ability, power or behaviour) be creative originations. The definition would then state: "A property (behaviour) of a complex system is said to be 'emergent' if realisation of it necessarily entails processes of creative origination within the system, and/or between the system and its interactions with an appropriate environment."

9.5.8 Given this revised definition of what qualifies as an emergent property, consider some possible candidates. An obvious one is inventiveness. But should it be taken to be an emergent property? Inventiveness is not usually thought of a property but as an ability, however this distinction shall be ignored and abilities – along with a powers, and distinctive kinds of behaviour – will be taken to be properties. The reason why inventiveness should be regarded as an emergent property according to the definition just developed is because manifestation of this property requires that the entity concerned – a person say – carry out creative activity and produce created outcomes. That is, *creative* origination must be going on not just *type-determined* origination, and it is this that makes prediction and reducibility not possible. There are several other kinds of familiar abilities that also qualify as being emergent according to the definition. For instance, learning (particularly in its more complex forms) necessarily involves the creative origination of such things as skills, knowledge, and understandings within the learner. And, to give a third example, the exercise of free will must be taken to be an emergent property because, according to the position adopted in this book, the free-will process necessarily entails creative origination. It may seem surprising that such familiar human behaviours as inventiveness, learning, and the exercise of free will count as emergent properties, but this does follow according to the reasoning just outlined.

9.6   The Problem of Irreducible Downward Causation

9.6.1   Closely connected to what has just been discussed is a related issue that in recent years has attracted much debate – namely, whether irreducible downward causation exists. Downward causation in its simplest form is the familiar idea that a system has properties that its components do not have and which may be such that they influence the components. Or, put more strongly, there may be cases in which the whole determines, to some significant extent, what happens to the parts. Roger Sperry, who among others has drawn attention to the idea, gave the example of a wheel rolling down a hill. He argued that the rollability of the wheel is a system property – not a property that any of its parts have but which belongs only to the whole wheel – and that this property may determine what happens to the parts. For example, the wheel's property of rollability may lead to its rolling down a hill and so transporting all of its part to a relatively distant location – something which its parts alone cannot achieve (Sperry 1969). However, this sort of downward causation is open to being reductively explained (at the type rather than the token level) in terms of the way the environment affects the individual parts and how these affect one another given that they are type-deterministically related to one another. A more interesting variant of this concept is that of irreducible downward causation. It is this stronger version of the concept that seems to have prompted Donald T Campbell to introduce the term "downward causation". (Campbell 1974) Many people deny that irreducible downward causation exists, while others believe that it does. What is lacking is a convincing naturalistic account of how irreducible downward causation can be possible. However, before indicating how independence indeterminism may help in providing such an account it is worth making a brief detour to consider the work of Helen Steward who, in her book *A Metaphysics for Freedom*, argues that the existence of irreducible downward causation would provide a solid basis for libertarian free will.

9.6.2   Steward develops a deeply and carefully argued case for agency being entirely natural but nonetheless something special in the world in that she sees the actions that agents give rise to as not being a necessary consequence solely of the properties and organisation of the neurological and other stuff of which an agent is constituted. What it seems she is arguing for is a form of agent causation. She writes:

> In the phenomenon of action, I have alleged, we see a situation in which a complex whole entity – an animal – is able to produce effects – in the first instance movements of and changes in its own body by means of which it is then able to bring about further effects in the world. But how can this be? Surely, movements and changes in the body that are of a physical sort are brought about by prior movement and changes in that same body, movements and changes that are also of a physical sort. [...] The question is how on earth a whole person or animal could manage to have effects on its own parts in such a way that the causation does not simply reduce to causation of parts on parts? (Seward 2012, p. 243)

How such irreducible causal influence may be realised she sees as a matter for science, and it is here that the weakness of her argument shows itself because science (with its current metaphysical orientation) has difficulty accepting irreducible downward causation. What is required is a new way of thinking about the world – one that has a natural place for irreducible downward causation – and independence indeterminism offers what is needed, as shall now be indicated.

9.6.3   Irreducible downward causation will exist when a REN-OIR is engaged in a process of creatively originating, eliminating, and modifying those parts of itself that are participating in realising such a process of creative self-alteration. The biological evolution of life by natural selection provides a good example because the evolution of new biological species by natural selection is, under independence indeterminism, understood to involve interactions among extant species with these species themselves having been creatively originated by the process of biological evolution by natural selection. That is, the actual species that exist at a given time are understood to play a key role in the process of biological evolution and therefore in the emergence of new species. Hence, species that have themselves been creatively originated by the process of evolution by natural selection play a key role, going forward, in that very creatively originative process itself.

9.6.4   Irreducible downward causation is commonly found in the realm of civilization. For instance, it is constantly at work in the evolution of human societies and in the evolution of technology because in both these cases what is creatively produced plays a part in the creative evolution going forward. But, unlike with evolution by natural selection, purposively directed creative activity plays a major part in the creative process within the realm of civilisation. For example, to varying degrees, irreducible downward causation is present within the evolution of all creative intellectual projects – like the one reported in this book – in that as ideas and understandings get creatively originated by the activity of the project they influence the future creation by the project of further ideas and understandings that then themselves become part of the project. There are many other examples of irreducible downward causation within the realm of civilisation. For instance, business firms manifest irreducible downward causation in that, to a greater of lesser extent, they creatively originate (e.g. by invention, construction, and selection) many of the things that get incorporated into what they are as a business – things such as the premises they use, the people they employ, the markets and regions they operate in, the products and/or services they offer, the relationships they have with their suppliers and customers, and the ways they organise themselves and operate internally. And these more or less creatively established parts of a business play an important role in its future creative activity (as well as, of course, in its non-creative direct-ive activities).

9.7 Independence Indeterminism and The Mind-Body Problem

9.7.1   Some general remarks were made in section 2.5 about how independence indeterminism may help resolve the mind-body prob-lem. And from what has been said above and elsewhere it should be clear that under independence indeterminism mind processes cannot in general be reduced solely to the prefigured properties and organ-isation of the brain and body of a person. Nevertheless, in spite of the argument having largely been made for the mind not being redu-cible to the body, it is worth using the position that has been de-veloped to provide a critique of a fairly mainstream view of the problem.

9.7.2   Jaegwon Kim, in his short article in *The Oxford Companion to Philosophy*, writes as follows.

The mind-body problem is the problem of giving an account of how minds, or mental processes, are related to bodily states and processes. [...] few philosophers now find the idea of minds as immaterial substances coherent or fruitful. There has been a virtual consensus, one that has held for years, that the world is essentially physical. [...] According to this physical monism (or 'ontological physicalism'), mental states and pro-cesses are to be construed as states and processes occurring in certain complex physical systems, such as biological organ-isms, not as states of some ghostly immaterial beings. The principle remaining problem for contemporary philosophy of mind, therefore, is to explain how the mental character of an organism or system is related to its physical nature.

The heart of contemporary physicalism is the primacy and priority of physical properties and the laws that govern them. The following 'supervenience thesis' is one way of expressing this idea: once all the physical facts about your body are fixed, that fixes all the facts about your mental life. That is to say, what mental properties you instantiate is wholly dependent

222

upon the features and characteristics of your bodily processes. (Honderich 1995, entry on 'The mind-body problem'.)

9.7.3   Independence indeterminism does not accept the supervenience thesis for two main reasons. The first reason is that it is widely agreed by scientists that many mind-brain processes run partly independently of one another while also having some interaction. This means that independence interactions are a common feature of the way the mind-brain operates, which in turn means that it does not operate as a deterministic system. Hence, it is not the case that 'once all the physical facts about your body are fixed, that fixes all the facts about your mental life' because the physical facts do not fully fix the course of your mental life – a course that, under independence indeterminism, is seen to be partly originated.

9.7.4   The second reason why independence indeterminism does not accept the supervenience thesis is that much of a person's mental life is significantly influenced by independence interactions the person has with their environment – interactions that include those that take place within social, cultural, linguistic, and symbolic domains in addition to interactions with the strictly physical world. Furthermore, many of these independence interactions are pattern-based rather than simple physical ones. So, given that independence interactions are de novo originated occurrences, it is not true that 'once all the physical facts about your body are fixed, that fixes all the facts about your mental life' because much of the course of your mental life is originated by independence interactions with things outside your body.

9.7.5   However, if all originated mind-brain events were type-determined originations then although it would remain true that a person's mental life was not wholly reducible to facts about their body, their mental life would nevertheless run in prefigured types of ways. However, under independence indeterminism it has been assumed that some mind-brain activity is creatively originative which means that, in a strong sense, it is activity that runs a course that is not reducible to facts about the body, or indeed anything else.

9.7.6   Kim's position and the critique of it just given are all very well but it might be thought that what has not been addressed is what many people would consider to be the central issue of the mind-body problem: namely, the problem of consciousness. The problem of consciousness is multifaceted, and although independence indeterminism has something to say about the possible ways in which, as a process, consciousness may operate, it can say nothing to help resolve what many people see as the heart of the problem: namely, how to reconcile the ineffable nature or conscious subjective experience with the effable nature of our understanding of the natural world. The reason why it cannot help with this facet of the problem is that independence indeterminism is a metaphysical thesis about the nature of the *effable* world – the world as it can be spoken about and explained. Conscious subjective experience is known to be utterly real to those who have this experience but nothing spoken about it, and nothing observed, measured, or probed that relates to it captures what it is like to actually have this experience. It is therefore a truly ineffable feature of existence. Of course, some people have denied that it is a real feature of existence simply because it is ineffable. A little more is said about consciousness in section 10.2, but this is too large a topic for it to be discussed extensively in this book.

9.8   The Arrow of Time

9.8.1   Most of the fundamental laws of physics (e.g. Newton's laws of motion, Maxwell's equations of classical electromagnetism, the equations of fluid dynamics, and Schrodinger's wave equation of quantum mechanics) are time-determinate laws and they permit the changes they describe to occur in reverse. However, it is only rarely that happenings that are time-reversals of one another are actually seen. What is usually seen are happenings that possess an intrinsic one-way directionality – something that is obvious once the change is depicted in a movie which is then played in reverse. The difficulty – the so-called problem of the arrow of time – is to explain why most real-world change has a one-way directionality when physics describes many basic kinds of change in a way that permits two-way directionality.

9.8.2   Attempts to resolve this problem often make use of the second law of thermodynamics. This law postulates that within a closed system (and the universe as a whole is generally taken to be a closed system in such discussions), any change that occurs produces either an increase in the total disorder (or entropy) of the system, or no increase at all. What the law forbids is a *decrease* in the overall entropy of a closed system. Now it logically follows from this that if a change in a closed system involves an increase in entropy then a reversal of this change must involve a decrease – something that would contravene the second law and so could not occur. This means that only those changes in a closed system that involve no increase in entropy can be reversed, which generally means that only those changes that do not involve any disordered dissipation of energy (which typically arises in the form of heat) are reversible. For example, a short movie of a pendulum suspended from an almost frictionless mounting and swinging in a vacuum – a setup that involves very little disordered dissipation of energy – looks almost exactly the same when played in reverse as when it is played in the forward direction. However, most real-world happenings involve some disordered dissipation of energy and therefore an increase in entropy, and so are not reversible. Nevertheless, in spite of the wide acceptance of the second law of thermodynamics, some physicists are still worried why it should be that when many of the basic laws of physics allow reversibility of change does it so rarely actually occur.

9.8.3   Under independence indeterminism there is a straightforward answer: namely, that because a de novo originated event (e.g. an independence interaction, or a quantum indeterministic event) arises indeterminately it has nothing definite to be reversed into, meaning that any change involving such events cannot be reversed. Furthermore, since it is assumed that independence interactions are very common, this means that irreversible change is going to be very common. However, it should be emphasised that independence indeterminism does not deny the truth of the time-determinate laws of change of physics because these are all sub-state laws and as such they say nothing about those aspects of existence that they do not refer to. Nor do these laws say anything about the occurrence of future interaction among independently running instances of change governed by such laws.

9.9   Naturalism Yes, Physicalism No

9.9.1   Independence indeterminism has a significance wider than discussed in the previous five sections because, while being a naturalistic metaphysics, it is incompatible with physicalism. There is no agreed definition of naturalism but the belief on which all versions are founded is that 'reality has no place for "supernatural" or other "spooky" kinds of entity.' (Papineau 2016) Physicalism, however, takes a narrower view and is 'the thesis that everything is physical, or as contemporary philosophers sometimes put it, that everything supervenes on the physical.' (Stoljar 2017). Physicalism and materialism are closely connected theses with physicalism being more general since physics includes non-material features of existence such as fields, forces, and electromagnetic waves. But current physics is incomplete so there are things yet to be included in physics. This suggests that it is what a "completed" physics says exists that should be taken as what is physical. Although not entirely satisfactory, this way of making clear what is meant by "physical" does a better job than relying only upon the common intuitive understanding that physical things are simply concrete or tangible things.

9.9.2   To say that independence indeterminism is compatible with naturalism but not with physicalism is a very large claim since almost all scientists, many philosophers, and a great many other people believe that the universe *is* wholly physical – for instance, Jaegwon Kim in discussing the mind-body problem (see 9.7.2) believes this. For most such people this belief is tacit and is so deeply rooted that for them any argument that denies it seems to be false for no other reason than it does deny it. Recall the case made in 1.1.10 for abandoning determinism and replacing it with independence indeterminism. In summary, three reasons were given. (1) That belief in true independence of change would be more difficult to abandon than belief in absolute determinism. (2) That the assumption of independence of change, upon which independence indeterminism rests, is much simpler and better supported by every-day and scientific evidence than are the assumptions upon which absolute determinism rests: namely, that existence consists of a succession of instantaneous total states of the universe deterministically connected one to the next by immutable laws of nature. And (3) that independence indeterminism helps resolve problems that absolute determinism brings with it, such as the problem of free will and the mind-body problem. Together these three reasons provide strong grounds for taking independence indeterminism very seriously indeed. Quite apart from the other two, reason (1) on its own really must be countered if absolute determinism, or any other form of determinism that denies independence of change, is to stand as an acceptable naturalistic metaphysics. However countering (1) is going to be very difficult because, to reiterate points already made (see 3.6.7, and 9.3.3), not only is independence of change tacitly assumed to be true by almost everyone in their ordinary doings, but it is assumed to be true by scientists because they believe themselves to be free agents – free to conduct and repeat observations and experiments as their interests and resources dictate. Furthermore, current physics only has laws that involve certain aspects (sub-states) of existence and not *every* aspect, and this implies there is independence of change since those aspects of existence not included in a law must change independently of those that are, otherwise these other aspects would have to be included in the law.

9.9.3   However, accepting the assumption of true independence of change means physicalism must be rejected for the following reasons. Firstly, the assumption implies that there is nothing in existence – either physical or anything else – that determines, links, governs, or describes how independently running changes are jointly changing (see 2.1.8). This means there is nothing in existence fixing whether or not future interaction will occur between such changes, which means that when such independence interactions do occur they will be de novo originated events – that is, events whose occurrence was not fixed by anything in prior existence. Hence, under this assumption, neither physics nor anything else can wholly account for all aspects of existence because the future course of existence cannot be fully accounted for, so physicalism must be rejected.

9.9.4   Accepting independence indeterminism means there are limits to what physics, and more generally science, can achieve. According to this metaphysics science cannot reliably and accurately predict the occurrence of future specific independence interactions. Nevertheless, science is extraordinarily successful in being able to account for a great deal of what goes on. According to independence indeterminism the reason for this is that almost all originations are type-determined (see 1.2.10, 1.5.1), and that at the type-level science can describe, explain, and predict much of the type-determined origination that takes place. What science cannot do is give reliable predictions of the details of single dated and located instances of type-determined origination. For instance, it cannot predict what specific oxygen molecules will bind with a particular haemoglobin molecule in the blood circulating through your lungs. The inability of science to predict the occurrence of specific instances of type-determined originations is generally explained by there not being available full knowledge of what is going on. It is rarely believed that true origination is involved. But once the assumption of independence of change is accepted then it must also be accepted that independence interactions are indeterminately occurring events (see 1.1.6) and that predicting them is not a matter of lacking knowledge because no such knowledge can possibly exist.

9.9.5 If the evidence was that everything that was originated was of a prefigured type then there would be a strong sense in which physicalism would be valid since the *types* of things that could exist in the future would be prefigured in past and present existence. However the evidence is that not all originations are prefigured but rather that some are creatively originated. That this is so may be denied but it seems difficult to do so with respect to biological evolution and the realm of civilisation since science is unable to predict such things as what new species will emerge in the future and what new human artefacts will be produced. Nevertheless, many people will probably continue to hold that this failure is a consequence of lacking the necessary knowledge and that were this available then what new species and what types of new artefacts were to emerge in the future would be apparent from examining past and present existence. Without a better understanding of how creative origination works it will be difficult to resolve this disagreement. Nevertheless, independence indeterminism holds strongly to the view that non-prefigured origination – i.e. creative origination – is a real feature of existence.

9.9.6 If naturalism is compatible with independence indeterminism and physicalism is not, what role might physics play that this new metaphysics accepts? It would accept, but have no reason for excluding other possibilities, that all interactions bottom out in (or supervene upon) interactions among entities that physics recognises as existing. But, as already argued (see sections 9.5 and 9.6), it would not accept that all happenings play out in ways that are solely a consequence of such physical interactions because it sees origination –

and creative origination in particular – making an essential contribution to at least some of what happens in the future: a contribution it sees as not being reducible solely to change that physics can account for. This means that under independence indeterminism physics may continue to be seen to play a very important role in existence, however not one that can account for the full future of existence.

9.9.7   It has been argued that creative origination is able to produce systems that are not prefigured – for instance, new biological species and new types of human artefacts. However, many of these created systems – particularly human created artefacts such as mobile phones or automobiles – do not themselves operate creatively and have system properties open to type-based explanation based on the physical organisation of the system's components. Nevertheless, according to independence indeterminism, the organisation underlying these systems will have been *creatively* produced and so not be reducible solely to physical interactions and prefigured types of originations. What this means is that there are many types of extant systems in the living and human realms whose emergence, as the *types* of things they are, physics cannot account for. And that this is so highlights the limitations of physicalism in being able to provide a complete account of the future types of things that may exist.

10   Factors In Human Free Will

10.1   Introduction

10.1.1   This chapter is included to help understand some of the main influences participating in human self-directed origination and human free-will processing. Much of the discussion highlights how different many of these factors are compared to those found in animals. Part of this difference appears to be attributable to human persons being more difficult to satisfy than animals because they have a greater variety of motivations and emotions, and experience more complex internal conflicts. Another apparent reason for the difference is that humans frequently engage in free-will processing to try to resolve conflict and indecision associated not only with their present situation but also with recalled, imagined or symbolically represented situations – something that animals do not appear to do to any great extent. Furthermore, human persons appear to have a more complex self and greater powers of self-examination, self-evaluation, and creative modification of the various parts of their self than do animals.

10.1.2   The remainder of this chapter consists of six sections. In each matters are discussed that are of great range and depth and for which much remains to be understood, and this means the treatment given is rudimentary – and sometimes somewhat idiosyncratic. Nonetheless, it would not be doing justice to explaining free will unless an attempt was made to identify some of the factors apparent in the human condition and way of being that makes the human manifestation of free will so different from what is observed in animals.

10.1.3   The first topic that is addressed is human consciousness and cognition. A start is made here because the remaining factors seem only to have the character and place in human life they seem to have because they are bound up with human cognitive and conscious processes. The second matter to be discussed is the concept of the human self – a topic that is returned to because of its central place in the account of human free will presented in this book. The third discussion concerns human lifestructure – something already mentioned (1.6.4) as playing a key role in the life of humans and the exercise of their free will. In the remaining three sections the human motivational, emotional, and executive sub-selves are discussed.

10.2 Human Consciousness and Cognition

10.2.1 Consciousness and cognition are dealt with together because they seem to be inextricably linked. As broad modes of cognitive activity humans share their basic perceptual, memory, attention, and learning capabilities with higher animals, although the ways these are expressed differ to some extent. Higher animals may have forms of consciousness that are similar to those of human persons in some respects – for example, their consciousness of their perceptual field may be similar – but the material upon which animal consciousness feeds, and the influence it has, seems to be much more limited.

10.2.2 However, regardless of any similarities there may be between human and animal consciousness, there is one thing that is highly relevant to the nature of the human condition and human free will, and that apparently greatly distinguishes us from animals, and this is the ability of human persons to engage in symbol-based thinking and action. Such thinking and action entails interaction with, and the production of, symbolic structures – structures composed of such things as utterances, gestures, performances, writing, pictures, diagrams, physical models, simulations, and mathematical and computer constructions and representations. Among other things, humans are able to interact with symbolic structures to stimulate thoughts and feelings about things, happenings, and states of affairs that are not currently present to their senses. These may include thoughts and feelings about past happenings and actions, possible future or potential happenings, and things and states of affairs that could not, did not, or do not exist in reality. To a considerable extent humans are able to interact with symbolic structures as if they were interacting with something real rather than symbolic – that is, the symbols as such tend to recede from human consciousness to be replaced by what, for them, they represent or mean. Symbolic interaction may stimulate ideas, memories, and imaginings, and it may activate emotions and motivations. Furthermore, through symbolic interaction people may sometimes engage in highly abstract forms of reasoning and logical analysis. With their capacity for symbolic interaction, humans have open to them worlds or domains quite beyond the here and now to which animals seem to be largely confined. And with the aid of symbolic interaction (mediated by written and spoken languages, and in many other ways), coupled with other human capabilities (particularly their high intelligence, imagination, creativity, and capacity for communication and cooperative directive activity), humans have collectively played the central role in the emergence of the realm of civilization.

10.2.3   The human capacity for symbol-based thinking and action seems to be at the heart of the difference between human persons and animals and it seems to be the basis of their ability to engage in what may be called "action-free thinking" – that is, thinking that is not directly tied to present or near-future action in the world. And it seems that human consciousness plays a major part in this sort of thinking. Some remarks have already been made about consciousness (see 9.7.6) and in what follow, given that it is too large a topic to deal with in much depth, only a few further points are made.

10.2.4   It is often assumed that human consciousness has two major features – one essentially private, and one public. (Note: it is being assumed that human consciousness is objectively real and that humans may lose it under certain conditions, such as when they are given a general anaesthetic.) The private feature of consciousness has no agreed label, but the terms "conscious subjective experience" (CSE), and "phenomenal consciousness" are both quite widely used. Conscious subjective experience is wholly personal and private and so cannot be shared by others. However, human persons each individually and completely privately know what it is like to have CSE, even though no-one can ever share or co-experience another person's. In spite of this, most people accept without question that human persons other than themselves have CSE, and they seem to reach this conclusion mainly because they recognise that other persons are in many ways like themselves, and because many words and phrases referring to aspects of conscious subjective experience are a familiar part of human languages.

10.2.5   The private/public difference between these two features of consciousness gives rise to one of the great questions regarding consciousness: namely, whether conscious subjective experience, as such, plays any part in influencing observable behaviour. On one side are those who insist that it does, and on the other are those who insist that it doesn't. Indeed, some who adopt this latter position take the view that CSE doesn't exist at all, and that all that exists is the behaviour that humans associate with the presence of CSE. In this book, and without making a case for it, it is simply assumed that CSE plays an important role in human life and that it does have a significant influence on the emergence and evolution of some observable human behaviours.

10.2.6 However, in adopting this position it is accepted that complex directive activity may be carried out without the person concerned having conscious subjective experience of the details of what they are doing. Nevertheless, it is also assumed that such behaviour requires that the individual concerned be able to sense, attend to, and process information about things and events relevant to the complex directive activity they are carrying out. There is no English word that specifically denotes this sensing, attending, information-processing activity which does not also carry connotations of there being accompanying conscious subjective experience. The word "awareness" is sometimes used but it is closely connected to definitions of consciousness: for example, *Webster's Dictionary* (1998) defines **conscious** as: 'Immediately aware of; mentally recognising, to some degree and extent one's own inner feeling and thought, or their subjective reference', and as 'Mentally alert, well aware of some object, impression, or truth'. Sometimes subjective conscious experience is said to be awareness of one's own awareness. But why should a first round of awareness (that is, of sensing, or attending, or carrying out information-processing) not be accompanied by the special quality of having subjective conscious experience, while a second round of it should? Ned Block introduced the term "access consciousness" (Block 1995) to denote those aspects of consciousness, separate from its phenomenal or CSE aspects, that contribute to the carrying out of activities of various sorts. But in using "consciousness" in the term "access consciousness", Block is, it would seem, not sufficiently separating the sensing, attending, information-processing aspect of consciousness from its subjective conscious experience aspect. What is needed is a form of words that makes no reference to "consciousness", and to that end the term "situationally sensitive" shall be used when an agent is merely sensing, attending to, and informationally processing aspects of its situation – or more accurately its circumstances (i.e. its environment and its own condition) – in order to carry out some directive activity.

10.2.7   The distinction being made between CSE and situationally sensitivity may be clarified by considering an occasion when a person has carried out some familiar task, or a part of such a task, without later being able to recall any details of what they did. To be specific, consider the complex directive activity involved in safely driving a car. People who are experienced drivers may sometimes find that they have driven for some period of time without being able to recall the details of their driving activity. This normally happens when they have been driving along a familiar route without any unusual incidents arising, and when their phenomenal consciousness has been occupied with matters other than driving – perhaps, for example, they may have been absorbed in thinking about some difficult decision or problem, or with reviewing or evaluating something they had done in the recent past. What this points to is that carrying out the complex directive activity of safely driving a car does not necessarily require that the directive system involved be making use of phenomenal consciousness. However, few people would doubt that in order to drive a car safely through traffic the directive system involved (whether it be a human driver or a computer-based automatic driving system) needs to be appropriately situationally sensitive. Once it is accepted that it is possible for complex human directive activity to be produced without the person having conscious subjective experience of what they are doing, the question arises whether all forms of human behaviour might be carried out without there being any accompanying conscious subjective experience. That is, could what are known as philosophical zombies exist? Could there exist beings behaviourally and socially indistinguishable from human persons that have no conscious subjective experience at all? Whether or not this is possible remains an open question – an open question that exposes the depth and difficulty of the problem of consciousness, or more broadly speaking, the mind-body problem.

10.2.8   However, the assumption being made in this book is that human persons do indeed have conscious subjective experience and that its presence plays an important role in some of their activity. One example of this role is that a person is only able to recall into phenomenal consciousness the details of carrying out complex directive activity – for instance, driving – if they were phenomenally conscious of these details when they carried out the activity. Freud drew attention to this apparent fact when he wrote: '[...] it dawns upon us like a new discovery that only something which has once been a *Cs.* [conscious] perception can become conscious [again]' (Freud 1962, p. 10). Are there other aspects of human functioning that seem to require the involvement of CSE? There seem to be many, but they all rest on subjective reports of such influence and not on objective evidence. For instance, most people believe that at least some of what they do is partly a consequence of their having phenomenally consciously thought about doing it. Indeed, one important contribution of phenomenal consciousness seems to be that it facilitates the emergence of creative rather than automatic or strongly prefigured responses. If this is so, then it may be that the special feel – e.g. the experiential richness or qualia-laden nature of conscious subjective experience – may help stimulate non-prefigured responses. But on the other hand, there seems to be no reason why creative activity within the mind-brain should necessarily require conscious subjective experience – after all, there is a good deal of evidence than much of the connecting-up and disconnecting that creative activity in the mind-brain entails happens unconsciously – i.e. without accompanying conscious subjective experience.

10.2.9   As a final point, in case it may be thought that conscious subjective experience is insignificant in human life, it is worth noting how few people would see any point in continuing to live faced with the certain prospect of living out their future without any subjective conscious experience at all. In fact some people make a "living will" in which they ask not to be resuscitated in the event that they are very unlikely to have any future conscious subjective experience. And the medical/legal position in some countries is that human life should not be artificially maintained for people who, on the basis of multiple expert opinion, are believed to have no subjective conscious experience, and no prospect of having any in the future.

10.2.10   Some cognitive activities that support and link with human consciousness and play an important part in human life deserve some mention since they play a part in the exercise of human free will and are much more highly developed in humans compared to animals.

Five broad types of such human cognitive activities will be discussed: semanticing, abstracting, imagining, inferencing, and valuing. Only a little will be said about each since this is not the place to attempt a fuller discussion. It should be borne in mind that while retaining some independence of operation, these cognitive activities, or processes, interact with and support one another.

10.2.11   Semanticing. There seems to be no English word for the cognitive activity of using (and producing) sign/meaning relationships. Animals have a weak form of this capability in that they are able to learn, and make good use of, some kinds of semantic relationships. Pavlov's famous experiments on the acquisition of conditioned responses showed that dogs came to learn that a relationship existed between their perception of a bell-ring and food. This is not a natural causal relationship – like the smell of meat being causally connected with the nearby presence of meat – and this points to the essential nature of semanticing: namely, that it is the process of learning, and making use of, non-naturally connected relationships between things. It is this capability, evolved to an extraordinary high level in human persons, that underpins the human ability to use language and engage in other forms of symbolic interaction.

10.2.12   Abstracting. This is the cognitive activity of using and creating classes, generalisations, and concepts. Animals certainly do this to the extent that they are able to respond to new instances of things in ways related to how they have responded to other instances of such types or classes of things in the past. However, the number of distinct classes that they may distinguish seems, relative to humans, to be quite limited – although animals are often able to make many fine distinctions within those areas of life that are important to them. In contrast, humans are able to distinguish and use a vast number of different classes, generalisations and concepts. And it seems this ability is coupled to their capacity for semanticing and thinking and communicating in symbolic terms. Humans are also able to use their abstracting capabilities to create and use classes, generalisations, and concepts that are based on classes, generalisations, and concepts themselves rather than on sensory information alone.

10.2.13   Imagining. This term is used to denote the mind-brain activity resulting in the spontaneous emergence, or the intentional summoning, of phenomenally conscious content without sensory

236

perception necessarily being directly involved. It draws strongly upon memory recall, but in its highly developed human form is not restricted to this since things may be imagined that have never been experienced by the person, may never have existed, or may be impossible in reality. Human imagination is often stimulated by sensory perception, but in a creative way so that what is imagined is not, for the person concerned, a prefigured consequence of what is sensed and perceived. Semanticing often accompanies human imaginative activity – as occurs, for example, when imagining what is written about in a novel. What comes into conscious subjective experience through imagining may lead to further imaginings, or to other cognitive activity, or more or less directly to motor action as in creative art activity (e.g. painting, sculpture, dance, or music).

10.2.14   Inferencing. In its simpler forms this cognitive process is carried out by higher animals, but in its more complex forms it seems to be confined solely to human persons. Typically, animals use inferencing when their current perceptions, coupled with relevant knowledge and experience, lead them to believe something exists (or has existed, or may exist in the future) which is not perceptually present. Being able to do this has great survival value. Inferencing becomes more powerful when it can be chained: that is with one inference being the basis for a second inference, and so on. Inferencing may be seen as a process in which the production of fresh content within the mind-brain is produced through making use of three types of links between existing content: those links with a natural basis (e.g. cause-and-effect, or contiguity); those with an abstract basis (e.g. shared class membership, conceptual connection, or similarity of some sort); and those with a logical basis (e.g. inductive or deductive). However, semanticing – i.e. the going from perception of a sign (or sign structure) to a meaning, and vice versa – is not included because semantic relationships do not require any natural, abstract, or logical relationship between the sign and the meaning. Also, imagining will not be taken to be a mode of inferencing – even though inferencing often plays a part in imagining – because again what is imagined need not have a natural, abstract, or logical link to what already exists in the mind-brain. Intuiting is a further means by which new mind-brain content may be obtained from existing content and it seems to involve both imagining and inferencing.

10.2.15   Valuing. This is a form of mind-brain activity that is carried out by animals but which humans have greatly developed and extended into a form of cognitive activity in its own right. In its basic form – the form humans share with animals – valuing is strongly linked to the emotional self, and the responses the emotional self has learned (or has received as part of its genetic inheritance) to associate with the perception of certain objects and situations. In animals, values seem largely to have a physiological and instinctive basis whereas with humans many have an abstract basis – as, for example, do some of the values associated with religious beliefs. Many of a person's abstract values come from their socialisation, but some may be more strongly self-created – for example, being based on personal experience and thought, and their own efforts to find a set of values with which they can deeply identify. Much human valuing uses codified and often institutionally-based values such as those made explicit in laws and regulations, or codes of practice, or that exist implicitly within the culture and ethos of a particular organisation or group. However it may be that some external and less personal values come to influence an individual in such a way that they so internalise and absorb them that they become part of their own personal value system.

10.2.16   It is assumed that the cognitive activities just outlined – together with the basic cognitive capabilities of sensory perception, attention, memory and learning, and coupled with the special form of human consciousness – help humans carry out many complex kinds of mind-brain activity. These include (but are not confined to) the human ability to cogitate, consider, contemplate, reflect, and understand; to analyse and explain; to review, and to plan; to evaluate and judge; to problem-solve, to innovate, invent and create; to deliberate, choose and decide; to make and follow instructions for executing complex directive activities; and to carry out calculations and formal manipulations within symbolic domains. Furthermore, it is assumed in the present work that a persons's processes of cognition coupled with their situational sensitivity and phenomenal consciousness, play a fundamental role in their social interactions, in conversing, in carrying out their ordinary daily activities; in the evaluation, re-evaluation, construction, re-construction, and maintenance of their lifestructure;

and in the operation of their motivational, emotional, and executive selves.

10.3 Some Further Comments about the Human Self

10.3.1   It has already been assumed (see section 1.6) that a human person is a human being who has undergone socialisation, and that the human self is primarily composed of motivational, emotional, and executive selves – parts that are assumed to coexist and interact with other distinguishable aspect of the self, such as a person's situ-ational sensitivity, phenomenal consciousness, cognitive processes, and their lifestructure. However, these assumptions are not univer-sally accepted and so in this section some other views are considered and related to those adopted in the present work.

10.3.2   Ulrich Neisser, a founder of cognitive psychology, sug-gests that humans have five kinds of what he calls self-knowledge (Neisser 1988). Self-knowledge may be thought of as the knowledge a person has upon which their sense of selfhood – or being an indi-vidual – is founded. The *ecological self* is a person's knowledge – usually expressing itself through situational sensitivity and/or phenomenal consciousness – of being in a particular place and environment and of being engaged in particular activity. It is what largely disappears when, generally on rare occasions, a person loses their bearings or be-comes temporarily disoriented. It seems humans share this kind of knowledge of their selfhood with higher animals, and possibly with quite lowly ones as well. The *interpersonal self* is a person's knowledge of how they see themselves as a participant in social situations and interactions. A person's phenomenal consciousness of having a self seems to depend greatly upon them having, at least during their early years, interpersonal interaction with other humans. Indeed, feral chil-dren generally lack the sense of self that children of the same age brought up in normal human society possess (Steeves 2003). A per-son's interpersonal self takes somewhat different forms depending upon who they are interacting with. For example, typically a person is one kind of interpersonal self in social interaction with their close family members, a somewhat different interpersonal self among their friends, and yet different kinds of interpersonal self in various sorts of formal social interactions. Many people, using their knowledge of their interpersonal self, engage in phenomenally conscious reflection upon, and evaluation of, their various presentations of it and as a result sometimes wish to change some aspects of how they present themselves socially. For instance, a person may wish to become more assertive, or more at ease meeting new people, or a better listener. A person's *temporally extended self* is the sense of selfhood they have that comes from being situationally sensitive to and/or phenomenally conscious of being an individual with a particular history and a particular expected future. A person's *private self* is the sense of their selfhood that they acquire when they engage in phenomenally conscious reflection about their conscious subjective experiences. This seems to take a little while to emerge since it appears that young children do not have powers of phenomenally conscious introspection. Finally, a person's *conceptual self* is the person they come to believe they are based upon what significant others (e.g. parents, teachers, friends, partners) have said they are, and upon ideas that they have picked up from various sources – for example, from popular psychology, or from personality tests they have taken. The concepts that a person develops of themselves may not be as others see them – indeed, some people are somewhat blind to the person others take them to be.

10.3.3 The various aspects of the human self that have been mentioned – both those adopted in this book and those that Neisser distinguishes – should not be thought of as being wholly distinct since they appear to co-exist and interact with one another. Although each person only knows about these various aspects of their self through phenomenally conscious thinking about them, it should not be thought that their operation necessarily requires the involvement of phenomenal consciousness because these various aspects of a person's self seem to run mostly subconsciously or unconsciously. Nevertheless, if a person does become phenomenally conscious of some of the aspects of their self, then this may have a significant influence upon how they operate and behave. For example, on occasions a person may become phenomenally conscious of some aspect of their personal history – such as a past failure to deal successfully with the kind of situation they are now in – and this may lead to an emotional response, such as heightened anxiety or embarrassment, which then affects their behaviour. Or, to give another example, on some occasion a person may become phenomenally conscious of a character trait that they believe they possess, and this may then influence how they conduct ourselves.

10.3.4 Interactions among aspects of a person's self seem to be a more or less constant feature of human wakeful existence. For instance, a person's knowledge of their ecological self tends to constantly give them a sense of place, time, and present ongoings which may have some influence on their activity and decision-making. A person's knowledge of their interpersonal self will, while they are in a particular sort of social situation, often have an influence upon the operation of their motivational, emotional, and executive sub-selves. And their awareness of being a temporally extended self with a past history and desired future may have an influence on the operation of their executive self.

10.3.5 There are many aspects of the human self that have not been mentioned. Perhaps the most important of these are human personality traits. Many theories and accounts of human personality have been proposed, but no consensus currently exists. However, there does seem to be quite widespread agreement among psychologists that there are five principle groups of personality traits – the so-called "Big Five" – which may be summarised as follows.

Openness

A tendency to value the aesthetic, intellectual, and imaginative side of life; a willingness to engage with the unconventional, the novel, and the complex; a tendency towards creativity and heightened curiosity; a tendency to be in touch with one's feelings.

Conscientiousness

A tendency towards self-discipline, fulfilling duties and commitments, and working to achieve things; a tendency towards perfectionism and compulsive working; a preference for planned rather than spontaneous activity; a tendency to avoid trouble and disruption.

Extraversion

A tendency to seek the company of others and the stimulation they may provide; a tendency towards positive, enthusiastic, and energetic engagement with the social world, and towards excitement in general. Intraversion, or low extraversion, is a tendency towards relative disengagement from the social world; towards a low-key, ordered and quiet way of life; and towards inner living.

241

Agreeableness
A tendency towards compassion, concern, and caring for others; to-wards generosity, helpfulness, cooperation and compromise; towards seeing the good side of human nature, and towards accepting human frailties.

Neuroticism
A tendency towards emotional instability and moodiness; towards the experiencing of negative emotions and moods (e.g. anger, hostility, anxiety, depression); towards interpreting situations and people as threatening or unfriendly; and a vulnerability to stress and an inability to cope calmly with minor problems and irritations.

10.3.6   A person's personality traits appear to have a strong genetic basis. To what extent a person's early life experiences and social-isation shape them is not certain, but some change does generally occur, and may continue throughout a person's life. Not all people are happy with their personality traits. Indeed, there is a thriving self-help industry that offers various means by which it is claimed a person may change some features of their personality and some of their traits and habits and acquire new ones.

10.3.7   Not mentioned explicitly in the above list of personality traits (but possibly subsumed under conscientiousness) is will-power. Will-power may be understood to be the capacity an agent to per-severe in the pursuit of a goal or the completion of a task when faced with setbacks, difficulties, competing and/or opposing motivations, and unpleasant emotions. Possessing strong will-power is something that the executive self may come to greatly value, and strengthening it may itself become a goal of the executive self. But will-power may well have a genetic basis meaning that some individuals are much more able to develop strong will-power than are others. Quite clearly, the strength of a person's will-power plays an important role in their free-will processing since it acts to support the continued pursuit of those goals and actions favoured by the executive self when there exist motivations and emotions that oppose their continued pursuit.

10.4 Human Lifestructure

10.4.1   Humans are social beings. Indeed, it has been assumed that without appropriate socialisation there would not be human persons but only human beings. This is not to deny the animal side of people; it is said to emphasise that people are not *simply* animals. Human socialisation takes place within an immediate family group, or some appropriate surrogate for such a group, and generally within a particular community and culture. But, particularly in the developed world of today, the life of many people is not confined to the community and culture within which they grew up. Indeed, nowadays many people have open to them an immense range of possible ways of living their lives, and in what follows it is assumed that it is such persons that are being discussed rather than those with little freedom and opportunity to fashion a lifestructure largely of their own creation.

10.4.2   The term lifestructure was introduced early on (see 1.6.4) to name the highly complex world within which a human person's self-evaluating executive self works and lives. It could have been said that a person's lifestructure simple *is* the world in which they live, and to some extent this is true. But this has not been done because the aim is to emphasise that it is both more than and less than this. It is *more* because a person's lifestructure includes the person's own take on the world and so encompasses all the idiosyncratic ways in which they have come to interpret it. Furthermore, a person's lifestructure includes things that belong to the person rather than their external world as such. And a person's lifestructure is also taken to be *less* than the world they live in because their idiosyncratic take on it leaves out much that they are not responsive to (i.e. neither situationally sensitive to nor phenomenally conscious of), or that in reality is different to how they think it is.

10.4.3   A person's lifestructure includes their social, cultural, economic, and political environment; their lifestyle, and the familiar routines of their life; their diet, eating habits, and food preferences; their partner, family, friends (and enemies), colleagues, and acquaintances; their home; their employment and/or other similar activity; their material possessions, financial assets, and their liabilities; their standing, status, and position within the various social groups they belong to; their interests including such things as their sporting and similar activities, hobbies, and leisure pursuits generally; their physical and psychological attributes and condition, including physical disabilities, compulsions, addictions and dependencies; their qualifications, skills, knowledge, and life experiences; their established values, life-hopes, projects, plans, goals and intentions; and their perceived duties, commitments, obligations, and responsibilities.

10.4.4 As an infant and child a person has relatively little control over much of their lifestructure. For instance, they are largely unable to choose where they live, what family they belong to, the culture they grow up in, and the opportunities made available to them for such things as travel, play, sports, and entertainment. However, there are some aspects of their lifestructure that a child often does have some control over: for example, such things as whom they make friends with, what leisure activities and entertainments they indulge in, and what foods they like. As a child they soon realise that their lifestructure makes many demands on them, and that parts of it limit and control much of what happens in their lives. And yet abandoning, or radically altering, the given aspects of their lifestructure seems not to be possible – although running away is always an option, but one that is only rarely pursued in earnest. As they grow up children demand, and are often freely given, more control over their lifestructure. For example, they will often be able to decide what subjects to specialise in at school and college, how to spend much of their leisure time, what to wear, and who to have as their boyfriend or girlfriend. As adolescents approach adulthood proper they tend to have greater and greater control over their lifestructure, although some aspects of it may still remain beyond their full control.

10.4.5 Some people, more or less constantly throughout their lives or only at certain periods, have a chaotic lifestructure – that is a life with little structure at all. But the great majority of people have a lifestructure which does have a good deal of complex structure and continuity to it. For example, consider the content and structure of a typical working-age adult's lifestructure in the modern developed world. It will often have several relatively distinct parts, such as a close live-in relationship with a partner and/or family, a home life, a working life, a leisure life, an extended-family life, a friendship life, and a community life. In addition, a typical adult is likely to have a large array of possessions – some personal such as clothing, some jointly owned with a partner and/or immediate family. Many of these possessions will be material objects of one sort or another – a home, furniture, a car, a mobile phone, a computer, TV, books, music, and so on. Others will be less tangible: such as having a page on one or more social network sites, and membership of clubs, societies, or social groups of various sorts; or such as having savings and spendable money, loans and overdrafts; and of course a multitude of other things like citizen rights, educational qualifications, skills, knowledge, and particular life experiences. Other less tangible possessions will include such things as their personal standing – for instance: in their family, among their friends, at work, within their community, and within the clubs and groups they belong to, and at their place of worship. Additionally, a typical adult in modern society will likely have more or less ready access to a great number of different services – for example: banking services, household utilities (e.g. electricity, water, sewerage, heating fuel, mobile and landline phone connections, internet access, insurance, security services), shops, restaurants, cinemas, theatres, travel services, and many, many others. But there is more. Typically, an adult will have their own specific obligations, responsibilities, duties, and commitments. And they will have their own values and standards of conduct that they have either acquired through their socialisation or through their own creative origination and which their executive self will normally feel constrained by and obliged to respect. And not to be forgotten, because this area is a major part of a person's lifestructure, are their life-hopes, ideals, longings, ambitions and projects, and their current goals and objectives. And, unfortunately, a typical person will usually have their own particular dissatisfactions, and perhaps their own feeling of entrapment – a feeling of not being free, or being unable to find true fulfilment in their lives, of being unable to reach self-actualisation.

10.4.6 Attention is being drawn to the concept of a person's lifestructure to help make sense of human free will, and in particular to help explain the very great difference between human and animal free will. Animals – social animals in particular – have lifestructures, but they are very much simpler than those that modern humans typically possess. Furthermore, the means by which animals may change their lifestructures are relatively limited and are mostly given genetically.

This is not the case with modern humans. Their capacity for creative origination, coupled with the tremendous range of resources, opportunities, and forms of lifestructure that seem to be available to many modern humans gives them an apparent freedom to change their lifestructure that goes far beyond what is available to any other living beings.

10.4.7   Human lifestructures – as the large and enormously complex things they typically are – have received relatively little scientific study, but their influence upon and place within people's lives has long been addressed within literature of all sorts, and within the performing arts. However, one piece of scientific work needs to be mentioned because the researchers involved recognise the concept of lifestructure in a similar way to how it has just been presented but with the difference that they were mainly interested in how a person's life structure changes over time, which is not a primary concern when using the concept in relation to the issue of human free-will.

10.4.8   The research was carried out by Daniel J. Levinson and his colleagues and was reported in their book *The Seasons of a Man's Life* (Levinson et al. 1978) Levinson had found that there was very little scientific discussion and research about the overall structure of a person's life and the major transitions that typically occur within it and so he set about establishing a research programme to investigate this aspect of the human condition. In the book Levinson et al. introduce and discuss at length the notion of a person's "life structure" – a concept that Levinson and his colleagues found gave coherence to their understanding of adult life as it is lived as a whole and how it changes through the years. The primary aim of the project was 'to create *a developmental perspective on adulthood in men*'. The project proper commenced in the late 1960s and ended in the mid 1970s. Some further work followed including that involving the lives of women. The initial investigation was of 40 men aged between 35 and 45 drawn from four occupational categories (industrial workers, business executives, university biologists, and novelists) who were living in North America. The study is therefore of specific sociocultural, and quite severely age-restricted, groups of men only and may be criticised for being too narrow to draw general conclusions.

10.4.9   Levinson et al. describe their conception of 'The Individual Life Structure' as a tool for analysing the fabric of a person's life. They consider that a person's life structure has three aspects: the sociocultural world in which they live, the satisfied and non-satisfied parts of their self, and the person's participation in the world. Regarding a person's self and their life structure they say:

The self includes a complex patterning of wishes, conflicts, anxieties and ways of resolving and controlling them. It includes fantasies, moral values and ideals, talents and skills, character traits, modes of feeling, thought and action. Part of the self is conscious; much is unconscious; and we must consider both parts. Important aspects of the self, initially formed in the pre-adult era, continue to influence a man's life in adulthood. We have to see how the person draws upon the self, or ignores it, in his everyday life. The self is an intrinsic element of the life structure and not a separate entity. (p. 43)

10.4.10   Levinson et al. recognize the deep and non-straightforward nature of many of the choices a person makes about their life structure – choices, for example, concerning 'work, family, friendships and love relationships of various kinds, where to live, leisure, involvement in religious, political and community life, immediate and long-term goals.' (p. 43) They see these sorts of choices (i.e. what is chosen) as constituting the primary components of a person's life structure and note that 'The components are not features of the self, such as motives and abilities, nor are they features of the world, such as institutions, groups and objects. [...] every choice is saturated by both self and world. To choose something means to have a *relationship* with it. The relationship becomes a vehicle for living out certain aspects of the self and engaging in certain modes of participation in the world.' (pp. 43-44) They suggest that at any given time one or two components (rarely three or more) of a person's life structure have a central place and strongly influence the way the person leads their life and the choices they make at that time. For example, a man who has been totally committed to work may start detaching himself from it and come to involve himself more in family and/or community life.

10.4.11   After discussing a major finding of the study – that the transformation of the subjects' life structures over time followed a similar pattern – Levinson et al. move on to talk about life structures in more general terms, noting that they are satisfactory according to the degree to which they are viable in society and appropriately serve the self, which means that life structures involve both society and a person themselves. The researchers recognise 'that often a person's life structure in only fairly satisfactory – typically, it works pretty well in the world, but does not wholly satisfy the person themselves [...]' and that it 'is never all of a piece. It contains some mixture of order and disorder, unity and diversity, integration and fragmentation. It is always flawed in some respects. It contains contradictions and gaps which can be modified only by basic changes in the structure itself.' (p. 54)

10.4.12   It is evident that a person's lifestructure has a very great influence on their doings. But their lifestructure only influences a person's actions through its relationship to and the affects it has upon other aspects of their self – specifically, from the viewpoint adopted in this book, upon their motivational, emotional and executive selves. So it is to further discussion of these aspects of a person that the last three sections of this chapter are addressed.

10.5   The Motivational Self

10.5.1   The dictionary definition of a **motivation** is that it is 'a causative factor; incentive; drive.' A broad psychological characteriza-tion is given in the following extract from a textbook on motivation theory and research:

> When the hypothetical man on the street asks, "What motiv-ates behaviour?" he is asking to have identified one or a com-bination of three kinds of things: (1) an *environmental determin-ant* which precipitated the behaviour in question [...]; (2) the internal *urge, wish, feeling, emotion, drive, instinct, want, desire, de-mand, purpose, interest, aspiration, plan, need,* or *motive* which gave rise to the action; or (3) the *incentive, goal, or object value*, which attracted or repelled the organism. (Cofer and Appley 1964, p. 5)

10.5.2   Of the three kinds of motivating factors identified above, members of the first and third groups are external while members of the second are internal. External factors only produce the effects they do because of the internal condition and nature of the person con-cerned, and in particular because these external factors stimulate or influence (via the person's mind-brain processes of perception, situational sensitivity, phenomenal consciousness, etc.) one or more of those factors that belong to the second group – factors that shall be referred to as the person's "motivations". For instance, according to this view, when a person is forced to do something under a threat of death they do it because those of their activated motivations that support compliance outweigh those that oppose compliance. Similarly, when a person responds in a particular way to an incentive – money, for example – they only do so because perception of the incentive activates mind-brain processes that stimulate motivations in the second group that then generate the response. There are human motivations in addition to those listed in (2) above. These include but are not restricted to life-hopes, ambitions, ends, goals, objectives, intentions, concerns, obligations, duties, commitments, responsibilities, aversions, and dislikes.

10.5.3 At any time there are active motivations, and latent or inactive ones. It is assumed that each of a person's motivations is supported by particular mind-brain sensitivities that, in conjunction with prevailing stimuli and mind-brain conditions and activity, may result in (some strength of) activation of the motivation. It is also assumed that an active motivation operates directively in the sense of being an initiator, supporter, sustainer, shaper, inhibitor, or destroyer of a person's contemplated or actual doings.

10.5.4 Unlike animals, human persons have many motivations that are not common to the species as a whole but are specific to the individual. These person-specific motivations include such things as an individual's particular responsibilities, duties, obligations and commitments; their personal ideals, and life-hopes; their various interests and concerns; and their particular current endeavours, projects, plans, goals, objectives, and intentions. However, there are several motivations – essentially biologically inherited ones – that it appears most humans possess. These motivations include the need for air, food and water, relief from bodily pain, for satisfaction of sexual arousal, and for self-preservation. But it seems other very commonly occurring types of human motivations – such as the need for esteem, and the need for creative expression – require human socialisation for their full emergence.

10.5.5 A view that has a long history is that all human behaviour is ultimately reducible to the influence of two fundamental motivations: the maximization of pleasure and the minimization of pain. Superficially, this view may appear to have a good deal of validity, but on closer examination it turns out to be rather inadequate. Firstly, it fails to easily explain why humans carry out a great deal of routine behaviour that does not directly involve either pleasure or pain. Secondly, because pleasure and pain come in a range of incommensurable kinds, it is difficult to see how maximisation and minimisation could actually work. For instance, how does one maximise across such different pleasures as those obtained from consuming delicious food, from solving a difficult problem, from communing with nature, or from having sex? And thirdly, this simple view fails to account for the manifest complexity of human motivational life. Given these weaknesses it is not surprising that many writers and researchers have attempted to give more complex accounts.

10.5.6   Early on in the history of psychology William James offered the following list of human motivations.

Saving – the desire to hoard.

Construction – the desire to build and achieve.

Curiosity – the desire to explore and learn.

Exhibition – the desire for attention.

Family – the desire to raise our children.

Hunting – the desire to find food.

Order – the desire for cleanliness and organization.

Play – the desire for fun.

Sex – the desire to reproduce.

Shame – the desire to avoid being singled out.

Pain – the desire to avoid aversive sensation.

Herd – the desire for social contact.

Vengeance – the desire for aggression.

(This list is given in Reiss 2000, pp. 7-8)

10.5.7   Later, William McDougall in his book *An Introduction to Social Psychology* (McDougall 1908/1924) proposed that the basic human conative instincts are those of: Acquisition, Construction, Curiosity, Flight, Pugnacity, Reproduction, Repulsion, Subjection, Self-display, Gregariousness, and Parental care. He accepted that subgroups of these may be active concurrently and so humans may have a large variety of complex influences on thought and action.

10.5.8   Henry Murray, drawing upon James's and McDougall's work, developed a sophisticated "need theory" in which he proposed – based on scientific research and observation – that humans have twelve physiological (or "viscerogenic") needs, and twenty-seven non-physiological (or "psychogenic") needs (Murray 1938). Murray took the human physiological needs to be for Air, Water, Food, Sex, Lactation, Urination, Defecation, Sensuous gratification, Rest and sleep, and the need to avoid and extricate oneself from Danger, Unpleasant stimuli, and excessive Heat and cold. His list of psychogenic needs is as follows.

Abasement – the need to punish oneself, or accept punishment from another.

Achievement – the need to succeed, to win, to overcome challenges.

Acquisition – the need to obtain resources and possessions.

Affiliation – the need for social acceptance, group membership, belongingness.

Aggression – the urge to fight or use force to defend, or to gain advantage.

Autonomy – the need for self-determination, for freedom of action.

Blameavoidance – the need to avoid blame or being singled-out.

Construction – the need to produce, build, and create.

Contravariance – the need to be unique, special, to be treated as an individual.

Counteraction – the need to defend and protect one's honour, dignity, respect.

Defendance – the need to justify one's actions, beliefs, and affiliations.

Deference – the need to follow a leader, to serve, to submit to power and authority.

Dominance – the need for power, for control over others, for the submission of others.

Exhibition – the need to be noticed, to be given attention.

Exposition – the need to be listened to, to be a source of information, to teach.

Harmavoidance – the need to avoid pain or injury.

Infavoidance – the need to avoid failure, shame, loss of status.

Nurturance – the need to nurture kin and helpless humans or animals.

251

Order – the need to organize, systematise, plan, and maintain an ordered life.

Play – the need for recreation, for entertainment, for carefree activity of all sorts.

Recognition – the need for social status, for respect.

Rejection – the need to create outsiders, the need for a "them" versus "us."

Sentience – the need to have aesthetic and sensuous experiences.

Sex – the need for sexual relationships and gratification of sexual arousal.

Similance – the need to empathise.

Succorance – the need for help when in distress; the need for protection.

Understanding – the need to analyse and explain.

10.5.9 Some of these psychogenic motivations may be understood to be partly or even wholly a product of a person's self-evaluating executive self as it grapples with how to satisfy and secure future satisfaction of the person's inherited or socially induced motivations and the many varied and changing motivations (such as ambitions, projects, goals) that it itself has established within the motivational self of the person.

10.5.10 According to Murray, needs have an unconscious as well as a conscious presence. He accepted that needs vary in their "prepotency", or relative power to command attention when activated. He took it that needs interact with one another in complex ways, including conflictual, competitive, and cooperative interaction, and that a person's doings are often devised by their executive self to serve more than one need while avoiding emotional disturbance and excessive opposition from other needs.

10.5.11 A more recent list of human needs and desires has been developed by Steven Reiss and his co-worker Susan Havercamp. The extensive research they conducted resulted in the following list of 16 basic human desires.

Power – the desire to influence others.

Independence – the desire for self-reliance.

Curiosity – the desire for knowledge.

Acceptance – the desire for inclusion.

Order – the desire for organization.

Saving – the desire to collect things.

Honor – the desire to be loyal to one's parents and heritage.

Idealism – the desire for social justice.

Social Contact – the desire for companionship.

Family – the desire to raise one's own children.

Status – the desire for social standing.

Vengeance – the desire to get even.

Romance – the desire for sex and beauty.

Eating – the desire to consume food.

Physical Activity – the desire for exercise of muscles.

Tranquility – the desire for emotional calm. (Reiss 2000, pp. 17-18). According to Reiss, these Basic Desires are actually families of related desires – for example, he takes the need for achievement to belong to the family of Power desires. Most of the desires he identifies are relatively unrelated to one another (although there are correlations, such as people with a strong desire for Power tend to have strong desire for Status). Reiss's list does not include physiological motivations because he is interested only in those desires that make a person the individual they are. Importantly, Reiss believes that people vary with respect to how significant these Basic Desires generally are for them, and he suggests that 'No two people have exactly the same potential for a particular desire' (p. 22), which, on his view, tends to accentuate the individuality of human persons.

10.5.12   Abraham Maslow argues against attempting to produce an atomistic list of human motivations and suggests that the fundamental human needs form a hierarchy in which the most prepotent needs – (the physiological needs) are at the base and the least prepotent (the self-actualisation needs) are at the apex. (Maslow 1954/1970, pp. 25-26) Maslow explains his idea of prepotency as follows.

> What this means specifically, is that in the human being who is missing everything in life in an extreme fashion, it is most likely that the major motivation would be the physiological needs rather than any others. A person who is lacking food, safety, love, and esteem would most probably hunger for food more strongly than for anything else. (pp. 36-37)

Maslow's hierarchy of fundamental human needs, ranked from most prepotent to the least, is as follows.

The *Physiological needs* – e.g. the need for food, water, warmth, sex.

The *Safety needs* – the need for 'security; stability; dependency; protection; freedom from fear, from anxiety and chaos; need for structure, law, limits; strength in the protector, and so on.' (p. 39)

The *Belongingness and Love needs* – marked, for instance, by missing one's friends, sweetheart, partner, children, etc.; and by hungering for a place in one's group or family.

The *Esteem needs* – the need for self-esteem, including the desire for achievement, adequacy, competence, and independence; the need for esteem from others, including the desire for attention, recognition, respect, dignity; the desire for prestige, status, fame and glory; the desire for influence, dominance, and power.

The *need for Self-Actualization* – the desire for self-fulfilment, the desire 'to become actualized in what [one] is potentially. [...] to become more and more what one idiosyncratically is, to become everything that one is capable of becoming'. (Maslow, p. 46) Maslow refers to these sets of needs as "fundamental" or "basic" but it is not clear if he believes they are all genetically given or just very commonly existing among socialised humans.

10.5.13   Before discussing the emotional self it is worth drawing attention to a set of human motivations that have not been mentioned because they are rarely explicitly included in lists of human needs. There does not seem to be a single word by which to refer to them collectively so the term "comfort motivations" shall be used. These motivations, or desires, are for comfort and pleasure in order to relieve, or displace from conscious subjective experience, such things as pain, distress, depression, anxiety, miserableness, and a sense of failure and inadequacy. Comfort motivations include urges and desires for such things as alcohol, drugs, sex, thrills, comfort-eating, and for engagement in such escapist activities as relaxed socialising, watching TV, or playing computer and other games.

10.6   The Emotional Self

10.6.1   The term "emotional self" shall be used to refer to the collection of "affective dispositions" that an individual human person possesses. Included in the use of this term are the various mind-brain systems by which affective dispositions become activated and influential in the thought and behaviour of a person. There is no widely accepted taxonomy of human affective dispositions although there is a general view that there are different kinds. However, in the following discussion, four major types are distinguished: *emotions*, *sentiments*, *moods*, and *body/mind conditions*.

10.6.2   Affective dispositions – and this is why they are *dispositions* – mostly lie dormant within human persons, but they may become activated and when they do they shall be referred to as affective *states*. Most affective states have a presence in phenomenal consciousness but not all do – e.g. some mood states, and some body/mind states to which a person has become habituated do not. The word "feeling" is often used to refer to the particular quality within phenomenal consciousness that is associated with an affective state and in the present discussion the word shall be used in this rather restricted sense.

10.6.3   Emotions are affective dispositions that when activated are accompanied by more or less marked physiological and psychological changes that are mostly governed by primitive and autonomous parts of the mind-brain. Emotional states are sometimes accompanied by, or stimulate, an urge to act in a particular manner and to this extent they have links to a person's motivational self. Physiological effects induced by emotional states include changes to glandular secretions, breathing-rate, heart-rate, posture, and facial expression. Psychological changes include the disruption of rational and evaluative thinking, heightened alertness, and narrowing of attentional focus.

10.6.4   *Webster's Dictionary* (1998) tells us that a **sentiment** is 'A mental attitude or response to a person, object, or idea conditioned entirely by feeling instead of reason.' Sentiments generally produce much milder feelings than emotions. Since sentiments are tied to objects they tend not to be innate although the feelings their activation arouse, if any, are usually of an innate type – and usually of an emotional type. Many of a person's sentiments will have been acquired as a result of having had one or more emotionally-charged direct encounters with instances of the type of thing in question. However people also acquire their sentiments through their socialisation and many culturally specific sentiments are acquired in this way and not through direct experience. Another way people establish sentiments is through generalisation: they propagate the sentiments they have about one type of thing to a much larger group of things – for ex-

255

ample, a person may have had a bad experience eating a curry in their childhood and in consequence decide that they don't like any 'foreign' food.

10.6.5   A mood state or condition differs from an emotion or a sentiment in that it is an affective state that is much more enduring. Indeed, a mood may become more or less detached from what initially activated it and become partially self-reinforcing. A mood colours a person's mind-brain activity in distinctive ways – for example, a person in a cheerful mood will tend to be mentally active and respond to situations and events in a positive and optimistic way, whereas a person in a depressed mood will tend to be mentally passive and respond in a negative and pessimistic manner. A mood also tends to make a person more likely than normal to produce particular sorts of emotionally-based responses – for example, a person who is in an ill-tempered or irritable mood is more likely to produce angry outbursts than someone in a placid or forgiving mood.

10.6.6   Body/mind states almost always have a more or less specific internal bodily (rather than mind-brain) source, and putting "body" before "mind" in "body/mind" is intended to emphasise this. Body/mind affective states include pain, hunger, thirst, nausea, bloatedness, sleepiness, fatigue, and various sorts of bodily unease such as those arising from postural discomfort, a full bladder, or an itch.

10.6.7   Emotions may be focused or unfocused – for example, a person may feel "anxious about the job interview tomorrow" or simply feel anxious in a non-focused way as when experiencing floating anxiety. Sentiments are always focused on some object or kind of thing. Moods are generally unfocused affective state, although they sometimes may have a consciously identifiable apparent cause. So, for instance, a person may just feel depressed and not know why, or, feel depressed for a specific reason, such as being depressed about their money problems. Body/mind affective states may be focused, as, for example, when a person has a pain in their foot, or unfocused as when they are feeling out of sorts.

10.6.8   Some activated emotions tend to encourage impulsive action, although some, such as extreme fear, tend to completely freeze or disable action. Strongly-felt emotions often disrupt the normal operation of a person's executive self, and sometimes in ways that may

256

lead them to make decisions that in a non-emotional state they would not make. Moods, since they are generally non-focused affective states, tend to be pervasive in their influence and tend to colour, negatively or positively, a person's whole outlook on the world and their doings within it. Body/mind affective states usually activate specific motivations which in turn tend to stimulate the performance of specific actions – such as scratching an itch, or finding a suitable place to urinate – aimed at relieving the physiological condition that is activating the body-mind affective state. Note however that the executive self may, to some extent at least, be able to control the execution of such actions, such as when a person tries to hold-off urinating until a more appropriate time, or (under medical advice, say) tries not to scratch an itchy patch of skin.

10.6.9 Since affective states often activate particular motivations, it might be thought that affective states in general do this, but this is only true in part. Some emotions do generally activate (or are co-activated with) specific sorts of motivation – for example, rage often stimulates a desire to lash out at something. But many emotions, sentiments, and moods do not produce specific motivations. For example, the emotion of feeling happy cannot be identified with the desire to carry out a *particular* action but, for instance, it may encourage a person to "let their hair down" and behave in ways that they may not usually allow themselves to do. Similarly, sentiments don't necessarily stimulate specific actions – for example, a negative sentiment towards a particular politician (activated, perhaps, by a news item) may not stimulate a person to take any particular action at the time, but it may reinforce this negative sentiment and give it increased influence in the self's production of some later action, such as how the person votes. And, to give an example relating to mood, being in a depressed mood may not necessarily produce specific types of motivations although it may well influence what motivations may become activated and the choices a person makes about what to do.

10.6.10 It is unclear whether humans share a set of basic types of emotion – or indeed, what exactly basic means within this context. A good many writers have proposed lists. For example, Paul Eckman, a major contemporary figure in the field, argues that all human emotions are basic because there are no compound emotions – i.e. no emotions composed of a two or more elemental emotions – and because all emotions 'evolved for their adaptive value in dealing with fundamental life tasks.' (Eckman 1994). Fundamental life tasks include such things as fighting, falling in love, escaping predators, and coping with loss. Eckman does however recognise that human emotions form clusters, and that there may be only a few types of these, for instance: Happiness, Sadness, Fear, Anger, Surprise, Disgust. Robert Plutchik, another notable figure in the field, suggested there are eight basic emotions: anger, fear, sadness, disgust, surprise, anticipation, trust, joy. But, unlike Eckman, he argued that a person may experience more than one basic emotion at a time so giving rise to a very large number of possible affective states (Plutchik 1991). But quite apart from whether or not there are basic emotions, there are certainly many words – in English at least – that refer to emotions or other affective states.

10.6.11 Affective states and the emotional self play an important part in the choice of a person's doings, and in influencing their execution. Given the physiological accompaniments of emotions and some other affective states, it seems that the emotional self has a long evolutionary history – certainly much longer than that of the executive self. It seems reasonable to assume that lower animals simply have two sub-selves: a motivational self mainly populated with genetically given motivations (e.g drives, and instincts), and an emotional self. However, higher animals do seem to have an executive self, but one that appears to be nothing like as complex as that possessed by human persons.

10.7 The Human Executive Self

10.7.1 The many special abilities of the mature human executive self have more or less been taken for granted so far, but it is worth listing some of them to indicate what a powerful and important part of a person it is.

Control – of behaviour and of some automatic and emotional responses and urges; powers of self-control, of anger management; the ability to suppress socially deviant or inappropriate behaviour; the ability to produce behaviour acceptable within given social conditions.

Directed or intentional learning – of skills, facts, knowledge, ideas, theories and ways of behaving.

Perseverance – the ability to continue with a task in spite of failures, fatigue, and lack of immediate reward or easy or early success.

Concentration – the ability to maintain situational sensitivity to, and phenomenal consciousness of, specific matters and doings; the ability to block out distractions and irrelevant sensory input; and the ability to overcome the urge to attend to competing motivations.

Foresight – the ability to anticipate near-term occurrences; the ability to 'read' the likely mental condition of others (i.e. to have a so-called "theory of mind"); the ability to predict the conditions and consequences likely to be associated with pursuing present doings and future goals and plans.

Rational decision-making – the ability to bring facts, reason and logic into play when carrying out decision-making; the ability to suppress or counteract the influence of emotions, moods, prejudices, and irrational motivations in decision-making.

Inventiveness, problem-solving and *creative thinking* – the ability to apply these forms of creativity in a directed way to a wide range of situations and endeavours.

Planning – the ability to carry out short- medium- and long-term planning and scheduling, and the evaluation and updating or alteration of plans in the light of anticipated and actual outcomes and changed circumstances and motivations.

Monitoring – of all sorts of things, happenings, and activities. For example, of one's actions, of one's success or failure in achieving objectives, of environmental circumstances, of the behaviour of individuals and groups, of the level and availability of resources, of one's bodily condition, and of one's thoughts and mind-brain state.

Meta-cognition – the ability to monitor and assess one's own self, including one's executive self, in order to learn about it and through this learning become, for example, a better learner, decision-maker, planner, thinker, group or team-members, and more in control of one's emotions and impulses.

Evaluation – of many sorts of things and activities: for example, of current circumstances, of anticipated and actual outcomes, of personal performance, of how others have treated one, of one's lifestructure, of one's aspirations, plans and hopes, and of one's values, views, knowledge and beliefs.

Judgement – for instance of what is true or false, satisfactory or unsatisfactory, right or wrong, good or bad, prudent or imprudent, better or worse, trustworthy or untrustworthy, safe or dangerous.

Flexibility – the ability to adapt to or cope with upsets, disruptions, and changes of circumstance.

10.7.2 These abilities draw upon the special cognitive capabilities and form of consciousness that human person's possess. They rarely operate in isolation since they not only interact among themselves but their execution takes place within the context of the influence of a person's motivational and emotional selves. Much of this interaction is not type-determined or prefigured and so, according to independence indeterminism, should be taken to be more or less creatively originative.

10.7.3 The idea of the executive self has been linked to Freud's concept of the ego (see 1.6.2), but a connection may be made to more recent work by linking the idea to Albert Bandura's "Agentic Perspective" in which he sees 'The capacity to exercise control over the nature and quality of one's life [as] the essence of humanness.' (Bandura 2001). He argues that this capacity depends mainly upon four core features of human agency, what he terms *intentionality, forethought, self-reactiveness,* and *self-reflectiveness.* He sees all of these features as necessarily involving situational sensitivity and phenomenal consciousness. In Bandura's terms, to have intentionality is to have a pro-active commitment to bring about certain consciously held ends or purposes; it is to possess 'considerable self-direction in the face of competing influences'. Bandura sees 'the power to originate actions for given purposes [as] the key feature of human agency'. He sees Forethought as underpinning this power since it allows a person to imagine, consider, and evaluate different futures; to choose among alternative goals; and to plan and guide action to achieve what they decide upon. Self-reactiveness is the ability of a person to be an effective self-motivator and self-regulator with respect to the pursuit and achievement of their intentions. Many human intentions have a more or less far-future payoff which requires that intermediate goals be identified and achieved if this payoff is to be realised. Often these intermediate goals will not have much rewarding payoff in their own

260

right – indeed, their pursuit may sometimes require that a person's executive self deny satisfaction to other motivations, and/or that the person undertake unpleasant activities. The final core feature of human agency that Bandura identifies is self-reflectiveness. He writes: 'People are not only agents of action but self-examiners of their own functioning. [...] Through reflective self-consciousness, people evaluate their motivations, values, and the meaning of their life pursuits. It is at this higher level of self-reflectiveness that individuals address conflicts in motivational inducements and choose to act in favor of one over another. Verification of the soundness of one's thinking also relies heavily on self-reflective means'. Bandura draws attention to the importance of 'perceived self-efficacy' – the beliefs a person holds about their ability, or inability, to achieve particular ends and purposes, He sees these beliefs as playing a pivotal role in shaping the course of a person's life and how they deal with setbacks.

10.7.4   A similar view to Bandura's, and which is also largely in line with the idea of the human executive self as presented here, is voiced by Roy Baumeister, Brandon Schmeichel, and Kathleen Vohs in their paper 'Self-Regulation and the Executive Function: The Self as Controlling Agent' (2007). The authors believe that self-regulation – 'the self altering its own responses or inner states' – can only be properly appreciated within a broader psychological context: that of the human self as a whole. They believe there are three basic features of the self. 'The first is reflexive awareness: Consciousness can be directed toward its source, so that just as people become aware of and learn about the world, they can also become aware of and learn about themselves.' The second is as a 'tool for connecting with others' and in so doing gaining increased reflexive self-awareness. And 'the third aspect of the self may be called its executive function, though it is also called the "agent" or "agentic aspect"' (p. 518) In addition to these three basic features, the authors argue that a proper appreciation of the human self requires that humans possess free will (at least of a sort that allows them to do as reason rather than passion dictates); and also that, uniquely among all natural beings that we know of, we recognise humans to be 'cultural animals'.

10.7.5   In section 7.6 the idea of human persons operating most of the time as self-evaluating executive controlling agents – or SEE-Cing agents – was introduced. It was remarked (7.6.2) that 'The superordinate objective (or prime directive) of an executive controller is to successfully organise (e.g. create, initiate, guide, coordinate, and terminate) directive activity to satisfactorily attend to a set of potentially conflicting tasks while doing so with limited resources and powers, with various constraints on its actions, and in the face of conflicting priorities and demands.' And later in the same section it was suggested that human persons may be understood to operate much of the time as self-evaluating executive controllers: self-evaluating in that, firstly, they can create their own methods and priorities for satisfying their genetically given motivations and their own self-created ends and purposes; secondly, that they can create their own criteria for what they believe makes them successful executive controllers; and thirdly, that they can carry out their own evaluation of their success/failure as executive controllers. A person's motivational self and their emotional self provide important feedback to the executive self on how it is performing. So, for instance, active motivations will signal their current level of satisfaction or dissatisfaction to the executive self; as too will be signalled the condition of their active affective states. But although a person operating in self-evaluating executive controlling mode is likely to be phenomenally conscious of this feedback, in being self-evaluating they do not have to respond to it if the criteria they have adopted for what they consider counts as success as an executive controller takes priority. So, for instance, if a person believes that pursuing some goal is important enough then they may be able to withstand strong influences directed at not pursuing the goal or not continuing its pursuit. For example, to succeed in carrying out a very dangerous mountain climb a person may need to overcome resistance from within themselves such as pain and fatigue, fear, and the feeling that they are doing something extremely foolhardy that threatens other things that are very important in their life such as their family.

10.7.6 Given that animals do not voluntarily undertake life-threatening endeavours of the sort just mentioned, it must be asked why humans do. Part of the answer seems to be that they do so to satisfy their esteem needs – for example, to prove their competence and bravery to themselves (and to others); to be able to excel in some area; to gain status and respect. But it also seems that they – the person they are in the guise of their executive self – may do so to prove to themselves their own capability and mastery as an executive controller able to achieve very difficult ends even when the pursuit of these is strongly opposed by other parts of their self.

10.7.7 The criteria a person holds for what counts as success seem to be a result of many influences. For example, influences from their socialisation, from their family and schooling, from the various peer groups they belong to, from media and cultural sources, from their own personal experiences, and from their own study and thinking. Some of the criteria may have been more or less uncritically (or even unknowingly) absorbed and therefore be only minimally of a person's own creation. But others – such things as their own specific ideals and life-hopes, some of their own standards and values, and their distinctive interests, hobbies, and projects – may be more strongly of their own creation.

10.7.8 In trying to manage how to satisfy a person's criteria for successful living – and achieve the associated projects and goals. they have adopted, or seek to adopt – a person's executive self is likely to have to pay most of its attention to managing and altering the person's lifestructure. For example, in striving to satisfy a person's esteem needs the executive self, working under the influences and constraints of the person's motivational and emotional selves, may come to adopt particular goals – career goals, say – whose pursuit will then have considerable influence on their lifestructure. However, it should not be thought that particular needs or motivations will always stimulate efforts on the part of a person's executive self to satisfy them because one strategy it may adopt – a strategy that makes sense from the perspective of the executive self's need to establish and maintain its perceived competence as an executive controller – is to deny the importance of certain needs, such as esteem needs. In achieving such denial not only does the executive self make its task easier but it gains a sense of power in being able to deny service to demands made of it. Thus, although taking on the world and trying to control it is one way by which a person's executive self may believe it is capable of satisfying the person's motivations, another way is for it to try to change the desires of the person so that they do not desire things that cannot be readily obtained or whose pursuit leads to unsatisfactory consequences. This, in part, is where the human possession of higher-order desires (see section 5.7) comes in: that is, a person's executive self seems to have the capacity to establish and pursue desires to desire differently.

10.7.9   In making some brief comments about how the nature of the human executive self may be understood, it is worth recalling the quotation from Levinson et al. (see 10.4.11), namely 'that often a person's life structure in only fairly satisfactory – typically, it works pretty well in the world, but does not wholly satisfy the person themselves [...]' and that it 'is never all of a piece. It contains some mixture of order and disorder, unity and diversity, integration and fragmentation. It is always flawed in some respects. It contains contradictions and gaps which can be modified only by basic changes in the structure itself.' This suggests that for some people (perhaps many) their executive self does not achieve full success, and this points to what seems to be a common feature of (at least modern) human life: namely that human persons are continual seekers, often seeking something more satisfactory than what they presently have. Or, in failing to find full satisfaction according to their own criteria and self-evaluations, indulging in activities to block dissatisfactions, perceived failings, fears, doubts, anxieties, and inadequacies through drink and drugs, or through engaging in various escapist or comfort-seeking activities.

10.7.10   The executive self is almost always a key participant in a person's free-will processing activity. Not only is the executive self a focus of much conflict but, in conjunction with human phenomenal consciousness and the cognitive capacities that persons possess, it plays a major part in the creative activity associated with the ARCS of free-will processing (see 1.5.4). However, a person's executive self is rarely the only participant in their free-will processing – their motivational and emotional selves usually also play important roles, and sometimes the interests of these other participants win out. When this happens, the executive part of the person – the part that seems to be most clearly identified with the "I" of first-personhood – may feel that its freedom or power has been overridden. But although such a feeling may well arise, this should not be taken to mean that a person has lost their free will because the other parts of their self also contribute to who they are as a person. What is being raised here are issues of human freedom – issues that deserve wider discussion, something which is done in the next and final chapter.

11 How Free Are We?

11.1 Introduction

11.1.1 Independence indeterminism tells us that we human persons have freedoms that we cannot possibly have under absolute determinism, nor under macroscopic determinism with micro-indeterminism. But the question remains: How free are we? In the light of the position that has been developed in this book, and the many points that have been discussed, in this final chapter various aspects of this question are addressed. A start is made by asking a slightly different question: How free am I? and by considering what the "I" of this question may refer to. Next, some points aimed at clarifying the general concept of freedom are discussed. This leads on to a return to one of the central issues of the free-will debate, namely: Could we have done otherwise than what we actually did? After this the question: To what extent are we able to live a self-created life? is considered. Next to be discussed is the question: Are we free enough to be moral agents? And the book ends by asking: Is the free will we have argued for worth having?

11.2 How Free Am I?

11.2.1 From one point of view it might be taken that the "we" of the question "How free are we?" stands for humans as a species but this invites an overly general answer. To expose a more subjective and individual perspective, it is useful to consider the related question: How free am I? and ask what or who the "I" refers to. The "I" could be referring to the whole human person who asks the question. But the "I" might be referring to some part of the person, and quite often this seems to be the case. For example, suppose that while discussing with a friend how a meeting had gone a person says: "I *was* trying really hard to keep my cool, but Bob was setting out to rile me and I finally lost it." In uttering this sentence does the person mean the "I" to refer to their whole self. Logically this doesn't make much sense since it seems it was a part of the person (their executive self) that was trying to keep control of another part of the person (their

265

emotional self). Consider another example: suppose someone says "What I would really like to do is quit my job and become a full-time artist." Again, logically speaking, the "I" cannot refer to the whole person because if the whole person would really like to quit their job then the whole person would indeed quit it. A more accurate but long-winded statement of their predicament would be for them to say something like: "Part of me longs for me to give up my job, but other parts of me resist this and at present they are the parts that win the struggle that is going on within me." Expressed like this it may then be asked: What is the part that longs to become a full-time artist? It seems it is an unsatisfied motivation – a life-hope, perhaps – and is part of the person's motivational self. However, if it is asked where this motivation came from it seems likely that the person's emotional and executive selves will have played an important role in its creation. Consider one further example, the sentence: "I didn't really want to go to the party, but I felt I had to." The various refer-ences of the word "I" in this sentence may be unpacked as follows: "I [at least one part of me] didn't really want to go to the party, but I [a different part, or parts, of me] felt I [me, the whole person] had to [go to the party]."

11.2.2   If it is accepted that in asking themselves How free am I? the "I" may refer to parts of a person's self rather than their whole self, then the three example sentences above may be restated to make this clear. So the first sentence – "I *was* trying really hard to keep my cool, but Bob was setting out to rile me and I finally lost it" – may be restated as "My executive self was trying really hard to control my emotional self from expressing my temper but Bob was setting out to rile me and my executive self finally lost control of my emotional self." And if the person were to ask themselves "How free was I?" with respect to this incident it is not clear how they should answer. Assume they were free from undue constraint, coercion, compulsion, and control so other aspects of their freedom may be considered. As things turned out, their executive self was not free enough to get its way since it lost out to the person's emotional self, so their answer to the question "How free was I" when "I" refers to their executive self must be "not free enough". But on the other hand, if they take the "I" of the question to refer to their emotional self (or rather the an-ger part of it) then their answer would be "free enough". Analysing

266

the second sentence – "What I would really like to do is quit my job and become a full-time artist." – in a similar way gives the person two "How free am I?" questions to answer: "How free am I to satisfy my motivation to become a full-time artist?" and "How free am I to resist becoming a full-time artist?" Given that the person has not actually become a full-time artist, their answer to the first of these questions must be "not free enough", and to the second, "free enough". With respect to the third sentence – "I didn't really want to go to the party, but I felt I had to." – the person again has two questions: "How free was that part of me that didn't want to go to the party?" – with the answer: "not free enough"; and to the question "How free was the part that wanted (i.e. felt duty-bound) to go to the party?" the answer is "free enough".

11.2.3   In this book free will has been taken to be the ability of an agent to self-directively originate satisfaction of their motivations, and to *self-creatively* resolve – through free-will processing – conflicts within their self about what to choose or what to do. But the capacity to exercise free will is only part of the more general concept of freedom, and in answering the question "How free are we?" some consideration should be given to this broader concept.

11.3   The Concept of Freedom

11.3.1   Two related but relatively distinct concepts are often distinguished. One of them is known variously as negative liberty, negative freedom, or freedom *from;* and the other as positive liberty, positive freedom, or freedom *to*. Isaiah Berlin, mainly talking of political or social freedoms, sees negative liberty as involved in the answer to the question 'What is the area within which the subject – a person or group of persons – is or should be left to do or be what he is able to do or be, without interference by other persons'. And he sees the concept of positive liberty as being involved in the answer to the question 'What, or who, is the source of control or interference that can determine someone to do, or be, this rather than that?' (Berlin 2002, p.169) One interpretation of positive freedom is that it is the freedom to act according to one's own free will, or for a group to act according, say, to what the majority wants. However, it may be that the chooser – the individual or the group – may be influenced in 'bad' ways: by irrational beliefs or base desires, for example. And it may therefore be argued that positive freedom actually entails something more: namely, having the power to override such bad influences by 'good' ones. But who or what determines the 'good' influences? Are they to be decided by a higher authority who ensures – through education, conditioning, brainwashing, or whatever – that individuals and groups possess them in such measure that they cannot be overridden. Or are they to be determined by the individual or group by their own processes – through creative self-determination, say? Exactly what constitutes positive liberty is therefore not an easy matter to decide because the question arises: What influences a person when they are creatively controlling and directing their own life? Is it biologically-based motivations, societal conditioning, peer pressure? Or do human persons have a way of truly transcending such influences? The view that is adopted in this book is that human persons have a considerable capacity for creative self-determination but that they remain influenced – directly and indirectly – by factors not of their own making, and that they can never completely transcend these influences.

11.3.2   Early on (see 1.4.7) attention was drawn to the freedoms necessary for voluntary action – namely, being able to choose and act free from undue constraint, coercion, compulsion, and control. To be free in this sense is to possess negative freedom. But possessing negative freedom does not necessarily mean that a person may enjoy a full measure of positive freedom. As Maslow points out (see 10.5.12), if a person's most prepotent needs remain unsatisfied – for instance, if their needs for food, warmth, and security of existence remain unsatisfied – then they shall likely spend most of their time working to satisfy these and shall have little opportunity to enjoy the satisfactions that may be had from attending to their less prepotent needs. With this in mind, it would be reasonable to add freedom from extreme poverty and insecurity of existence to what is required in order to possess negative freedom.

11.3.3   Many (but by no means all) persons in the modern world are able to live much of their life free from undue constraint, coercion, compulsion, and control, and also free from poverty and insecurity of existence. Indeed, some people have most of the wide-ranging freedoms enshrined in such aspirational statements as the Universal Declaration of Human Rights. Additionally, some people have sufficient disposable income and free time to be able to pursue many projects and interests that are not open to those who lack these re-sources. Nevertheless, although some people may have all of these freedoms, they may be severely limited in what they may do because they suffer from serious disability or illness. However, considering only those persons who have full negative freedom in the sense just outlined, does this mean that they have full freedom? Clearly not if they lack positive freedom.

11.3.4 The power to "make our own fate" is at the heart of what positive freedom is about, and it has been argued that independence indeterminism offers a thoroughly naturalistic way of understanding how human persons are such that to some significant extent many of them may achieve this. Furthermore, as just noted, many people in the modern world have more or less full negative freedom, and so it might seem that they have a very full measure of positive freedom. However, human persons do not have ultimate freedom because they cannot completely detach themselves from their genetic inheritance, nor from the influences of their early socialisation, and nor from other influences not of their own making. And having available a huge variety of things that a person may possibly do does not mean that they are free to do these things because many of their contem-plated doings, although desired by certain parts of their self, will be unacceptable to other parts. Hence, doubts remain about just how much positive freedom humans actually have even if they have a good measure of negative freedom. This issue will be returned to shortly (see section 11.5) but first one of the central questions in the free-will debate deserves to be further discussed.

11.4   Could We Have Done Otherwise?

11.4.1   In Chapter 1 (see 1.4.13) a distinction between indiffer-ently originative free will and self-originative free will was made and it was stated that it was the latter sort that would concern us in this book. There are two reasons for not trying to explain indifferently-originative free will: firstly, because there is little scientific (or even every-day) evidence that humans actually possess an Indifferent Will, and secondly because what comes at all close to it tends to be classified as a kind of mindlessness – as, for example, when a person says "I really don't know what came over me". However, there is one aspect of the Indifferent Will that has played an important part in the history of the free-will debate and this is that it gives its possessor the power to choose to do something completely uninfluenced by any factors external to their Indifferent Will. An agent who possesses and uses such a power seems to have a special form of responsibility for what they then do because nothing at all other than this wholly independently operating part of themselves is responsible for their actions. But one consequence of the infinite regress argument (see section 5.5) is that no natural agent can be the sole and completely independent creator of their Indifferent Will, and so they cannot be held *ultimately* responsible for what it does.

11.4.2 It has earlier been suggested (see 1.4.14) that if a psychological agent is self-directively and creatively originating their choices and doings then, because anything that is creatively originated is not wholly prefigured, they could (in a significant rather than a marginal sense) have chosen otherwise. But this point requires more discussion because there are two senses of the word "could" and only one sense is being used – and it is not necessarily the sense that is generally meant when discussing positive freedom, moral responsibility, and similar matters.

11.4.3 Formally, "could" is the past tense of "can" which means "to be able to". However, it is also used as an auxiliary verb with several meanings – in particular it is used to express possibility as, for example, in the sentences "It could be you!" (an advertising slogan used to launch the UK National Lottery in the 1990s), and "There could be a recession next year". By making use of this possibility interpretation the claim that "free will means that, in a given situation, an agent *could* have done otherwise than what they actually did do" becomes the claim that "free will means that, in a given situation, an agent *might* have done otherwise than what they actually did do." This latter claim is more readily realisable than the former because the agent need not possess the *ability* to do otherwise; minimally, all that is required is that the processes that produce their action (or inaction) run indeterministically.

11.4.4 But is the "ability" meaning important when talking about whether an agent "could have done otherwise"? It seems that it may be, since, for instance, it does not appear that a quantum indeterministic process has the *ability* to "do otherwise" even though such a process *might* have turned out otherwise than it did. Like many common words that people generally have little difficult in using, the word ability is a tricky one to define. Dictionaries say **ability** is the 'state of being able; physical, mental, legal, or financial power to do.' And that **able** means 'having adequate power; competent; qualified.' Synonyms for **ability** include 'aptitude, capability, capacity, cleverness, competency, dexterity, expertness, faculty, power, qualification, readiness, skill, talent'. Clearly, ability is a concept that is strongly connected with human persons and human life, but it is also recognised that it has non-human and indeed non-biological meanings.

11.4.5 Whether or not it is correct to say that the free-will process as it is understood according to independence indeterminism means that an agent engaged in such a process has the *ability* to do otherwise, may be an open question. But as a creatively originative process it is necessarily one that might have turned out differently from how it actually did because its outcome is not prefigured. And since there seems nothing particularly odd about saying that human persons have the *ability* to carry out free-will processing, it doesn't seem unreasonable to say that they do indeed have the *ability* to do otherwise. And this is the position that is being adopted in the present work. Nevertheless, the extent to which a person (or more generally, a psychological agent) may "do otherwise" seems to vary a great deal. Indeed, some forms of being able to "do otherwise" are so weak that they cannot reasonably be counted as involving the exercise of free will at all. This point needs a little more discussion.

11.4.6 Often what a person actually does in a decision situation is fairly predictable – except for fine details – and when this is the case it would seem there is no significant sense in which they could have done otherwise. However care must be taken, as the following incident from the author's own experience indicates. I was once talking to some friends about free will and I related an episode that had occurred a short while earlier on holiday when I had been faced with choosing an ice-cream from a stall offering many enticing varieties and I had experienced indecision about what to choose. When I told my friends that, after a good deal of deliberation, I ended up choosing vanilla they burst out laughing saying "we knew that's what you would choose, Mike." This outcome was obvious to them because they knew of my non-adventurous nature in such matters, and they were not at all surprised that I had ended up acting "true to form". Indeed, examples like this seem to provide good ammunition for those who seek to establish that our experience of exercising our free will is nothing but an illusion – as, for instance, Wegner (see section 5.2) has argued. But care must be taken. I believe I certainly was in a condition of genuine indecision and this being the case, under independence indeterminism, it was possible for me, in that specific situation, to have acted "out of character". In fact, prior to this occasion and in similar situations I had occasionally acted out of character in that I had made 'adventurous' choices regarding food, so it seems it was not impossible that I might have done so in the situation in question.

11.4.7 Under independence indeterminism, and using the account of the factors that tend to influence the human free-will process that were discussed in the previous chapter, it should not be difficult to explain what was probably going on within me when I was in a condition of indecision over what ice-cream variety to choose. It seems that what was involved was a relatively weak form of creative origination involving interaction among conflicting and competing motivations – motivations stimulated within me by the situation, and by the process of deliberation itself. In saying that the process was creative in the situation concerned is to say that there was nothing within me – no existing 'machinery', or routines, or pre-established rules – that type-determined the course of the decision-making process taking place. Rather, various aspects of my self – for example, a motivation to be more adventurous, a motivation to not look a fool by taking too long to make a decision, my emotional self producing increasing embarrassment because of my indecision, and my executive self trying to work out what to do to best handle the situation – interacted in a mildly creatively originative fashion and eventually the action of choosing vanilla was produced. It has earlier been argued (see 1.5.7) that such creatively originative interaction is a feature of all conflictual or competitive processes when there is no machinery or set of rules in place that type-determines the way the interaction will proceed and what the outcome will be. And this may be so even when it is apparent what the outcome is likely (but not certain) to be.

11.4.8   Such creative decision-making is to be contrasted with the great deal of more or less automatic decision-making which humans continually carry out. Such automatic decision-making occurs, for example, when a person is driving, or navigating their way through a crowd when walking about, or dealing with routine matters at work, or carrying out some activity which is very familiar to them, or doing innumerable other everyday things. The decision-making is automatic when a person has in place well-developed routines for deciding between the alternatives that arise, and nothing occurs that de-rails the smooth execution of these routines. However, when such decision-making does not go smoothly some sort of creative activity is required – albeit usually of a relatively weak form. But if such a weak form of creativity fails to overcome the problem the person may resort to stronger forms, and even possibly to carrying out full-blown free-will processing to work out what to do.

11.4.9   However, under independence indeterminism and given the apparent nature of human persons it would be incorrect to say that when humans are operating automatically they "could *not* have done otherwise" because humans are not automata: indeed, many mind-brain processes not connected with a person's automatic performances may be active within them at the same time, and these may, in a non-prefigured way, interrupt their automatic activity and lead them to "do otherwise" than automatic execution of the process would allow. For example, while driving in a more or less automatic fashion something not to do with a person's driving may enter their phenomenal consciousness and prompt them to break into the automatic process. For instance, they may suddenly remember that they failed to make a certain phone call before they left which they decide requires, say, that they stop the car and make the call before continuing their journey. What this means is that, in general, a person may be able to "do otherwise" even when they are apparently operating automatically.

11.4.10   There is another way in which, even when a person is operating more or less automatically, they could (might) have done otherwise: namely, that they might make an error in performing an action. Although making an error, or of things not working out as expected, usually has a negative value it should not be thought that this is always so because sometimes, by making use of their creative cap-

273

abilities, errors and unexpected outcomes can be useful to a person. For instance, there are several examples of important advances in science being initiated by a researcher questioning why something unexpected happened rather than just ignoring it as something having gone wrong – Henri Becquerel's discovery of radioactivity, and Alexander Fleming's discovery of penicillin are notable examples. And to show that this can be so in much more mundane cases it is worth mentioning an incident that occurred to the author. Many years ago, I was trying to explain to my aunt and some of my cousins how my struggle to find a naturalistic explanation of free will was going. Having got myself into quite deep water, and in trying to make clear what I was getting at, I made a slip and used the words "independence interaction" instead of "independence indeterminacy". I recognised I had made a slip – because at that time the phrase "independence interaction" had not consciously occurred to me and so was not at all part of my vocabulary – and I corrected it and did not think more about it at the time. However, on the drive home this slip came back into my phenomenal consciousness and I began to think that actually the phrase "independence interaction" was very useful since I needed a term for referring to interactions between things that, prior to their interaction, had been running (at least in some ways) independently of one another. The slip I made does not seem to have been a pure accident. Rather, it seems that my speech production system – a system that runs fairly automatically most of the time – in working to translate my thoughts into speech came up with "independence interaction" as a reasonable way of linguistically expressing what was not yet a fully formed idea in my phenomenally conscious thinking. If this was so then the slip was not actually really a slip at all but an unconsciously operating part of my mind-brain producing something that later, in a phenomenally conscious way, I recognised as having considerable value. Errors of this sort that stimulate creatively originative processes in a person's mind-brain are not uncommon when someone is learning new things or thinking things out for the first time or when engaged in some other creative activity, and they provide further evidence that a person's mind-brain is, among other things, a richly creative domain.

11.4.11   There is another point that needs to be addressed, which is whether human persons can only "do otherwise" because of the indeterminacy of events in their environment. One of the important features of the traditional idea of free will is that the Indifferent Will may make an undetermined choice at any moment. That is, it may "do otherwise" at any instant in time and not via a process – i.e. something necessarily spread out in time. Self-originative free will, on the other hand, is understood to be a process, and although the final product of this process – a decision being reached, or an action being taken – may apparently arise suddenly it is not something that is produced in an instant but over some period of time, sometimes a lengthy, and possibly very lengthy, period of time. During a period of free-will processing external events may arise that may influence the course of the originative process involved, and it might be argued that a person is only able to "do otherwise" because of such events. Although such environmental independence interactions are an important source of originative occurrences during free-will processing they are not the sole source because many independence interactions within and between various parts of the self and the mind-brain of the person concerned will be taking place as well, and although many of these will be chance interactions not all of them will be because some will be a consequence of the person's self-directed creative activity.

11.4.12   It has just been emphasised that exercising self-originative free will is understood to be a process. When this process is very short-lived there is generally not much time for a lot of creative change to take place and the creative activity seems mainly to be confined to creative interaction between conflicting or competing parts of the self. But when a free-will process takes place over a long period creative origination may take place in all the four areas of the ARCS of the human free-will process. For instance, alternatives that were initially under consideration and strongly supported by reasons may get completely overthrown and replaced by their opposites. This may be illustrated by an incident that arose during the author's work on the present project – a project that has been going on for many years and which has involved a great deal of free-will processing.

11.4.13   Several years ago I was trying to find out what I had on some old 5.25-inch floppy discs relating to my thinking on free will. The first file I managed to recover contained the following piece of writing.

19th September 1993

Consider a Meccano set and a person locked in a room using the Meccano set to make constructions. Is the future of the contents of the room determined? We might readily agree that every construction (and all the learning and change to the person) is derived from what was in the room at the start. In other words we are probably happy with the assumption that the room contains the source of everything that subsequently happens within it. Yet we could still feel uncertain that what actually happened in the room was determined at the start. I want to show why this uncertainty is well grounded and indeed develop a system of ideas which will make it seem utterly reasonable that the future of the room is not determined.

I think this example puts my problem very clearly.

In accepting that what happens in the room is in some sense derived from what the room contains at the start we are limiting the space of all possible futures for the room. This may be an effectively infinite space but it is certainly not a completely unconstrained space. We can go further than this and allow that all change that takes place to be fully determined in the sense discussed above [and not included in this extract, but in line with Laplace's account (see 3.2.6)]. Is it still the case that the future of the room is not determined? I want to argue that it is.

Let me be clear about what I am not claiming. I am not claiming that the future that actually came about contains instances of indeterminism and that because of this it was not determined at the start. I want to assume, although it may not be true of the world in light of our understanding of quantum indeterminacy, that the future that actually occurs in the room is fully determined when looked back [at] as a sequence of events. This follows from our assumption that every event (i.e. change) is determined.

276

I seem to have so restricted things that my argument cannot be won. I leave myself a difficult argument to construct but I think, in setting the conditions as I have, that I have avoided most of the grounds that the determinists have for rejecting previous arguments for an open future. What I have done is give the determinists most of their fundamental assumptions, assumptions that are very well supported by our experience of the world.

How will my argument go? The key idea is to question what is in the room at the start and to argue that this is insufficient to determine the full future of the room. This seems to be a nonsense since I am accepting that everything in all the possible futures of the room is contained within the room at the start. Surely it must follow that the room at the start does contain sufficient to determine the full future of the room given that this future must belong in the space of all possible futures. My argument rests on a vital distinction. I want to distinguish between what is in real existence in the room at the start from what is in the room but not in real existence. This non-real contents of the room, its potential, not being real is not properly in the room at the start. Yet, because some of this potential will be actualised and become the future that occurs, it is proper to say that all that may be derived from the room is contained within it, even though much of this contents is not real within the room at the start. But this argument seems to be playing with the idea of real and non-real; this distinction must be justified before we can go any further.

11.4.14 A few points are worth making. First, it should be clear that in 1993 I was strongly wedded to determinism and simply could not bring myself to abandon its basic assumptions. Indeed, I had much earlier been pleased that the computer simulation model of police detective decision-making that I produced as part of my PhD research (Elstob 1975) was 100 per cent deterministic with no random or statistical "fudge factors". Second, and in opposition to my strong attachment to determinism, it seems that I was also convinced that there must be a way forward that would provide a means of escape from the devastating consequences determinism has for the possibility of free will. In other words, there was a good deal of conflict within my mind-brain. Third, and what is perhaps most interesting about this piece of writing, was that I was trying to see "possibility" or "potential" – what later I came to refer to as passive existents, or "no-things" – as somehow existing in but not being a real part of the room until this possibility became actualised through the special powers of a person or similarly creative agent. This half-formed idea later crystallised into the notion of indeterminately changing joint-change (see 2.1.8). Fourth, the present work makes clear that I did eventually resolve the conflicts within my thinking and that I did re-lease myself from the grip that determinism had over me – which il-lustrates that creative origination can not only produce what is not prefigured but can produce outcomes whose emergence was posit-ively opposed by some of the things that existed. Finally, it is worth saying that absolute determinists would deny that my efforts over the years have involved any creative origination at all. Rather, they would insist that although I was still very largely a determinist in 1993, the world (including my mind-brain) at that time was set upon an entirely fixed course that would eventually lead to my abandoning that view and to my producing the present work. Of course independence in-determinists do not accept this view and would insist that I have in-deed been involved in a long creative process whose outcome was neither predetermined nor prefigured. And so independence inde-terminists come up with a very definite "No" in answer to the ques-tion "Is the future of the contents of the room determined?" be-cause they accept that the person in the room may carry out self-dir-ected creative origination in producing some of their Meccano con-structions.

11.5   The Self-Created Life

11.5.1   To be able to self-directively create important aspects of their life is one of the greatest freedoms that humans possess and it is understood to come with the capability of human persons to carry out creative origination – a capability, it seems, that humans have in far greater measure than any other natural beings (or artificial entities) that we know of. Higher animals are able to live a self-originated life to the extent that they are able to originate satisfaction of their motivations. However, their motivations tend to be fairly directly related to their species-specific needs and drives, and most of the time they engage in largely genetically-determined (and so relatively type-determined) directive activities to satisfy them. They engage in creative origination to the extent that they are able to learn and to carry out problem-solving but what they do not appear to do is create the sort of elaborate and distinctly individual lifestructures that are common among humans.

11.5.2   Although many humans do actively work to create a lifestructure that they may rightly claim is their own, not all people are able to do so. Indeed, in some societies even today the structure of a person's life is largely set for them by their family and community. For instance, what work they do, where and in what conditions they live, their economic conditions, their social position, and who they might marry are all largely decided by others according to long-established traditions. There have always been rebels – in the sense of those who go against what family and community expect of them – but it is only in relatively recent times that it has been common for many individuals to largely be in charge of creating the major features of their lifestructure. This freedom is not an unalloyed blessing as it often brings with it much angst – for instance: the angst of indecision, the angst of forestalled hopes, the angst of dissatisfaction with their lot, the angst of possibly losing what they already have, and the angst of envy.

11.5.3   Before going further, something needs to be said about the nature of the creative origination involved in "making our own future" since very often what people originate does not seem to be particularly novel from an external perspective. Creative origination is understood to arises when the types of outcomes and/or things that are originated are not prefigured within the domain concerned. For a person, the domain is themselves and their own lifestructure – not the human race at large, nor even their family and community, except to the extent that these constitute parts of their lifestructure. Many things are largely prefigured in a human being's life such as their overall biological development and ageing, their basic needs and drives, and that they will (almost certainly) undergo socialisation and become a human person. Some things are partially prefigured in that they are concomitants of their socialisation – things such as their language, how to conduct themselves socially, and certain values and beliefs. These things may change as the person lives their life, but initially they are givens. But other aspects of a person's lifestructure are not prefigured. It is these non-prefigured aspects that may be creatively originated and they include such things as the friends a person makes, the special interests they develop, what leisure pursuits appeal to them, and what aspirations and life-hopes they form. As a person grows up, and providing they have the necessary negative freedoms, more aspects of their lifestructure becomes open to them to choose – things such as the job or work they do, where they live, and who they share their life with. However, even though there may be a range of options open to them this does not mean they are necessarily free from external influences in what they choose. Society at large, family, friends, and many other external factors – TV, movies, books, advertising, for instance – may influence what they choose and what they seek to become, and what they want to change about themselves and their current lifestructure. This means that although each person may originate things of a type not prefigured within themselves, and so will carry out creative origination of these things relative to themselves, much of what they create will, relative to society at large, be of a more or less familiar general type and so, relative to this larger domain, may not be regarded as having been creatively originated. It is for this reason that most lifestructures do not, from the outside, seem to be particularly novel.

11.5.4   Although many people in the modern world have sufficient negative freedom to create their lifestructure according to their own preferences not all of them do. This doesn't mean that such people don't have any choices, but rather that they have only a severely restricted range of choices. But being restricted in this way is sometimes a sort of freedom in its own right: a freedom from indecision; a freedom from the pain of having, through exercising their self-originative free will, made bad decisions; and a freedom to blame others for their lack of satisfaction and fulfilment.

11.5.5   Given that independence indeterminism allows people, under the directive influence of their self, not only to originate many aspects of their life, but to *creatively* originate some of them, it must be asked to what extent people are free of external influences and biologically inherited givens in doing this? That is, are human persons ultimately products of nature and nurture alone? If they are, then no matter how creative they may be in responding to the influence of nature and nurture, these factors will be the real drivers of a person's life and it shall have to be accepted that humans have much less freedom than otherwise might be thought. But are humans indeed ultimately products of nature and nurture alone? Determinism says they must be, indeed they must be a necessary consequence of conditions existing long before they were born. Independence indeterminism gives a very different answer because, while acknowledging the influence of nature and nurture, it sees a person's life as being influenced as well by partly self-created criteria for what for them makes for a successful life.

11.5.6 There is no English word that stands for the self-directed striving of a person to create and fulfil their own criteria for a successful life but the little-used word "nisus" may be pressed into service. The *Oxford English Dictionary* tell us **nisus** is a noun of action meaning 'effort, endeavour, impulse', and *Webster's Dictionary* (1998) says it means 'The exercise of power in acting or attempting to act; an effort, endeavor, or exertion.' But in looking for a suitable word I had the additional motive of wanting one that starts with the letter "n" so that it would be possible to state, in a memorable way, that under independence indeterminism there are three (not two) major sources of influence on the life of each person: namely nature, nurture, and nisus. The introduction this third major source of influence immediately changes the basis of many of the discussions that presently take place about whether nature of nurture is the dominant factor in a forming a person's life.

11.5.7 It is all very well to say that a person's nisus is an important influence on their path through life but do people, even under independence indeterminism, have the capability to create some of their own criteria for success and so some of their own motivations? If they don't have this capability – if all their motivations are ultimately derived from biological and socially determined givens – then they have a severely limited ability to shape their lives according to their own self-created criteria since any shaping shall be done to serve (biological and social) criteria not of their own making. However, in understanding human persons to be operating most of the time as self-evaluating executive controlling agents – SEECing agents – it seems that they do have some freedom to shape their lives in ways that are not ultimately dictated by their nature and nurture. The key here is the human capability for self-evaluation. With this capability humans are, in significant ways, able to escape from both their nature and nurture to create for themselves motivations – e.g. values, ideals, life-hopes, projects, ends and purposes – that derive from their own self-created and self-adopted criteria for what they believe counts as success in their lives. And with the power of the executive self to override or sideline the demands of a person's biological and socially determined motivations, it seems humans, in some significant measure at least, do have just such a freedom.

11.6 Are We Free Enough to be Morally Responsible Agents?

11.6.1 The free-will debate has long been concerned with whether humans are sufficiently free to be ultimately responsible for their actions. The infinite regress argument (see section 5.5) suggests that they can never be totally free from influences not of their own creation and so cannot be *ultimately* responsible. It might seem that possession of an Indifferent Will would make humans ultimately responsible because it is not influenced by anything external to itself. However, humans do not choose to possess their Indifferent Will (if indeed they have one), and its fundamental indifference to influences makes it insensitive to moral sanctions. Given that nothing can make natural beings such as humans *ultimately* responsible, and given that, by and large, people do believe themselves to be fully-fledged moral agents, a lesser basis needs to be sought for them having this belief.

11.6.2 It is very widely accepted – by compatibilists as well as most other participants in the free-will debate – that a person cannot be held morally responsible for an action if they could not have done otherwise. This is the so-called Principle of Alternate Possibilities (PAP) and it has already been discussed at some length (see sections 5.8 to 5.10). Under absolute determinism the whole history – past, present, and future – of the universe is fixed, which means no agent could have done otherwise than they did. This does not mean that codes of conduct cannot exist in such a universe, nor that measures

282

to encourage their adoption must be ineffectual since such things might be part of the way the predetermined history of the universe unfolds. This means that absolute determinism is incompatible with the Principle of Alternative Possibilities in spite of arguments to the contrary (see section 5.9).

11.6.3   It has been argued that under independence indeterminism agents who carry out free-will processing may be taken to be involved in self-directed creative origination in producing their choices and doings, and in consequence could (might) – in a strong sense – have done otherwise than they did (see section 11.4). This means that when so operating such agents qualify as moral agents to the extent that alternative possibilities of a significant sort are genuinely open to them. However, there is a problem: to possess moral agency is to possess a special ability – what may be referred to as "moral intelligence". That is, the agent must be able to use the abstract ideas of right and wrong, and other moral concepts, to figure out what would count as morally correct conduct in situations with which they are unfamiliar. At present (since no machines with moral intelligence have been built) it is only human persons of sound mind and of sufficient maturity that are thought to have this ability. Animals are generally thought not to have it. And although it is usually recognised that most young human children have the inherent capability to acquire moral intelligence, it is generally acknowledged that until they grow up and have sufficiently developed this ability they should not be counted as full moral agents. Certainly, animals, young children, and to a limited extent some machines, can learn to respond in the 'right' way to certain types of situation, but they do so without an appropriate appreciation of the *moral* rightness of what they are doing. So, for example, a dog may be trained not to steal food from the table, but it cannot understand the abstract concept: "It is wrong to steal". And the same is true for a very young child.

11.6.4   With these two conditions – alternative possibilities and moral intelligence – assumed to be satisfied, does it follow that a person is morally responsible for their actions? It seems that it is generally believed that they are. And this is believed in spite of it being accepted that often some relevant features of the person's self that led them to act as they did may not be of their own creation. However, people and human societies do often excuse a person of moral responsibility when they believe that an "objective attitude" towards them should be adopted and, in Peter Strawson's words, be treated as 'psychologically abnormal – or as morally undeveloped' (see 5.6.2).

11.6.5   Is there much more to say about moral agency under independence indeterminism? Not really. Providing they believe that they could have done otherwise (in the ways that have been discussed) then most people would probably be prepared to face the music for what they have actually done. It may be that a person's moral code does not accord with that of the society they are in, but then most people would accept that there is little they can do other than leave and find a community with codes more in line with what they believe. The required possession of moral intelligence presents few difficulties, other than a need for a better understanding of what mind-brain capacities it rests upon and how these may be developed adequately within members of a community. Rather, the difficulty with the possession of moral agency only comes to the fore when people really do believe that they and other humans have no capability to "do otherwise". And although the extent to which a society is morally justified in using particular punishments in an attempt to enforce its laws and codes of conduct does raise important and difficult questions, it is not an issue directly related to whether humans are moral agents.

11.7   Is the Free Will That Has Been Argued For Worth Having?

11.7.1   It might be thought that the kind of self-originative free will that independence indeterminism makes possible offers a very incomplete sort of freedom because human persons cannot fully escape the nature that evolution has created for them. If a naturalistic metaphysics existed that was able to explain that humans possessed indifferently originative free will, would such a freedom be more worth having? In one sense it might be because it would be a kind of freedom that transcends the influences that biological and social factors impose on a person. But is this the sort of freedom people really want? It seems not because, as mentioned earlier (see 1.4.11), few people would wish for such an alien-seeming freedom – a freedom that might lead them to say such things as "I don't know what came over me", or "I hardly felt it was me making the choice".

11.7.2   Is there a sort of free will that most people would see as better than either of these two alternatives? And if so, what might it be like? One possibility would be a sort of free will in which a person's executive self had complete rather than only limited power to override their emotional and motivational selves. Would this sort of free will be preferred? Probably not, as long as a person's motivational and emotional selves remained active because the continual non-satisfaction of these parts of their being would not be compatible with them living a fulfilled life. What about a sort of free will that enabled a person to choose and act in the world in such a way that they could live a life of unbroken happiness? If such a free will was possible there seems to be little to be said against it, but – putting aside an artificially induced state of happiness – at present such a form of free will is not available to us. Indeed, the best that seems available to us is the sort of self-originative free will that has been described in this book. But perhaps all that can be claimed for it is that this sort of free will seems more worth wanting than that which determinism is able to offer.

11.7.3   However, is free will worth wanting at all? Might human persons be better off without free will? In this book it has been argued that free will is, among other things, a means by which a psychological agent is able, through self-directed creative means, to resolve conflicts and indecisions within themselves when they have no prefigured means for doing so. All of us know that such difficult-to-resolve conflict and indecision is rarely a happy experience. Might, then, life be better if our nature was such that the internal conflicts and indecisions that arose within us could, rather like animals, always be resolved by prefigured means? We must all answer these questions for ourselves.

References

Ackoff, R. L. and Emery, F. E. *On Purposeful Systems.* London: Tavistock Publications Limited, 1972.

Aune, B. *Metaphysics – The Elements.* Oxford: Basil Blackwell Ltd. 1986.

Austin, J. L. 1956. '"Ifs" and "Cans."' *Proceedings of the British Academy.* Reprinted in J.L. Austin, *Philosophical Papers,* third edition edited by J.O. Urmson and G.J. Warnock. (Oxford: Oxford University Press, 1979.) pp. 205-232.

Ayer, A. J. 'Freedom from Necessity'. *Philosophical Essays* by Professor Sir Alfred Ayer. (London: Macmillan, 1954.) pp. 271-284.

Baer, J. Kaufman, J. C. and Baumeister R. F. (eds.) 2008. *Are We Free.* (Oxford: Oxford University Press.)

Baggini, J. 2015. *Freedom Regained: The Possibility of Free Will.* (London: Granta Books.)

Bandura, A. 2001. 'Social Cognitive Theory: An Agentic Perspective', *Annual Review of Psychology,* 2001, 52. pp. 1-26.

Baumeister, R., Schmeichel, B. and Vohs K. 2007. 'Self-Regulation and the Executive Function: The Self as Controlling Agent'. *Social Psychology: Handbook of basic principles* (Second edition), eds. A. W. Kruglanski & E.T. Higgins. (New York: Guilford.) pp. 516-539.

Bell, J. S. 1985. This quotation appears in the Wikipedia article on Bell's theorem (as of 21st September 2015). It is based on the edited transcript of the radio interview with John Bell of 1985. (See also Davis and Brown 1986.)

Bergson, H. 1911. *Creative Evolution.* (Authorized translation by Arthur Mitchell. London: Macmillan & Co. Ltd., 1911.)

Berlin, I. 2002. 'Two Concepts of Liberty' *Isaiah Berlin – Liberty.* ed. Henry Hardy. (Oxford: Oxford University Press.)

Bishop, R. C. 1999. 'Chaos, Indeterminism, and Free Will'. In *The Oxford Handbook of Free Will,* ed. Robert Kane. (Oxford: Oxford University Press, 2002.).

Block, N. 1995. 'On a Confusion About a Function of Consciousness.' Behavioral and Brain Sciences 18 (2): 227-287. 1995.

Bobzien, S. 1998. *Determinism and Freedom in Stoic Philosophy.* (Oxford: Oxford University Press.)

Campbell D. T. 1974. '"Downward causation" in Hierarchically Organised Biological Systems', in Studies in the Philosophy of Biology, F.J. Ayala & T. Dobzhansky (eds.). (Macmillan Press, 1974). pp. 179-186.

Catholic Encyclopedia 1909. http://www.newadvent.org/cathen/06259a.htm (Accessed 2nd December 2016.)

Churchland, C. 2006. 'Do We Have Free Will?' *New Scientist*, No. 2578, 18th November 2006. pp. 42-45.

Cofer, C. N. and Appley, M. H. 1964. *Motivation: Theory and Research*. (New York: John Wiley & Sons, Inc.)

Davies, P. C. W. and Brown, J. R. 1986. *The Ghost in the Atom: A Discussion of the Mysteries of Quantum Physics* by Paul C. W. Davies and Julian R Brown. (Cambridge, England: Cambridge University Press, 1986/1993. pp. 45-46.)

Dennett, D. C. 1978. 'On Giving Libertarians What They Say They Want'. *Brainstorms: Philosophical Essays on Mind and Psychology*. (Brighton UK: Harvester Press.)

Dennett, D.C. 1984. *Elbow Room – The Varieties of Free Will Worth Wanting*. (Oxford: Clarendon Press.)

Dennett, D. C. 2003. *Freedom Evolves*. (London: The Penguin Group 2003.)

Doyle, B. 2011. *Free Will: The Scandal in Philosophy*. Cambridge. Mass.: I-Phi Press.

Eckman, P. 1994. 'All Emotions are Basic' in *The Nature of Emotions – Fundamental Questions* eds. Paul Eckman and Richard J. Davidson. New York, Oxford University Press, 1994.

Elstob, C. M. 1975. 'The simulation of criminal detection activity'. Unpublished PhD thesis, University of Surrey, Guildford, England.

Elstob, C. M. 1976. 'A Cybernetic Analog for Human Behavior,. Proceeding of the *Third European Meeting on Cybernetics and Systems Research*, Vienna, Austria, 20-23rd April 1976. pp. 97-104.

Elstob, C. M. 1984. 'Emergentism and Mind'. *Cybernetics and System Research 2*, R. Trappl (ed.), 83-88. Elsevier Science Publishers R.V. (North-Holland) 1984.

Elstob, C. M. 1986. 'Indeterminism in System Science'. *Cybernetics and System '86*, R. Trappl (ed.), 79-86. D. Reidel Publishing Company 1986.

Elstob. C. M. 1988. 'Beyond the Machine Model'. *Cybernetics and System '88, 2*, R. Trappl (ed.), 93-100. Kluer Academic Publishers, 1988.

Fitzgerald, E. 1936. *Rubaiyat of Omar Khayyam*, Rendered into English Verse by Edward Fitzgerald. London: The Richards Press, 1936. Stanzas LXXVII - LXXIX. The Second Edition of the Translation. p. 59.

Frankfurt, H. G. 1969. 'Alternate Possibilities and Moral Responsibility.' *The Journal of Philosophy*, 66/23 (1969), 829-839. Reprinted in: *Free Will* second edition, ed. Garry Watson. (Oxford: Oxford University Press, 2003.) pp. 167-176.

Frankfurt, H. G. 1971. 'Freedom of the Will and the Concept of a Person', *Journal of Philosophy*, 68/1 (1971) 5-20. Reprinted in *Free Will* Second Edition, ed. Gary Watson. (Oxford: Oxford University Press, 2003.) pp. 322-336.

Freud, S. 1933. *New Introductory Lectures on Psychoanalysis*.

Freud, S. 1962. *The Ego and the Id*, Trans. Joan Riviere. Revised and newly edited by James Strachey. (London: Hogarth Press and the Institute of Psycho-Analysis.)

Harri-Augstein S. and Thomas, L. 1991. *Learning Conversations*. (London: Routledge.)

Harris, S. 2012. *Free Will*. (New York: Free Press.)

Henson, R. 2015. 'Experimental loophole-free violation of a Bell inequality using entangled electron spins separated by 1.3km.' R. Henson, et al. http://arxiv.org/abs/1508.05949

Hobart, R. E. 1934. 'Free Will as Involving Determination and Inconceivable Without It.' *Mind*, XLIII, No. 169 (January, 1934), pp. 1-27.

Hobbes, T. 1651. *Leviathan*, Ch. XXI 'Of the Liberty of Subjects'. Reprinted in *Classics of Western Philosophy* 3rd Edition, ed. Steven M. Cahn. (Cambridge, Indianapolis: Hackett Publishing Co., 1977.) pp. 501-502.

Honderich, T, 1988. *A Theory of Determinism: The Mind, Neuroscience, and Life-Hopes, Part I*. (New York: Oxford University Press.)

Honderich, T. 1993. *How Free Are You?* (Oxford: Oxford University Press.)

Honderich, T (ed.). 1995. *The Oxford Companion to Philosophy* 1995. (Oxford: Oxford University Press.)

Inwagen, P. van. 1983. *An Essay on Free Will.* (Oxford: Clarendon Press.)

James, W. 1923. 'The Dilemma of Determinism,' *The Will to Believe and Other Essays in Popular Philosophy.* (New York: Longmans, Green.)

Kane, R. 1996. *The Significance of Free Will.* (New York: Oxford University Press.)

Kaptian, T. 2002. 'A Master Argument for Incompatibilism?' in *The Oxford Handbook of Free Will*, ed. Robert Kane. (Oxford: Oxford University Press, 2002. pp. 127-157.)

Kim, J. 1971. 'Causes and Events: Mackie on Causation.' *Journal of Philosophy*, 68 (1971), pp. 426-441. Reprinted in *Causation and Conditionals*, ed. Ernest Sosa. (Oxford: Oxford University Press, 1975.) pp. 48-62.

Kohler, W. 1928. *The Mentality of Apes.* English translation, Harmondsworth, England: Penguin Books. 1957.

Lamont, C. *Freedom of Choice Affirmed.* USA 1967. (London: Pemberton Books, 1971.) Included quotation from: Anatole France, *A Mummer's Tale.* Translation by Charles E. Roche (New York: Gabriel Wells, 1924) p. 10.

Laplace, P. 1820. *Theorie analytique des probabilites* 3rd ed., Paris. Translation as quoted in a footnote in Ernest Nagel, *The Structure of Science.* (London: Routledge & Kegan Paul. 1961.) p. 281.

Levinson, D. J., Darrow, C. N., Klein, E. B., Levinson, M. H. and McKee, B. 1978. *The Seasons of a Man's Life.* (New York: Ballantine Books Random House Inc.)

Limborch, P. 1713. *A complete system or body of divinity, both speculative and practical, founded on scripture and reason*, trans. William Jones, second edition, 2 vols. Quoted in: *Of Liberty and Necessity* by James, A. Harris. (Oxford: Clarendon Press, 2005.) p. 22.

Lorenz, E. 1972.
http://eaps4.mit.edu/research/Lorenz/Butterfly_1972.pdf

Lucretius. *On the Nature of the Universe.* (Harmondsworth, England: Penguin Classics, 1951.)

Mackie, J. L. 'Causes and Conditions' *American Philosophical Quarterly*, 2.4 (October 1965), 245-255 and 261-264. Reprinted in *Causation and Conditionals*, edited by Ernest Sosa, (Oxford: Oxford University Press.) 1975. pp. 15-38.

Maslow, A. H. 1954. *Motivation and Personality* second edition. (New York: Harper & Row, 1970.) Original edition 1954.

McDougall, W. 1908. *An Introduction to Social Psychology*. (London: Methuen & Co. Ltd. Nineteenth edition, 1924.) p. 45. First edition 1908.

McKenna, M, 2015 *Stanford Encyclopedia of Philosophy*, entry on Compatibilism.

Mele, A. R. 2014. *Free – Why Science Hasn't Disproved Free Will*. (New York: Oxford University Press.)

Miles, J. B. 2015. *The Free Will Delusion – How We Settled for the Illusion of Morality*. (Leicester: Matador – Troubador Publishing Ltd.)

Moore, G. E. 1912. *Ethics*, Vol 52 Home University of Modern Knowledge. Available as a digital download from various sites on the internet.

Murray, H. A. 1938. *Explorations in Personality*. (New York: Oxford University Press.)

Neisser, U. 1988. 'Five Kinds of Self Knowledge', *Philosophical Psychology*, Vol. 1. Issue 1. 1988. pp. 35-59.

Nietzsche, F. 1886. *Beyond Good and Evil*. 21. Quoted in 'The Buck Stops – Where?', an interview with philosopher Galen Strawson. www.naturalism.org/strawson_interview.htm. (Accessed 28th June 2015)

Nietzsche, F. 1889. *Twilight of the Idols*. (Section 7: The Error of Free Will). Reprinted as *Twilight of the Idols* and *The Anti-Christ*. Trans. and commentary by R.J. Hollingdale. (Harmondsworth, England: Penguin Books. 1968) p.53.

Oerton, R. 2012. *The Nonsense of Free Will*. (UK: Matador Books.)

Papineau, D. 2016. "Naturalism". *The Stanford Encyclopedia of Philosophy* (Winter 2016 Edition), Edward N. Zalta (ed.), URL = <https://plato.stanford.edu/archives/win2016/entries/naturalism/>.

Peterson, J. L. 1981. *Petri Net Theory and the Modeling of Systems*. (Englewood Cliffs, NJ: Prentice-Hall Inc.)

Pico dela Mirandola, Giovanni. 1486. *Oration de Hominis Didnitate – Oration On the Dignity of Man*. Translated by Elizabeth Livermore

Forbes. In *Bartlet's Familiar Quotations*. 16th edition. Boston: Little Brown and Co.

Pilcher, H. 2013. 'No great flakes'. *New Scientist* 21/28 December 2013, No 2948/2949, pp. 70-71.

Plutarch. *Plutarch's Morals*. Boston: Little, Brown, 1870, Vol. III. p.129. Quoted in Charles Lamont, *Freedom of Choice Affirmed*. USA 1967. Reprinted London: Pemberton Books 1971. p. 13.

Plutchik, R. 1991. *The Emotions: Revised Edition*. (Lanham, USA: University Press of America.)

Popper, K 1982, *The open universe – an argument for indeterminism*. (London: Hutchinson.)

Rees, M. 1997. *Before the Beginning*. (UK: Simon & Schuster.) Quote from The Free Press paperback edition, 2002.

Reiss, S. 2000. *Who Am I: The 16 Basic Desires that Motivate our Actions and Define our Personalities*. (New York: Berkley Publishing Co.) Reprinted Penguin Putnam Inc, 2002. pp. 7-8.

Rescher, N. 1996. *Process Metaphysics: An Introduction to Process Philosophy*. (New York: State University of New York Press.)

Russell, B. 1918. 'On the Notion of Cause', Chapter IX, in *Mysticism and Logic (and other essays)*, Republished Harmondsworth: Penguin Books.1953. p. 175.

Russell, E. S. 1945. *The Directiveness of Organic Activities*. (Cambridge: Cambridge University Press, 1945.)

Steward, H. 2012. *A Metaphysics for Freedom*. (Oxford: Oxford University Press.)

Skinner, B. F. 1971. *Beyond Freedom and Dignity*. (Harmondsworth, UK: Penguin Books, 1975.) First published in the USA 1971.

Sperry, R. W. 1969. 'A Modified Concept of Consciousness', *Psychological Review*, 1969, Vol. 76, No.6, pp.532-536.

Stoljar, D. 2017. "Physicalism". *The Stanford Encyclopedia of Philosophy* (Winter 2017 Edition), Edward N. Zalta (ed.), URL = <https://plato.stanford.edu/archives/win2017/entries/physicalism/>.

Strawson, G. 1994. 'The Impossibility of Moral Responsibility'. *Philosophical Studies*, 75/1-2, 5-24. Reprinted in: *Free Will – Second Edition*, ed. Gary Watson. (Oxford: Oxford University Press, 2003.) pp. 210-228.

Strawson, P. 1962. 'Freedom and Resentment', *Proceeding of the British Academy*, 48(1962), 1-25. Reprinted in: *Free Will* – Second Edition, ed. Gary Watson. (Oxford: Oxford University Press, 2003.) pp.72-93.

Steeves, H. P. 2003. 'Human Animals at the Divide: The Case of Feral Children' Between The Species III, August 2003. http://digitalcommons.calpoly.edu/bts/>

Thomas, L. F. and Harri-Augstein, E. S. 1985. *Self-Organised Learning: Foundations of a Conversational Science for Psychology*. (London: Routledge & Kegan Paul, Reprinted by Routledge 1993.)

Tinbergen, N. 1953. *Social Behaviour in Animals*. London: Chapman and Hall.

Tse, P. U. 2013. *The Neural Basis of Free Will: Criterial Causation*. (Massachusetts, USA: MIT Press.)

Turner, M. n.d. "Pilot wave theory, Bohmian metaphysics, and the foundations of quantum mechanics" The TCM Group, Cavendish Laboratory, University of Cambridge. Available at: www/tcm.phy.cam.ac.uk/~mdt26/PWT/lectures/bohm7/pdf

Twain, M. 1883. *Life on the Mississippi*. Reprinted London: Oxford University Press, 1962. p. 246.

Wallas, G. 1926. *The Art of Thought*. (New York: Harcourt, Brace and Company, 1926). Republished UK, Tunbridge Well: Solis Press. 2014.

Watson, G. 1975. 'Free Agency.' *The Journal of Philosophy*, 72/8 (1975), 205-20. Reprinted in: *Free Will* second edition, ed. Garry Watson. Oxford: (Oxford University Press, 2003.) p. 341.>

Webster's Dictionary 1998. *The New International Webster's Comprehensive Dictionary of the English Language – Deluxe Encyclopedic Edition*. (Naples, Florida: Trident International.)

Wegner, D. M. 2002. *The Illusion of Conscious Free Will*. (Cambridge USA: The MITPress.)

Weir, M. K. 1984. *Goal-Directed Behaviour*. (London: Gordon and Breach.)

Weir, M. K. and Wale, A. P. 2011. 'Revealing non-analytic kinematic shifts in smooth goal-directed behaviour'. *Biological Cybernetics*, (2011) 105:89-119.

Woodfield, A. 1976. *Teleology*. (Cambridge, UK: Cambridge University Press.)

Wolf, S. 1990. *Freedom Within Reason*. (New York: Oxford University Press.)

Index

Appley, M.H, 10.5.1
ARCS of free-will processing, 1.5.4, 8.1.2, 10.7.10, 11.4.12
Aristotle, 3.1.2, 5.5.1
Arrow of time, problem of §9.8
Arrow paradox, 9.2.3
Artefact, 9.2.10, 9.9.5/7
"Artificial directiveness", §7.4
Artificial intelligence (AI), 1.5.3, 8.4.2
Artificial,1.1.7, 2.3.11, 8.2.2
Assumption of independence of change, see Independence of change, assumption of
Aune, B, 5.8.3
Austin, J.L, 5.9.2
Authorship emotion, 5.2.9
Autonomous, 7.3.2, 9.2.9, 10.6.3, see also: Agent, autonomous
Autonomy, 1.4.11, 7.3.3, 10.5.8
Awareness, 2.3.8, 2.4.3, 5.2.4-6, 5.7.6, 10.2.6, 10.3.4, 10.7.4
Ayer, A.J, 5.8.3

Baggini, J, 8.4.10
Bandura, A, 10.7.3
Baumeister, R, 10.7.4
Behaviourist, 8.4.2
Beliefs, 1.1.10, 2.1.4, 3.6.6/7, 5.4.4, 10.2.15, 10.5.8, 10.7.1/3, 11.3.1, 11.5.3
Bergson, H, 9.2.3/4
Berlin, I, 11.3.1
Big bang, 3.4.9
Billiard balls, 2.1.9/10, 6.4.4-8
Biology, 1.6.5/6, 2.3.10, 8.5.3, 9.2.9, 11.5.7
Bishop, R, 4.4.4
Bobzien, S, 1.3.2
Body/mind states, 10.6.2/6
Bohm, D, 3.5.7
Bell's Theorem and J.S. Bell, §3.5
Block, N, 10.2.6
Brain, 1.2.5, 1.4.7/8/12, 2.5.3-5, 5.2.4/5/7, 5.5.6, 5.9.5, 8.3.3, 9.2.11, 9.7.1 see also Mind-brain

Butterfly effect, 4.4.3

Calculus, infinitesimal, 9.2.4/5
Campbell, D.T, 9.6.1
Catholicism, 1.3.7, 5.5.2
causa sui, 5.5.2/3
Causal, 1.1.5/7, 1.2.3/8, 1.3.6, 1.4.12, 1.7.2, 2.1.5/6/9, 2.5.5, 3.3.2/9,
  §4.3, 4.7.2, 5.2.7, 5.3.3, 5.4.2/11, 5.5.1, 5.9.5, 6.2.5-7, §6.5, 6.6.1,
  9.2.11, 9.3.5, 9.6.2, 10.2.11
Causal chains/links, 1.2.3, 1.3.6, §4.3, 4.7.2, 5.4.11, 9.3.5
Causal networks, gaps within and between, Preface, 1.1.4/7, 3.6.8,
  6.1.4, 9.1.2
Causation, 3.3.2, 9.2.11
Causation, agent, see Agent causation
Causation, criterial, §5.4, 5.8.1
Causation, downward, see: Downward causation
Causation, pattern-based, §5.4
Cause, 1.2.3, 1.3.3/6, 1.4.5/7/10, 1.7.2, 3.1.4, 3.2.3/6/8, §3.3, §3.4,
  3.6.2/6, 4.3.1-3/5, 5.2.7, 5.4.11, 5.5.1, 6.1.4, 6.5.2, 9.2.11, 10.6.7
Cause, conspicuous 3.3.6/7/9
Cause, full 3.3.6-10
Cause and effect, 3.1.4, 3.2.3, §3.3, §3.4, 6.52, 9.2.11
Cause and effect, law of 1.7.2, 3.1.4, 3.2.8, 3.3.9, 3.6.2, 6.1.4, 9.2.11
Cause and effect, temporal gap 3.3.9/10
Chance, 1.1.2/6/9, 1.2.3, 1.5.6, §2.2, 2.3.1-5/12, 2.5.10, 3.4.6, 3.6.4,
  4.1.1, 4.2.3, §4.3, 5.3.3, 5.5.2/6, 5.7.6/7, 5.10.6, 7.2.2-6, 8.2.2,
  8.3.6/9/10/15, 8.4.2/14, 9.3.6, 9.6.3/4, 11.4.11, see also Inde-
  terminism
Chance origination, 1.1.6, 1.1.9, 1.5.6, 2.2.2, 2.5.10, 3.4.6, 9.3.6, see
  also Undirected independence interactions
Change, condition-determinate, 3.3.3-5
Change, continuous, 9.2.4/5
Change, discontinuous, 9.2.5
Change, disruption to, 2.1.11
Change, independence of, see Independence of change
Change, synchronous & non-synchronous, 2.1.5-11, 3.3.5, 6.2.5-7,
  §6.5, §6.6
Change, time-determinate, see Time-determinate, (change/laws, etc),

Chaos/chaos theory, §4.4
Character, human, 1.3.7, 1.4.5/13, 5.5.2. 8.4.15, 9.7.2, 10.3.3, 10.4.9, 11.4.6
Chemistry/chemical, 1.1.4, 1.5.1, 2.2.1/3, 4.4.2, 4.6.5/6, 7.4.1, 7.5.3, 8.3.3/16, 9.2.9
Child/children, 5.6.2, 5.7.5, 10.3.2, 10.4.4, 10.5.6/11/12, 10.6.4, 11.6.3
Chimpanzees, insight learning, 8.4.4-11
Chrissipius, 1.3.2
Churchland, P, 1.4.12, 2.5.5, 9.2.11
Circumstances, 1.2.2/5, 1.3.7, 1.4.9/13, 1.5.1, 2.2.1, 2.3.6/7/9/12, 2.5.9/10, 4.3.2, 5.3.4, 5.9.5, 7.2.4-7, 7.3.2-6, 7.5.4/7, 7.6.3, 10.2.6, 10.7.1
Civilization, see Realm of civilization
Clark, T, 9.2.11
Clocks, 3.3, 4.6.5, 6.2.5, 6.3.7, 6.5.3/4, §6.6
Clockwork, 1.2.7, 3.5.5, 4.6.6
Coercion, 1.4.7, 5.9.3/5, 11.2.2, 11.3.2/3
Cofer, C.N, 10.5.1
Cogito model, §5.3
Cognition/cognitive, 1.6.2, 8.4.8, 10.1.3, §10.2, 10.3.1, 10.7.2/10
Comfort motivations, 10.5.13
Compatibilism compatibilists, 1.3.2-6, 1.4.4, 3.1.4, 3.4.1/6, 5.6.1/5/7, 5.7.8, §5.8, 5.9.1, §5.10, 11.6.2
"complete picture", 4.2.3, 4.7.2, 6.5.2
Complex adaptive systems, 4.6.4
Compulsion, 1.4.7, 10.4.3, 11.2.2, 11.3.2/3
Computer, 1.2.5, 2.4.3, 3.6.9, 4.1.1, 4.2.1, 4.4.3, 4.6.5, 7.6.1, 8.4.10/13, 9.2.9, 10.4.5, 10.5.13, 11.4.14
Concentration, 10.7.1
Conditioning, 8.1.2, 11.3.1, operant 8.4.2
Conflictual-competitive-cooperative interaction, 1.5.4/5/7, 2.4.2:4, 4.6.1, 8.3.20, 10.5.10, 11.4.7

Conflict/indecision, 1.4.15/16, 1.5.3/5, 1.6.4, 2.3.2, 10.1.1, 10.4.6, 11.4.7, 11.5.2/4
Conflict/indecision, blanking of 1.4.16, 1.6.4, 10.5.13, 10.7.9

Creative origination, Preface, 1.1.1/2, 1.4.14, §1.5, 1.7.4, 2.3.2, §2.4, 2.5.6-10, 3.6.9, 4.6.1, 5.4.9, 6.4.8, 6.6.6, 7.5.9, 7.6.4/6, Ch8, 9.1.3, 9.2.10, 9.5.7/8, 9.9.5-7, 10.1.1, 10.4.4/6, §11.4, 11.5.1/3/4, 11.6.3

Creative origination, degrees of, Low-end §8.3, Mid-rang §8.4, High-end §8.5

Creative origination, directed, 1.1.2, 2.5.7, 5.4.10, 7.5.9, 8.4.14/15, 8.5.3, 9.1.2/3, 9.6.4, 10.7.1, see also Creative self-directed origination

Creative origination and chance, 1.5.6, 8.2.2

Creatively originative processes, 1.5.1-8, 5.4.6, 5.5.7, 5.9.6/7, §8.3, 8.4.14/15, 9.6.3, 11.4.5/10, 11.5.5

Creative self-determination, 1.1.1, 11.3.1

Creative self-directed origination, 11.4.2, 11.5.5/6, 11.6.3, 11.7.3

Criterial causation, see: Causation, criterial

Criterial decoders, 5.4.11/12

Criteria, for success in life, 1.6.4, 7.6.3-6, 10.7.5-8, 11.5.7

CSE, see: Conscious subjective experience

Culture/cultural, 1.5.3, 2.4.8, 5.10.4, 7.6.4, 8.2.7, 8.4.12, 9.7.4, 10.2.15, 10.4.1/3/4, 10.6.4, 10.7.4/7

"dated and located", 2.1.4, 3.6.2, 6.2.5, §6.3, 6.4.7, 6.5.3, 7.2.6, 8.2.1, 9.3.2/3, 9.9.4

De Broglie, 3.5.7

Decision-making/ decision process, 1.2.4/5, 1.3.3, 1.4.14, 5.2.10, 5.3.3, 5.3.5, 5.4.3, 7.5.5, 10.3.4, 10.6.8, 10.7.1, 11.4.7/8/14

de novo origination, 1.2.4/5/9, 1.3.6, 1.5.6, 5.1.2, 5.3.6/7, 5.4.13/15, 5.5.6/7, 5.10.9, 7.2.2, 7.3.2/3/7/8, 9.4.3, 9.5.5/7, 9.7.4, 9.8.3, 9.9.3

Deliberated/deliberation, 1.5.5, 5.7.5, 10.2.16, 11.4.6/7

Dennett, D, 1.3.3, 5.10.5-8

Dependence interactions/relations, 1.1.7, 3.6.3/4/6, 4.1.1, 4.7.1, 6.1.5, 6.2.5, 8.3.1, 9.3.5/6, 10.4.3

Desires, 1.3.2, 1.4.11, 3.4.5, 5.1.2, 5.5.2, §5.7, 5.10.3, 8.4.12/13, 10.5.1/6/11-13, 10.3.4, 10.6.9, 10.7.8, 11.3.1, see also Motivation

Determinism/determinists, §1.1, §1.3, 1.4.5, Ch3, 4.2.3, §4.5, 5.3.6, 5.4.3, see also: Absolute determinism

Determinism, adequate, see "adequately determined"

Determinism, logical, 3.1.2/3

Determinism, macroscopic, 1.2.8/9, 2.1.10, 3.6.2, 4.1.1, 4.2.2/3, 4.4.1, 4.7.1/5, 5.3.1, 5.8.2, 11.1.1
Determinism, near, 1.2.8
Deterministic, Preface, 1.1.5/6/7, 1.2.5/7-9, 1.3.3/6, 2.1.11, 2.4.3, 2.5.5, 3.1.3, 3.2.3, 3.4.7, 3.6.1/2/6, 4.1.1/2, 4.2.1, 4.3.4, 4.4.3, 4.5.1/4/6, 4.6.5, 4.7.1-3, 5.1.2, 5.3.5/6, 5.4.12, 5.5.6, 5.6.7, 5.9.7, 5.11.4/7, 6.3.4, 6.4.1/3/7, 7.3.3/4/7/8, 8.3.1, 9.2.11, 9.7.3, 9.9.2, 11.4.14
Determinists and Absolute Determinists, 2.5.8, 3.6.4, 5.4.3, 6.5.2, 7.3.1, 11.4.13/14
Determinists, hard, see Hard determinists
Directed happening, 7.2.3-9
Directed (and non-chance) independence interactions, 1.1.9, 1.3.6, 2.3.2/6, 2.4.9, 5.4.10
Directedness/directiveness, 7.2.3-5/9, 7.3.1, §7.4
Directed origination, 1.1.2, 1.1.9, 1.2.5/6, §2.3, 2.5.7/10, 6.6.6, Ch7, see also Self-directed origination, Creative origination, directed
Directed outcome, 1.1.9, §2.3, §7.2, §7.3, 7.4.1/2, §7.5, 7.6.1/2, 8.3.15/18, 8.4.7, 10.2.2/6, 10.7.5, 11.4.11
Directive activity, 1.1.9, §2.3, 4.3.5, 7.2.4-9, §7.5
Directive system, 1.1.9, §2.3, §2.4, 5.4.3/4, 5.10.8, 7.2.4/6/9, §7.3, 7.4.1/2, §7.5, 8.2.2, 10.2.7
Disruption, 1.5.5, 2.3.12, 4.6.4, 7.5.4, 8.3.1, 10.3.5, 10.6.3, 10.7.1
"dominoes world", 1.3.3
Downward causation, §9.6
Doyle, B, §5.3
Drives, 1.6.3, 10.5.1, 10.6.11, 11.5.1/3/5, see also: Motivation

Eckman, P, 10.6.
Ecosystem, 2.5.9
Ego, 1.6.2/3, 10.7.3
Einstein, A, 1.2.7, 3.4.8, 3.5.2, 4.5.1
Effect, 3.3.6, full, 3.3.6, conspicuous, 3.3.6 see also cause and effect, and cause and effect law of
Emergent, 1.1.5, 1.3.6, §9.5
Emergentism/emergentists, 2.5.8/9
Emergent properties, §9.5

tion: snowflake production 8.3.5, meiosis 8.3.6-16, Jumbled table-top and creative origination, 8.3.19, System properties: mobile phone 9.3.5,9.5.2, Downward causation: rolling wheel 9.6.1, Open future: Meccano constructions in a locked room 11.4.13

Executive control, 2.3.8, 5.4.10, 5.10.5, §7.6

Executive self, 1.5.5, 1.6.3/4, 5.4.8/10, 5.10.5, 7.6.2/3, 10.3.4/7, 10.4.2/5, 10.5.9/10, 10.6.8/11, §10.7, 11.2.1/2, 11.4.7, 11.5.7, 11.7.2

Existence, 1.1.4/7/10, 1.2.8, 1.5.6/8, 2.1.8, 2.4.2, 2.5.9, 3.1.2/3, 3.3.6/8, 3.5.5, 3.6.7, 4.5.1/3/6, 4.7.5, 6.1.3/4/5, 6.4.3, 8.5.3, 9.4.1, 9.5.3, 9.7.6, 9.8.3, §9.9

Existence, indefiniteness of, Preface, 3.6.8, 9.1.2

Extraversion, 10.3.5

Family, 1.5.5, 4.6.3, 8.4.12, 10.3.2, 10.4.1/3/4/5/10, 10.5.6//11/12, 10.7.5/7, 11.5.2/3

Far-future, 3.6.3-5, 6.1.5/6, 10.7.3, see also: Near-future.

Fate, 1.2.2/5, 1.4.5/14, 3.2.1-3, 7.2.3

Fate, "making our own", 1.1.1/2, 1.2.2/3, 1.3.4, 1.4/14, 11.3.4

Fermat's principle, 7.4.1

Finite state machine, 4.5.4

First cause, 1.2.3

Foresight, 10.7.1

Frankfurt Cases, 5.9.3-8

Frankfurt, H, §5.7, 5.9.3-8, 5.10.3

Freedom, 1.2.6, 1.3.2/7, 1.4.11, 5.3.3, 5.4.14, 5.5.2, 5.6.1, 5.7.1/6, 5.10.4/7, 7.6.4, 8.4.2/10, 9.6.1, 10.4.1/6, 10.5.8/12, 10.7.10, 11.1.1, 11.2.2/3, §11.3, 11.5.1/2/4/5/7, 11.7.1

Freedom, negative, §11.3

Freedom, positive, §11.3

Free will, (main entries) 1.1.1, 1.2.2/6, §1.3, §1.4, 1.6.5, 3.2.3, 3.3.12, 3.4.5/6, Ch5, 9.5.8, §11.7

Free-will debate, Preface, 1.2.4, 1.3.2, 1.4.14, 1.6.1, 5.1.1/2, 5.2.6/10, 5.5.2, 5.8.1, 5.9.3, 11.1.1, 11.3.4, 11.4.1, 11.6.1/2

Free will, indifferently originative, 1.4.13, 5.8.1, 9.2.11, 11.4.1/11, 11.6.1, 11.7.1

Free will, originative, 1.4.13, 3.4.5/6, 5.9.7

Free-will process/processing, 1.4.14-16, 1.5.4-6/8, 1.6.3/4, Ch5, 7.5.5, 7.6.3/6, 8.1.2, 9.5.8, 10.1.1, 10.3.7, 10.4.7, 10.7.10, 11.2.3, 11.4.5/7/8/11/12,
Free will, self-originative, 1.4.13, 5.1.2, 5.3.6, 5.4.4/15, 5.8.1, 11.4.1/11/12, 11.5.4, 11.7.1/2
Free will, standard positions §1.3,
Free will, theological, 1.2.6
Freud, S, 1.6.2/3, 10.2.8, 10.7.3
"fusion indeterminacy", 5.5.7/8,

Geiger counter, 1.2.9, 4.4.4
Genes/genetic, 1.3.5, 2.4.8, 5.7.7, 7.5.8, 7.6.2-6, 8.2.2/4, 8.3.7-16, 9.2.10, 9.6.3, 10.2.15, 10.3.6/7, 10.4.6, 10.5.12, 10.6.11, 10.7.5, 11.3.4, 11.5.1/5
God, 1.2.5-7, 2.1.6, 5.2.2, 5.5.2
Goal, 1.1.9, 1.6.3, 2.3.3-5, 5.10.6, 7.2.1, 7.3.4, 7.5.4, 7.6.2, 8.4.7-12, 10.3.7, 10.4.3-5/10, 10.5.1/2/4/11, 10.7.3/5/8
Goal-directed activity/behaviour, 2.3.4/7, 7.2.1/9, 8.4.8, see also Directive activity

Habit/habitual, 1.4.14, 1.5.5, 5.4.4, 7.6.2, 8.1.2, 10.3.6,10.4.3, 10.6.2
Hamilton's principle, 7.4.1
Hard determinists, 1.3.5, 1.4.6, 5.9.1
Harri-Augstein, S, 2.4.5
Harris, S, 9.2.11
Heisenberg's uncertainty principle, 9.1.2
Henson, R, 3.5.4
Hidden variables, 3.5.2/3
Higher-order desires, 5.1.2, §5.7, 5.9.3, 5.10.3, 10.7.8
Hobart, R.E, 1.4.11
Hobbes, T, 1.3.2
Homeostasis, 2.3.10, 7.5.3
Honderich, T, 1.2.8, 1.4.6
Human being, 1.6.1, 2.3.8, 5.6.2, 5.7.7, 8.3.7, 10.3.1, 10.4.1, 10.5.12, 11.5.3
Human person, 1.4.16, 1.3.3/4, 1.6.1-4, 2.3.8, 2.4.8, 5.4.4/5, 5.6.3, 5.7.6/7, 5.10.4, 7.1.1, 7.6.4, 8.1.2, 9.1.3, 8.4.2/4/13, 8.5.1, 10.1.1/2/4, 10.2.4/7/10, 10.2.7/8/11/14, 10.2.1, 10.3.1, 10.4.1,

10.5.4, 11.2.1, 11.3.1/4, 11.4.4/5/9/11, 11.5.1/3/5/7, 11.6.3,
  11.7.1/3,
Human realm, 1.5.2/3/7/9, 2.5.9, 7.5.1, 9.9.7
Human self, 1.1.1, §1.6, 10.1.3, §10.3, 10.7.4
Hume, D, 3.3.8

"I" of first-personhood, 10.7.10, 11.1.1, §11.2
Id, 1.6.2
Idealists, 6.1.3/4
Illusionists, 1.3.5
Illusion of free will, 3.6.7, §5.2, 9.2.11, 11.4.6
Imagining, 1.5.8, 2.1.6/8, 2.4.3, 5.3.4, 5.4.8/10, 6.44/7, 7.3.8, 8.4.8,
  10.1.1, 10.2.2/10/13/14, 10.3.5, 10.7.3
Incompatibilists, 1.3.5/6, 5.6.1/5/7
Indecision, see Conflict/indecision
Indefiniteness of existence, see Existence, indefiniteness of.
Independence indeterminism, Preface, §1.1, 1.2.1/10, 1.3.6, 1.4.13,
  1.5.1/2/6/8, §1.7, Ch2, 3.1.3, 3.2.6, §3.6, Ch4, 5.3.7, 5.4.5/10,
  5.5.7, 5.10.8, §6.1, 6.2.3, 6.4.8, 6.5.1, 6.6.6, 7.3.7/8, 7.4.1, 8.2.1,
  8.3.1/4/16, Ch9, 10.7.2, 11.1.1, 11.3.4, 11.4.5-7/9/14, 11.5.5-7,
  11.6.3/5, 11.7.1
Independence indeterminism v. determinism, 1.1.10, §3.6, 6.1.5/6,
  §9.3
Independence indeterminism, wider significance, §2.5, Ch9
Independence indeterminists, 3.6.4, 5.4.3, 6.1.5, 7.3.1, 11.4.14
Independence interaction(s), §1.1, 1.5.1/6, 2.1.6-11, Ch2, §3.6, 4.1.1,
  §4.2, §4.3, 4.6.6, 4.7.1/2, 4.7.4/5, 5.4.10, 5.5.7, 6.1.5/6, 6.4.8,
  7.2.2, 7.3.2, §8.3, 9.4.3, 9.5.5/6, 9.7.3/4, 9.8.2/3, 9.9.3/4, 11.4.10
Independence interactions, anticipation of, 3.6.2/4, 6.1.5, 7.5.5, 10.7.1
Independence interactions, directed: see Directed independence in-
  teractions
Independence interactions, non-directed see: Undirected independ-
  ence interactions
Independence interactions, type-determined, 1.5.1, 2.2.1, 2.3.2/8,
  2.5.9, 3.6.2/6, 4.1.1, 4.7.1, 9.5.5, 10.7.2
Independence of change, assumption of, §1.1, §2.1, 3.6.4, 4.5.3, 4.7.1,
  Ch6, 7.1.4, 7.3.9, 9.1.2, 9.3.3, 9.8.3, 9.9.2-4
Independence of change, conditions for, 2.1.5, 6.5.1

Independence of change, true, Preface, 1.1.3/9, 2.1.3/4, 6.5.2, 9.3.2, 9.8.3

Independence of change, type and token, §6.3, 6.4.7, 9.3.2

"independent causal chains", §4.3

Indeterminately changing joint-change, 2.1.8, 11.4.14, see also, Joint-change

Indeterminism, 1.1.2, 1.4.11, 3.4.7, 3.6.1, 4.2.2/3, §4.3, 4.4.4, 4.6.6, 5.2.9, 5.3.35/7, 5.4.11, 5.5.6, 11.1.1, 11.4.13

Indeterminism/indeterminacy, macroscopic, 1.2.8/9, 3.6.1, 4.1.2, 4.3.6, 4.7.1/5, 5.5.6, 8.3.1

Indeterministic, 1.1.3, 1.2.5/9, 1.4.7, 2.1.11, 3.5.1, 3.6.1/4, 4.1.1, 4.2.2/3, 4.6.6, 4.7.5, 5.3.5, 5.4.12, 6.1.5, 7.3.7, 9.2.10, 11.4.3, see also, Event, quantum indeterministic

Indeterministic, quantum, 1.2.5/9, 1.3.6, 1.5.1/6, 2.5.8, 3.5.11, 4.4.1/4, 5.5.5/6, 5.8.1, 5.10.9, 6.3.4, 6.4.8, 8.3.4, 9.2.11, 9.5.5, 11.4.4, see also, Event, quantum indeterministic

Indifferently originative free will, see Free will, indifferently originative

Indifferent Will, 1.4.9-13, 5.7.6, 9.2.11, 11.4.1/11, 11.6.1

Inferencing, 10.2.10/14

Infinite regress, 5.5.2/4, 5.7.67, 11.4.1, 11.6.1

Influence relations, §4.6, 9.3.5/6, 9.9.7, see also RENOIR

Initial conditions, 2.4.3, 4.2.3, 4.4.1/3/4

Input(s), 2.2.3, 2.5.3/4, 3.3.3, 4.4.1, 4.5.4-6, 5.4.11/12, 7.3.7, 9.3.5, 9.5.4/5, 10.7.1

Input/output relations/interactions, 9.3.6, 9.5.4/5

Instant, 1.1.3/10, 1.4.7, 3.2.6, 3.4.8, 4.5.4, 4.7.4, 5.3.3, 6.4.4/5, 9.2.4/6, 9.4.2/3, 11.4.1

Instantaneous state (of the world/universe), 1.1.8, 2.1.2, 3.3.10, 3.4.4/7-9, 6.4.2, §9.2, 9.3.2, 9.9.2

Instinct, 1,4,14, 1.6.2/3, 2.4.5, 7.6.2, 8.1.2, 10.2.15, 10.5.1/7, 10.6.11

Intentions, 1.6.3, 9.2.11, 10.4.3, 10.5.2/4, 10.7.1/3

Internal states, 4.5.4-6

Intuition/intuitively, 3.2.8, 3.4.2/4, 5.2.9, 6.1.4, 6.5.1, 7.2.1, 8.2.1/4, 9.4.1, 10.2.14

INUS condition, 3.3.7/8

Inventiveness/invention, 1.5.3, 2.4.4, 2.5.9, 8.2.6, 8.3.18, 8.4.10/13, 9.5.8, 10.7.1

Inwagen, van P, §3.4, 4.3.3, 6.4.2, §9.2, 9.4.3

James, W, 3.2.5, 3.4.1, 6.5.2, 10.5.6/8
Joint-change/joint change 2.1.5/8, 2.5.5, 3.6.4, 4.3.2, 5.4.5, 6.1.5,
    6.5.1/4, 7.3.8, 9.1.2, 9.9.3, 11.4.14
Judgement, 5.10.3, 8.3.2, 10.7.1

Kane, R, §5.5, 5.8.1
Kim, J, 3.3.2, 9.7.2, 9.9.2
Kohler, W, 8.4.4-11
Knowledge, 1.2.1, 1.5.2/3, 1.6.4, 2.1.4, 2.3.4/7, 2.4.7/8/10, 3.6.2,
    4.2.1/3, 4.3.2, 5.10.1, 6.1.5, 6.5.2/3, 7.2.5/6, 7.5.5, 8.3.3,
    8.4.4/8/12, 9.5.8, 9.9.4/5, 10.2.14, 10.4.3/5, 10.5.11, 10.7.1

Lamont, C, 3.2.7
Language, 1.3.3, 4.3.4, 7.5.9, 8.4.12, 10.2.2/4/11, 11.5.3
Laplace, P-S, 3.2.6, 11.4.13
Laws of Nature, 1.1.3/10, 3.2.6/7, 3.4.3/4/7, 4.2.3, 4.3.3, 4.7.4, 6.4.1-
    3/8, 9.2.1/7/8/11, 9.3.2, 9.4.3, 9.5.5, 9.9.2
Laws of science/physics, 1.1.4, 1.2.1/7, 2.1.6, 3.4.8, 4.1.1, 4.5.1/2,
    9.2.5, 9.3.3, §9.8
Learning, 1.3.3, 1.5.2/3, 2.3.7, 2.4.2/4/5/8/9, 4.6.4, 5.4.4, 7.5.4/6,
    8.2.6, 8.3.18, §8.4, 9.5.8, 10.2.1/10/11/15/16, 10.5.6, 10.7.1/4,
    11.4.10/13, 11.5.1, 11.6.3
Learning, directed, 2.4.5, 8.4.12, 10.7.1
Learning, insight, 8.4.4-11
Learning, trial-and-error, 8.4.2-5
Learning to learn, 2.4.5
Le Chatelier's principle, 7.4.1
Leibniz's principle of sufficient reason, 3.1.4, 3.6.2
Leucippus, 3.2.2
Levinson, D.J, 10.4.8-11, 10.7.9
Libertarians, 1.3.5/6, 1.4.13, 3.1.4, 3.4.6, 5.2.9, 5.6.5, 5.8.3, 5.9.6,
    5.10.5/9
Liberty of indifference, 1.4.7, 5.8.1, see also Free will, indifferently
    originative
Libet, B, experiments, 5.2.6-8

Life, (biologically related references), 1.2.8, 3.3.4, 4.6.6, 7.5.9, 8.2.2, 8.3.6, 9.2.10

Life-hopes, 1.6.3, 10.4.3/5, 10.5.2/4, 10.7.7, 11.5.3/7

Life, realm of. See Realm of life

Lifestructure, 1.6.4, 2.4.8, 4.6.5, 10.1.3, 10.2.16, 10.3.1, §10.4, 10.7.1/8, 11.5.1:4

Life structure, 10.4.7-11, 10.7.9

Limborch, P. van, 1.4.9

Living will, 10.2.9

Lockstep, 1.1.3/6, 2.1.3/4/7, 3.4.8, 3.6.4/6, 4.3.5, 6.1.5, 6.4.5, 9.8.3

Lorenz, E, 4.4.3

Luck, 1.2.2/9, 5.10.7

Lucretius, 3.3.2/3

Mackie, J.L, 3.3.7

Macroscopic determinism, see: Determinism, macroscopic

Macroscopic indeterminism, see Indeterminism/indeterminacy, macroscopic

Macroscopic origination, 1.2.10, 8.3.1

Macroscopic level/realm/world, 1.2.8/9/10, 1.2.10, 2.1.10, 3.6.1, 4.3.6, 4.4.4, 4.7.1

"make our own fate", see Fate, "make our own"

Maslow, M, 10.5.12, 11.3.2

Material, system, etc, 1.4.8/12, 2.2.2, 2.5.3, 3.5.7, 4.5.6/7, 4.6.1/2/4/5/7, 5.10.1, 7.3.7. 9.9.1

McDougall, W, 10.5.7/8

McKenna, M, 1.4.4

Meiosis, 8.3.6-17

Mele, A.R, 1.4.7, 3.1.2, 5.2.8

Metaphysical, 1.2.7, 1.3.7, 1.7.2/4, 2.1.4, 3.3.8/11/12, 3.4.7/8/10, 3.6.1/4/6, 4.1.1, 4.3.2/4, 4.7.2/5, 5.5.2, 6.1.2-4, 6.3.2, 6.5.1, 9.1.1/2, 9.2.7/11, 9.3.1, 9.6.2, 9.7.6

Metaphysics, 1.1.2/3/6/10, 1.2.1, 1.3.7, 1.5.6, 2.5.1, 3.1.3, 3.6.9, 4.6.7, 5.4.10, 5.6.5, 5.10.9, 6.1.4, 6.2.4, 6.6.6, 9.1.1/2, 9.2.8, 9.3.4, 9.4.3, 9.6.1, 9.9.1/2/4/6, 11.7.1

Metaphysics, naturalistic, 1.1.2, 1.1.2, 2.5.1, 3.6.1/9, 4.6.7, 5.10.9, 6.1.2, 6.6.6, 9.1.1/2, 9.3.4, 9.9.1/2, 11.7.1

Metaphysics, process, 1.1.8, 1.4.7, 3.2.6, 5.3.4, 6.2.3

Nature, 1.1.8, 1.2.1/8, 3.2.6, 3.3.9, 3.5.5/6, 4.3.4, 4.5.1, 6.2.3, 7.6.4, 9.2.10, 11.5.5-7, see also Laws of nature
Near-future, 3.6.2/3/4/6, 6.1.5, 10.2.3, see also: Far-Future.
Need(s), 1.6.2, 2.3.7, 8.4.11, §10.5, 10.7.6/8, 11.3.2, 11.5.1/3, see also Motivation
Needs, prepotent, 10.5.12, 11.3.2
Neisser, U, 10.3.2-4
Neuroticism, 10.3.5
Newton/Newton's laws, 4.4.3, 4.5.1/3, 6.4.4, 9.2.4, 9.8.1
Nietzche, F, 5.5.1/2
Nisus, 11.5.6/7
NMDA receptors. 5.4.13
Noise, §5.3, 5.4.11/13
Nondeterministic, 4.1.1, 4.2.1
Non-necessitated self-determination, 1.4.6/7/14/15, 2.3.3, 3.2.3, 8.1.2
"no-thing", 2.1.8, 11.4.14
"now", 3.4.8, 6.3.3
Nurture, 7.6.4/5, 10.5.8, 11.5.5-7

Oerton, R, 9.2.11
Omar Khayyam, 3.2.4
Ontological reductionism, §9.4
Open-loop, 7.5.5/6/7
Openness & open future, Preface, 1.1.2/5/7, 1.4.7, 10.3.5, 10.4.13
Optimists, 5.6.1, see also Compatibilists
Originated event, see Event, originated
Origination, §1.1, §1.2, 2.5.10, 5.3.6
Origination, chance, Chance origination
Origination, creative, see: Creative origination
Origination, directed: see Directed origination
Origination, fresh or de novo: see de novo origination
Origination, self-directed, see Self-directed origination
Origination, stale: see Stale origination
Origination, type-determined: see Type-determined origination
Originative free will, see: Free will, originative
Originative process, 1.2.4, 1.4.14, 1.51-5, 5.3.5, 5.4.3/6, 5.5.5, 5.9.6, 8.2.1, 8.2.1, 8.3.3/4/19, 11.4.11

Process metaphysics, see Metaphysics, process
Process peripherals, 2.5.3
Property/properties, 1.2.4/9, 1.3.3, 2.5.4/8/9, 3.1.2, 3.5.1, 4.1.1, 4.5.2/6, 5.4.13, 5.5.6, 6.2.2, 8.2.2, 8.3.2/19, 9.3.5, §9.5, 9.6.1/2, 9.7.1/2, 9.9.7
Propositions, 3.1.2-4, 3.3.11, 3.4.4/5, 4.3.3/4, 9.2.1/3/6/7
Psyche, 1.6.2
Psychological agent, 1.2.2, 1.4.1/8/10, 1.5.6/7, 2.5.4/6, 4.6.7, 5.3.6, 7.6.1/2, 11.4.2/5, 11.7.3
Purposeful, 2.3.8, 2.4.8, 5.10.8
Purposes (ends and purposes), 1.6.3, 5.4.12, 5.5.1, 8.4.12, 10.7.3/5, 11.5.7
Purposive system or agent, 1.1.9, 2.3.3-5, 2.3.8, 2.4.2, 7.2.9, 7.3.3, 8.3.20, 19.1.3

Quantum entanglement, §3.5
Quantum indeterminism/indeterminacy, 1.2.5/8/9, 1.3.6, 1.4.7, 1.5.1/6, 2.5.8, 4.3.6, §4.4, 4.5.6, 4.7.1/4, 5.1.2, §5.3, §5.4, §5.5, 5.8.1, 5.10.9, 6.3,4, 6.4.8, 8.3.4, 9.2.8/10, 9.4.3, 9.5.5, 11.4.4/13
Quantum physics & quantum mechanics, 1.2.7/8/9, 1.5.6, 3.4.7/9, 3.4.9, §3.5, 4.1.2, §4.4, 4.5.2, 6.4.8, 7.4.1, 9.2.9, 9.8.1

Radioactive nuclei, 1.2.9, 4.4.4
Randomness, 1.3.1, 1.5.6, 2.4.3, 3.2.2/3, 4.2.1, 4.3.5, 5.3.3-6, 5.4.1/11-15, 5.5.6/7, 6.3.7, 8.3.7/10-19, 9.5.6, 11.4.1
Random numbers, 1.2.9, 5.3.6, 6.3.4, 8.3.4
Reactive attitudes, §5.6
Readiness potential, 5.2.5
Realists, 6.1.3/4
Realm of artificial, 8.5.3, 9.1.3
Realm of biology/life, 1.5.2, 2.5.9, 7.5.1/3/7, 8.2.7, 8.5.3, 9.2.5, 9.9.7
Realm of civilization, 3.6.9, 6.6.2, 7.4.3, 8.2.7, 8.4.14, 8.5.3, 9.1.3, 9.2.10, 9.6.4, 9.9.5, 10.2.2
Realm of technology, 1.5.3, 2.4.10, 6.6.4, 7.5.1, 7.6.1, 8.2.7, 8.5.3, 9.6.4
Real world, 4.2.1, 6.1.3/4
Reason view, 5.10.4/5
Reconcilists, 5.8.3, see also Compatibilists

Reductionists, reducibility, 1.2.7, 1.3.6, 2.1.2, 2.5.4/8/9, 6.4.8, 8.9.4, 9.3.5, 9.4.3, §9.5, 9.7.1/5, 9.9.7, 10.55

Rees, M, 9.2.9

Reiss, S, 10.5.11

Relatively Enduring Network Of Influence Relations, see RENOIR

Relativity, theory of, 3.4.8, 3.5.2, 4.7.4, 6.3.3, 6.6.5, 9.2.9

Renaissance, 1.2.7

RENOIR, §4.6, 6.2.3, 7.2.4, 8.2.1/2/5/6, 9.3.5, 9.5.3, 9.6.3

Representations, 1.4.11, 8.4.8/14, 10.1.1, 10.2.2

Rescher, N, 1.1.8

Responsible/responsibility, 1.4.3/4, 3.2.7, 5.2.9, 5.3.3/5, §5.5, §5.6, 5.7.8, 5.8.2/3, 5.9.3, 5.9.5/6/7, §5.10, 10.4.3/4, 10.5.2/4, 11.4.1/2, §11.6

Responsibility, moral: see moral responsibility

Responsible, ultimate: see ultimate moral responsibility,

Russell, B, 3.3.9

Russell, E.S, 7.2.9

Schmeichel,B, 10.7.4

Schrodinger/Schrodinger's wave function, 3.5.7, 4.5.2, 6.4.8, 9.8.1

Science, Preface, 1.1.4-8, 1.2.1/7-9, 1.4.12, 1.5.4/6, 1.7.3, 2.1.6, 2.2.2, 3.2.6, 3.3.11, 3.4.6-10, 3.5.1, 3.6.6, Ch4, 5.1.2/3, 5.2.8, 5.3.1, 5.5.5, 5.8.1, 6.4.8, 8.2.7, 8.3.1, 9.1.2, 9.2.5/8/9/11, 9.3.1/3/4, 9.6.2, 9.7.3, 9.9.2/4/5, 11.4.7/8, 10.5.8, 11.4.1/10

Scientists, 1.3.4, 1.4.12, 2.5.5, 3.2.6, 3.6.1/4/6, Ch4, 5.2.9/11, 5.3.1, 5.4.1/10/15, 6.1.3, 6.2.2, 9.1.2, 9.3.3, 9.4.1/3, 9.7.3, 9.9.2

SEECing agent, 7.1.1, 7.6.4, 7.6.4/6, 10.4.2, 10.7.5, 11.5.7

Self, 1.4.10, §1.6, §10.3

Self-created ends and purposes, values, etc. 10.2.5, 10.7.5

Self-created life, §11.5

Self-determination, 1.1.1, 1.4.5/14, 8.1.2, 10.5.6/8, 11.3.1, see also Creative self-determination, Non-necessitated self-determination

Self-evaluation, 1.3.3, 1.6.4, 5.10.5, 7.6.4-6, 10.1.1, 10.4.2, 10.5.9, 10.7.5/0, 11.5.7

Self-directed creative origination, see: Creative origination, directed

Self-directed origination, 1.2.3/5-7, 1.3.6, 1.4.5/13/14, 2.5.7, 3.4.6, 5.2.1, 5.10.5

Self-organised learning, 2.4.5

Self-originative free will, see Free Will, self-originative
Semantics/semanticing. 3.3.2, 10.2.11-14
Sentiments, 10.6.1/4/7/9
Situational sensitivity, 5.4.3, 10.2.6/7, 10.3.1/2, 10.4.2, 10.5.2,
    10.7.1/3
Skinner B.F, 8.4.2
Snowflakes, production of, 8.3.5
Socialisation, 1.2.4, 1.3.2, 1.6.1/3, 5.5.4, 7.6.5, 10.2.7/15, 10.3.1/6,
    10.4.1/5, 10.7.7, 11.3.1/4, 11.5.3/5
Society, human, 1.3.2, 5.5.2, 5.6.6, 7.6.5, 8.4.2, 9.6.4, 10.3.2, 10.4.5/11,
    11.6.4/5
Socrates, 5.10.1
Space-time, 6.3.3, 9.4.1
Sperry, R, 9.6.1
Spooky, "spooky action at a distance", §3.5, 4.6.2, 9.9.1
Stale origination, 1.2.4/9/10, 7.3.7
Steward, H, 9.6.2
Strawson, G, 5.5.3
Strawson, P, §5.6
"stretches of change", §2.1, 3.6.4, 4.3.2, Ch6, 7.3.2/5/6, 9.3.2/3
Subconscious, 5.2.1/10, 8.4.10, 10.3.3, see also Unconscious
Sub-state determinism, §4.5
Sub-state laws, 6.4.3-5, 9.2.8, 9.3.3, 9.8.3
Sufficient reason, principle of: see Leibniz,'s principle of sufficient
    reason.
Super-ego, 1.6.2
Superordinate objective, 7.6.2, 10.7.5
Supervenience, 9.7.2-4, 9.9.1/6
Symbol/symbolic 4.5.4, 5.4.1, 9.7.4, 10.1.1, 10.2.2/3/11/12/16
Synchronous/synchronicity, see: Change, synchronous & non-syn-
    chronous
System, directive, see: Directive system
System Determinism and deterministic systems, 1.1.5/6, 2.5.5, 4.1.2,
    §4.5, 4.6.5, 4.7.1, 9.7.3
System, functional, §4.5, §4.6 7.3.3/7/8, 9.3.5
System, material, see Material, system, etc.
System property, 9.6.1

Technological civilization, 2.4.10, 8.5.3
Theory of Everything, 9.2.9
Theory of mind, 10.7.1
Thermodynamics, second law, 1.3.3, 9.8.2
Thermostat/home heating system, 1.1.9, 7.2.9, 7.3.4-6, 7.5.1/2, 8.3.3
Thinking, see Cognition/cognitive
Third party, influence, 2.1.5/6/9, 6.5.1-3
Thomas, L, 2.4.5
Thorndike, E, 8.4.2
Time, 3.4.8, 6.3.3, §6.6, §9.8
Time-determinate (change/laws, etc), 2.1.9-11, 3.3.3-5, 3.4.9, 3.6.6,
    4.3.2-5, 4.5.1-2, 4.7.3/4, 6.4.4/5/8, 6.5.4, 8.3.1, 9.8.1/3
Total-state, 3.2.6, 3.3.10, 3.4.7/8, 4.3.2, 6.4.2-4, 9.2.7/8, 9.4.3, 9.9.2
Tse, P, §5.4
Twain, M, 2.2.4
Two-stage models of free will, 5.3.3
Type boundaries, 8.2.3/4, 8.3.2
Type-determined independence interactions, see under Independence
    interactions
Type-determined origination, etc. 1.2.10, 1.4.14, 1.5.1, 2.2.1,
    9.5.5/6/8, 9.7.5, 9.9.4
Type independence of change, §6.3, §6.4
Type/Token distinction, 6.2.1, §6.3, 6.4.1/7, 6.5.1/2, 8.3.15, 9.3.2,
    9.6.1

Ultimate responsibility, §5.5, 5.6.5, 11.4.1, 11.6.1
Unconscious, 1.4.8/15, 1.6.2, 2.4.8, §5.2, 8.4.10/13, 10.2.8/14, 10.3.3,
    10.4.9, 10.5.10, 11.4.10
Undirected independence interactions, 1.19, 1.3.6, 1.5.6, §2.2, 5.5.7
Universe (the), see also: Existence, Preface, 1.1.2/5/10, 1.2.4-7,
    1.3.3/5/6, 1.4.7/17, 1.7.2, 2.1.1/3/4, 2.5.1, 3.1.3, 3.2.5/6,
    3.3.1/6/11, 3.4.8/9, 6.2.4, 6.3.2, 6.3.3-5/9, 6.5.1, 7.2.3, 8.5.3,
    9.1.2, 9.2.7/8/10, 9.3.1-3, 9.8.2/3, 9.9.2, 11.5.3/7, 11.6.2

Values/valuing, 1.2.1, 1.3.3, 1.4.13, 1.6.2/-4, 5.10.3-5, 6.4.5, 7.6.5,
    8.4.12, 10.2.10/15/17, 10.3.2, 10.4.3/5/9, 10.6.3, 10.7.1/7,
    11.5.3/7
Vohs, K, 10.7.4

Voluntary/voluntariness, 1.4.6/7, 2.3.3, 3.2.3, 4.7.3, 5.2.5-7, 5.5.1, 5.9.7, 5.10.1, 8.4.10, 10.7.6, 11.3.2

35546432R00184

Printed in Poland
by Amazon Fulfillment
Poland Sp. z o.o., Wrocław